Free but Not Equal

Free but Not Equal

THE MIDWEST AND THE NEGRO DURING
THE CIVIL WAR

V. JACQUE VOEGELI

THE UNIVERSITY OF CHICAGO PRESS, CHICAGO & LONDON

Standard Book Number: 226-85925-8

Library of Congress Catalog Card Number: 67-25531

THE UNIVERSITY OF CHICAGO PRESS, CHICAGO 6063

The University of Chicago Press, Ltd., London W.C. 1

To My Mother and Father

Contents

⚜{1}⚜

Background for Conflict

On the eve of the Civil War, the great majority of Americans believed in the innate superiority of the Caucasian race and were determined to maintain white supremacy. Whether by slavery, by restrictive laws, by public opinion, or by subtle discrimination, the Negro in the United States was usually doomed to a life of subordination.[1]

Except for the South, the Middle West—Ohio, Indiana, Illinois, Iowa, Michigan, Wisconsin, and Minnesota—was the region most firmly committed to white supremacy. To most midwesterners, Negroes were biologically inferior persons to be shunned by all respectable whites. In 1858, George W. Julian, an Indiana abolitionist, described the character and strength of this feeling when he lamented: "Our people [of Indiana] hate the Negro with a perfect if not a supreme hatred."[2]

With these articles of faith, the Middle West wove the doctrine of racial discrimination into its legal and social fabric. Ohio began this tradition with the passage of stringent anti-Negro laws in 1804; the other states of the region later followed suit. Except for Ohio, where many of the harsher features of the state's Black Laws were repealed in 1849, the immense popularity and rapid growth of political democracy and three decades of pre-Civil War antislavery agitation brought little relaxation of the restrictions that bound men of color. In an outburst of indignation at the Fugitive Slave Law of 1850, Ohio, Wisconsin, and Michigan devised personal liberty laws to nullify the federal statute; but they failed to match these humanitarian gestures by ameliorating the condition of Negroes within their own society. Amid the conflict over the expansion of slavery

1

and the sectional tension of the 1850's, the Midwest steadily refused to grant equality to the Negro. During this decade, Ohio and Indiana approved constitutions denying the vote to Negroes. In a series of popular referenda, Michigan (1850), Iowa (1857), and Wisconsin (1857) decisively turned down proposals to extend the ballot to Negroes. The legislatures of Iowa in 1851, Indiana in 1852, and Illinois in 1853 adopted laws making it a crime for Negroes to settle in their states.

As the nation girded for war in 1861, state constitutions and statutes reflected the racism that had always existed in the Middle West. The severity of the discriminatory legislation varied, but every state imposed legal disabilities upon its black residents. All seven states barred Negroes from suffrage and from the militia.[3] In Illinois and Indiana there were no provisions for the education of colored children; Negroes were not permitted to testify against white persons in court.[4] Iowa, Ohio, and Illinois excluded men of color from jury service.[5] Interracial marriages were forbidden in Michigan, Ohio, Indiana, and Illinois.[6] Ohio denied Negroes the benefits of poor relief and provided for racially segregated public schools.[7] Exclusion laws carrying severe penalties prohibited Negroes from settling in Indiana, Illinois, and Iowa.[8]

Negroes fared no better in social relationships than in civil and political rights. They were lumped together at the lowest level of a society governed by a color-caste system. Though there were variations in social practices, colored people were generally the victims of segregation and ostracism.[9] Public opinion apparently enforced the dictates of an unwritten code which demanded the rigorous separation of the races. In 1854 an Indiana newspaper editor wrote that Negroes "suffered severely" from the "terrible and irresistible" law of public sentiment. "Under its rule, they are constantly subject to insults and annoyance in traveling and the other daily avocations of life; are practically excluded from all social privileges, and even from the Christian communion."[10]

Here and there, a spirit of moderation eased their plight. A few districts in Ohio's Western Reserve allowed colored children to attend white schools and sometimes permitted Negroes to vote and to hold office. Oberlin, Antioch, and Otterbein colleges in Ohio admitted Negro students.[11] In Iowa and in most parts of Illinois and Indiana the exclusion laws were not enforced. Free Negro immigrants and fugitive slaves found havens of refuge in Quaker settlements in Indiana, Ohio, and Cass County, Michigan.[12] Nevertheless, islands of racial toleration were rare in the Midwest.

Broad differences of opinion on slavery separated the two major political parties in the section, but, almost without dissent, Democrats and Republicans alike recognized and appealed to racial prejudice.[13] Rent by dissension over the slavery expansion issue, midwestern Democrats were united in their contemptuous opinion of the black race. In fact, part of their refusal to embrace the tenets of antislavery was the product of Negrophobia, for many Democrats who despised slavery viewed free Negroes as an even greater evil.

The attitudes of the Republicans were more complex. The Republican party of 1860 was a diverse organization of abolitionists, "conscience Whigs," antislavery Democrats, Free-Soilers, and Know-Nothings, chiefly bound together by a single idea—opposition to slavery in one way or another. In this coalition, the avowed abolitionists and radical antislavery men—those who aimed at the immediate and total destruction of slavery—were in the minority. A much larger group, men of moderate and conservative views, were content to prevent slavery from spreading into the western territories and to hope it would eventually disappear peacefully. Though the motives and goals of the Republicans were a curious mixture of idealism and avarice, their party was essentially founded on a moral principle. With widely varying intensity ranging from zealous hatred to apathetic distaste, most Republicans viewed slavery as an immoral system that violated the precepts of Christianity and humanity, as well as the natural rights of man. Yet, despite an aversion toward "the peculiar institution," their attitude toward the Negro as a human being closely resembled that of the Democrats. Though feeling more sympathy for slaves than did most Democrats, a majority of the Republicans nevertheless believed implicitly in the inferiority of the black race; their abhorrence for human bondage went hand in hand with their abhorrence for living among large numbers of Negroes.

The pronouncements of Abraham Lincoln in the ante bellum years most clearly defined the limitations of the moral principle of the Republican party. Fused in Lincoln were two seemingly discordant strands of thought—a sense of outrage at slavery and

3

a belief in white superiority—that were often blended in the antislavery intellect. An eloquent exponent of the Declaration of Independence, Lincoln repeatedly held that all men were equal in their right to "life, liberty, and the pursuit of happiness." With equal sincerity, he insisted that physical differences between the two races forbade political and social equality, and he favored "having the superior position assigned to the white race."[14]

In reconciling the lofty phrases of the Declaration of Independence with the doctrine of white supremacy, Lincoln drew a commonly made distinction between natural and political rights. According to the most popular moral interpretation of the antislavery gospel, all men were entitled to God-given or natural rights. Usually enumerated among these were the rights of each man to be free, to enjoy the fruits of his labor, to have a family, and to acquire and hold property. In the Middle West, political and social rights were seldom, if ever, included in this category, for they were not endowed by God; they were regarded instead as secular privileges to be conferred by the community upon the worthy. In the 1850's few prominent midwestern Republicans claimed publicly that Negroes either had earned or were capable of exercising such responsibilities. Undoubtedly, there were some political leaders in the region who genuinely desired complete equality for all men but remained silent in order to preserve party strength and unity. Yet most Republicans of every rank opposed equal rights because they shared in traditional midwestern attitudes toward Negroes. In fact, the Republicans' skill in appealing to morality and racial pride contributed greatly to their success in the Middle West. By condemning slavery as a moral wrong, by urging free western territories for white men, and by pledging devotion to white supremacy at home, they swept to victory in the elections of 1860.[15]

The outbreak of the Civil War in April of 1861 increased the virulence of midwestern racism. Armed conflict brought the fear that the chaos of war or federal emancipation could loosen the bonds of slavery and allow southern Negroes to move into the Middle West. Democratic papers sounded the warning. Even before Fort Sumter was fired upon, the Columbus, Ohio, *Crisis* had cautioned that in event of war Ohio would probably become the "general resort of all free blacks." In May of 1861 the Detroit *Free Press* complained that the city was being overrun by Negroes. The Republican press was also concerned. On June 5, 1861, the Chicago *Tribune* puzzled over what could be done with the slaves fleeing into federal lines. Though it offered no answers, the *Tribune* ruled out some possibilities: slaves could not be allowed to remain in the South to be re-enslaved after the withdrawal of federal troops; they could not be brought North to compete with white labor; and they could not be taken into the territories because of the expense. If war continued for another year, the *Tribune* concluded, the Negro question would become the paramount problem facing the nation.[16]

The prospect of an inundation by Negroes touched a raw nerve in the section where even a minute black population was considered an imposition. Prior to war, state exclusion laws, federal fugitive slave acts, an unfriendly white populace, and southern slavery itself had held the number of Negroes in the Midwest to fewer than one per cent of the total population.[17] Now, for the first time, midwesterners were confronted with the possibility of a massive Negro immigration which could radically alter the existing racial settlement. Farm workers and unskilled city laborers feared that the release of southern slaves would bring a horde of Negroes into the Midwest to reduce wages, drive native laboring men from their jobs, and associate with the lower classes of whites. Since they performed much of the unskilled labor, German and Irish urban workers were especially fearful of Negro competition.[18] Persons residing near the slave states, many of them of southern birth or descent, also lived in dread of a Negro ingress, feeling that they would bear the brunt of the invasion. Before the war, this fierce antagonism to Negroes had led the reformer, Theodore Parker, to complain that public opinion in southern Ohio and Illinois was keeping the slaves from leaving northern Virginia and Kentucky.[19] But the opposition to a possible Negro influx was not confined to any ethnic group, political party, class, or particular part of the Midwest. Most midwesterners wanted their section kept free from Negroes.

In the summer of 1861 fears of a Negro inflow heightened as a few Republicans began a campaign against slavery. "Slavery is the cause of the trouble that is upon us, and we shall never have peace until the accursed institution is wiped out," announced the radical Cleveland *Leader*. The equally militant Chicago *Tribune* suggested the wisdom of freeing the slaves in the Confederacy; and even the moderate Columbus *Ohio State Journal* acknowledged that the federal government might be forced to resort to emancipation to quell the rebellion. During a special session of the United States Congress (July–August, 1861), a small number of radicals eagerly clamored for slave confiscation and emancipation.[20]

Angered and alarmed by these gestures, the Democratic press in the Middle West flayed the emancipation heresy. Though they had a host of constitutional and political objections to slave liberation, much of their resistance to abolition was born of racial animosity. Democratic journals explored the social and economic consequences of emancipation and Negro immigration and told of the ruin and degradation that would follow in the wake of the black tide. An editorial in the Cincinnati *Enquirer* denounced a measure, then before Congress, proposing to confiscate slaves employed in Confederate service. "The hundreds of thousands, if not millions of slaves it will emancipate will come North and West, and will either be competitors with our white mechanics and laborers, degrading them by the competition, or they will have to be supported as paupers and criminals at the public expense." Samuel Medary, energetic patriarch of the Democratic party in Ohio and acid-penned editor of the Columbus *Crisis,* asked if freedmen would take the places of southern whites or drive out the white laborers of the North. Ohio's mechanics and farmers were not prepared to "mix up *four millions of blacks,* with their sons and daughters. . . ." From the Chicago *Times* came the complaint that emancipation would flood the North with "two or three million semi-savages."[21]

These arguments were not new. Southern defenders of slavery and northern opponents of abolition had long used the fear of a mass migration of free Negroes into the North to combat the antislavery movement. Henry Clay had played upon these apprehensions in 1839, Senator Robert J. Walker of Mississippi and some northern congressmen had deftly probed the same vein in 1844 in the debate over the annexation of Texas, and Democratic politicians had made use of similar pleas in the 1850's and in the election of 1860.[22] Yet, in 1861, with slavery in real jeopardy for the first time, these appeals took on added meaning. By warning of the pestilential effects that emancipation would have on the Midwest, the Democrats partly removed the slavery debate from its usual midwestern setting of moral and legal abstractions and made the destiny of the

Negro race a burning practical problem affecting the well-being of the region.

Faced with this dilemma, Republican leaders weighed the problem of emancipation. The influential Chicago *Tribune,* edited by Dr. Charles H. Ray, one of the earliest midwestern advocates of wartime emancipation, flatly admitted, "The greatest ally of slaveholders in this country is the apprehension in the Northern mind that if the slaves were liberated, they would become roaming, vicious vagrants; that they would overrun the North, and subsist by mendicancy and vagrancy; and that from the day they were made free, they would cease to work."[23] The *Tribune* then brought forth a solution destined to become the Republican panacea for many of the ills of emancipation. Drawing upon a theme that had long been stressed by antislavery men—by evangelical abolitionists, by Frederick Douglass, the Negro abolitionist, and by the Western Reserve Antislavery Convention of 1842—the *Tribune* reasoned that northern fears of Negro immigration were groundless. Why should the freedmen leave their homes, a pleasant climate, and "the prospect of wealth and independence, to seek a strange country, a forbidding climate, penury, and starvation." Not only would the freed slaves remain in the Cotton Kingdom, the *Tribune* prophesied; Negroes already in the North would emigrate to a more hospitable section, the free South.[24] Thus, emancipation would at once remove slavery from the South and most of the Negroes from the Middle West. For the remainder of the war antislavery spokesmen would echo parts or all of this hoary line.

On the surface, the Middle West's anxieties were chiefly economic, growing from a belief that black immigrants would either compete with white labor or become costly thieves and paupers. With the region in the throes of business depression, these apprehensions were powerful forces in 1861. But economic adversity only aggravated the section's fears; racial antipathy had deeper and more enduring roots than this.

The newspapers of the Midwest best revealed the complex nature of anti-Negro feeling in 1861. Throughout the year the Democratic press vilified the black race and reinforced the widely held stereotype of the Negro as a lazy, shiftless, vicious, and biologically peculiar being. According to Democratic editors, free Negroes were innately indolent or criminal. If they should stay in the South, they

7

would reduce that fertile region to a waste; on the other hand, if they should come North, they would blight and degrade the Midwest. A particularly vitriolic critic of Negro character was the Chicago *Times,* edited by Wilbur F. Storey, recognized as one of the ablest and most caustic journalists in the section. "There is in the great masses of the people a natural and proper loathing of the negro, which forbids contact with him as with a leper," stated the *Times* in a typical editorial. Moreover, it said, this feeling ought to be encouraged. From far back in the past "the negro, with his woolly hair, thick lips and idiotic countenance, grins upon us . . . with the same half-human, half-beastly leer which characterizes him now."[25]

Republican editors were more charitable; they did not abuse or reproach the black race. Yet most of them failed to defend men of color from their assailants and made no attempt to convince the Midwest that colored persons were responsible and desirable residents. Part of their failure to plead for the Negro stemmed from an unwillingness to wear the "nigger party" label; more important, they had little confidence in the ability of the Negro. Republican journals frequently referred to colored people as "Sambo," "Cuffie," and "niggers," and derisively mocked their dialect.[26] The most influential Republican paper in Indiana expressed contempt for Negroes when it cautioned against using blacks for soldiers. "Certainly we hope we may never have to confess to the world that the United States Government has to seek an ally in the negro to regain its authority." In an editorial on the future of the black man, the Milwaukee *Sentinel,* a moderate Republican publication, voiced similar disdain when it predicted, "Let slavery release its grasp from him, and he will shuffle from the stage with the utmost celerity; and . . . sink quietly into the pit—a most unimportant and unobserved spectator, troubling no one."[27]

Despite wide differences of opinion on slavery and on the Negro, the friends and foes of liberation agreed on one point: Negroes were not wanted in the Midwest. And they correctly judged popular opinion. In addition to the "penury and starvation" which the Chicago *Tribune* promised southern Negroes, midwesterners discouraged immigrants by less subtle methods. Black refugees moving into the region were often met by antagonistic whites and by the federal Fugitive Slave Law. A leading Missouri newspaper commended the citizens of Illinois for their aid in capturing slaves escaping from Missouri. In hostile southern Illinois runaway slaves were rapidly arrested and restored to their owners in Kentucky. Negroes were made so unwelcome in Cairo that one fugitive surrendered himself there to be returned to the South. The Democratic Cairo *Gazette* proudly quoted him as saying that four days free in Cairo were worse than four years in bondage. In Quincy, Illinois, a resident who for eighteen years had passed for white was kidnapped and taken back to his master in Missouri. The indignant Quincy *Whig* reported that the wife of the kidnapped man said, "If [he] *was* a nigger, and had deceived her, he deserved his fate."[28]

Negro residents of the Middle West also felt the lash of hardening public opinion. A group of irate whites in Hocking County, Ohio, tarred and feathered three Negroes for making remarks which "they did not relish very well" and then ordered several families in a nearby community to leave within six months. Though the Democratic Columbus *Crisis* ostensibly deprecated this violence, it admonished all northern Negroes "to confine themselves to their proper sphere during these exciting times, or their lives will not be worth a copper." In Milwaukee a lynch mob, shouting "Kill the damned niggers!" and "Damn the niggers and abolitionists!" broke into the jail, hanged a Negro prisoner accused of murdering a white man, and attempted to lynch another Negro who managed to escape.[29]

Until late fall, 1861, the debate over emancipation and the Negro was largely confined to the few Republican papers endorsing liberation and to their Democratic critics. Congress had met in the summer of 1861, and both political parties solemnly pledged to leave slavery alone. With only two dissenting votes in the House and five in the Senate, Congress approved resolutions defining its war aims: war was being waged to preserve the Union; not for the purpose of interfering with the rights or established institutions of the states.[30] Throughout most of the rest of the year these objectives remained intact. But in December, 1861, with Congress about to reconvene, a group of determined Republicans moved toward Washington eager to change all that.

Notes

1. This conclusion is drawn chiefly from Leon F. Litwack, *North of Slavery: The Negro in the Free States, 1790–1860* (Chicago: University of Chicago Press, 1961). See also Thomas F. Gossett, *Race: The History of an Idea in America* (Dallas: Southern Methodist University Press, 1963), pp. 54–122 and *passim*.

2. Quoted in James Albert Woodburn, "Party Politics in Indiana during the Civil War," *American Historical Association Report for the Year 1902*, I (1903), 226. Parts of the material in chaps. i–iv are drawn from my article, "The Northwest and the Race Issue, 1861–1862," *Mississippi Valley Historical Review*, L (September, 1963), 235–52.

3. Franklin Johnson, *The Development of State Legislation concerning the Free Negro* (New York: n.p., 1918), pp. 96, 98–99, 104, 126, 128, 163, 206; Emil Joseph Verlie (ed.), *Illinois Constitutions* (Springfield: Illinois State Historical Library, 1919), p. 80; Charles Kettleborough, *Constitution Making in Indiana* (3 vols.; Indianapolis: Indiana Historical Commission, 1916–30), I, 358; Leola Nelson Bergmann, "The Negro in Iowa," *Iowa Journal of History and Politics*, XLVI (January, 1948), 21; *Compiled Laws of . . . Michigan* (2 vols.; Lansing: Hosmer and Kerr, 1857), I, 73; *Revised Statutes of . . . Wisconsin . . . , 1858* (Chicago: W. B. Kerr, 1858), p. 343; *General Laws of . . . Minnesota . . . , 1858* (St. Paul: E. S. Goodrich, 1858), p. 232.

4. Emma Lou Thornbrough, *The Negro in Indiana: A Study of a Minority* (Indianapolis: Indiana Historical Bureau, 1957), pp. 123, 161–63, 166–67; Mason M. Fishback, "Illinois Legislation on Slavery and Free Negroes, 1818–1865," *Transactions of the Illinois State Historical Society*, January, 1904, pp. 425–26. See also U.S., Department of Interior, *Report of the Commissioner of Education . . . for the Year 1870* (Washington, D.C.: Government Printing Office, 1875), p. 112.

5. Bergmann, "The Negro in Iowa," p. 21; George H. Porter, *Ohio Politics during the Civil War Period* (New York: Columbia University, 1911), p. 20; *Illinois State Journal* (Springfield), January 23, 1865.

6. *Crisis* (Columbus, Ohio), February 28, 1861; *Compiled Laws of . . . Michigan*, II, 950; Johnson, *State Legislation*, pp. 98–99; Fishback, "Illinois Legislation . . . ," p. 422.

7. Porter, *Ohio Politics during the Civil War Period*, p. 20; Eugene H. Roseboom, *The Civil War Era, 1850–1873* (Columbus: Ohio State Archaeological and Historical Society, 1944), pp. 193–94.

8. Kettleborough, *Constitution Making in Indiana*, I, 360, 363; Verlie (ed.), *Illinois Constitutions*, p. 98; Johnson, *The Development of State Legislation . . . ,* pp. 102–3.

9. Litwack, *North of Slavery*, pp. 64–112; Thornbrough, *The Negro in Indiana*, p. 143; Henry Clyde Hubbart, *The Older Middle West, 1840–1880: Its Social, Economic, and Political Life and Sectional Tendencies before, during, and after the Civil War* (New York: D. Appleton-Century, 1936), p. 45.

10. *Standard* (Fort Wayne), 1854 (date of issue not given), quoted in *Indiana True Republican* (Centreville), December 8, 1864. See also Thornbrough, *The Negro in Indiana*, pp. 143, 153; Hubbart, *The Older Middle West, 1840–1880*, p. 45.

11. Roseboom, *The Civil War Era, 1850–1873*, pp. 193–95.

12. Thornbrough, *The Negro in Indiana*, pp. 47–50; Harold B. Fields, "Free Negroes in Cass County before the Civil War," *Michigan History*, XLIV (December, 1960), 375–83; John Mercer Langston, *From the Virginia Plantation to the National Capitol; or, The First and Only Negro Representative in Congress from the Old Dominion* (Hartford: American Publishing Company, 1894), pp. 137, 141–42, 144–45, 168.

13. Litwack, *North of Slavery*, pp. 267–79.

14. Roy P. Basler (ed.), *The Collected Works of Abraham Lincoln* (9 vols.; New Brunswick, N.J.: Rutgers University Press, 1953), II, 256; III, 16, 79–80, 145–46, 179, 220–22.

15. See Litwack, *North of Slavery*, pp. 267–76, and Richard Hofstadter, *The American Political Tradition and the Men Who Made It* (New York: Vintage Books, 1949), pp. 111–17.

16. *Crisis* (Columbus, Ohio), February 7, 1861; *Free Press* (Detroit), May 29, 1861; *Tribune* (Chicago), June 5, 1861.

17. In 1860 the number and percentage of Negroes in each state were: Illinois: 7,628 (0.4); Indiana: 11,428 (0.9); Ohio: 36,673 (1.3); Wisconsin: 1,171 (0.2); Minnesota: 259 (0.1); Michigan: 6,799 (0.9); Iowa: 333 (0.2). U. S., Department of Commerce, *Negro Population: 1790–1915* (Washington, D.C.: Government Printing Office, 1918), pp. 44, 51.

18. See Frank L. Klement, *The Copperheads in the Middle West* (Chicago: University of Chicago Press, 1960), pp. 13–14, 33; Wood Gray, *The Hidden Civil War: The Story of the Copperheads* (New York: Viking Press, 1942), pp. 23, 65.

19. Parker to Salmon P. Chase, March 9, 1858, *Diary and Correspondence of Salmon P. Chase* (Washington, D.C.: Government Printing Office, 1903), p. 478.

20. *Leader* (Cleveland), June 19, 1861; *Ohio State Journal* (Columbus) quoted in *Crisis* (Columbus, Ohio), July 11, 1861; *Tribune* (Chicago), August 10, 1861; *Enquirer* (Cincinnati) quoted in *Herald* (Dubuque), July 27, 1861; T. Harry Williams, *Lincoln and the Radicals* (Madison: University of Wisconsin Press, 1941), pp. 26–27.

21. *Enquirer* (Cincinnati) quoted in *Herald* (Dubuque), July 27, 1861; *Crisis* (Columbus, Ohio), July 11, August 22, 1861; *Times* (Chicago), October 8, 1861.

22. *Congressional Globe,* 25 Cong., 3 sess., Appendix, p. 358; Henry Clay to Calvin Colton, September 2, 1843, in Calvin Colton (ed.), *The Private Correspondence of Henry Clay* (New York: A. S. Barnes, 1856), pp. 476–77; *Letter of Mr. Walker of Mississippi, Relative to the Annexation of Texas . . .* (Washington, D.C.: Globe Office, 1844), pp. 11–13; *Tribune* (New York), February 4, 1864; Louis Filler, *The Crusade against Slavery, 1830–1860* (New York: Harper, 1960), p. 178; Sterling D. Spero and Abram L. Harris, *The Black Worker: The Negro and the Labor Movement* (New York: Columbia University Press, 1931), p. 13; Bernard Mandel, *Labor: Slave and Free; Workingmen and the Anti-Slavery Movement in the United States* (New York: Associated Authors, 1955), pp. 67–68; Litwack, *North of Slavery,* pp. 268–69.

23. *Tribune* (Chicago), August 10, 12, 1861.

24. William Dexter Wilson, *A Discourse on Slavery: Delivered before the Anti-Slavery Society in Littleton, N.H., February 22, 1839* (Concord: Ara McFarland, 1839), pp. 49–50; Filler, *The Crusade against Slavery, 1830–1860,* p. 224; Frederick Douglass to Thomas Auld, September 3, 1848, in Philip S. Foner (ed.), *The Life and Writings of Frederick Douglass* (4 vols.; New York: International Publishers, 1950–55), I, 339; George M. Weston, *The Progress of Slavery in the United States* (Washington: n.p., 1857), pp. 127–28; Mandel, *Labor: Slave and Free,* p. 68; *Tribune* (Chicago), August 10, 12, 1861; William H. and Jane H. Pease, "Antislavery Ambivalence: Immediatism, Expediency and Race," *American Quarterly,* XVII (Winter, 1965), 690.

25. *Times* (Chicago), August 2, 1861.

26. *Tribune* (Chicago), September 6, November 2, 1861; *Sentinel* (Milwaukee), November 27, 1861.

27. *Journal* (Indianapolis), November 26, 1861; *Sentinel* (Milwaukee), December 11, 1861.

28. *Republican* (St. Louis), October 24, 1861, quoted in *Times* (Chicago), October 28, 1861; *Times* (Chicago), June 26, 1861; *Gazette* (Cairo), June 20, 1861; *Whig* (Quincy), June 11, 1861, quoted in *Tribune* (Chicago), June 14, 1861.

29. *Crisis* (Columbus, Ohio), May 23, 1861; *Times* (Chicago), September 10, 1861.

30. Edward McPherson, *The Political History of the United States, during the Great Rebellion* (2d ed.; Washington, D.C.: Philip and Solomons, 1865), p. 286.

❧ 2 ❧

Emancipation, Race, and Politics

When the United States Congress convened on December 2, 1861, the Republicans served notice that the objectives of the war were changing. Acting under the influences of political expediency, military necessity, moral urgency, and adroit radical leadership, they quickly launched an onslaught against slavery. In December, the House refused to reaffirm its resolution limiting the purpose of the war to the preservation of the Union; congressmen offered resolutions calling for emancipation; and a drastic slave confiscation bill was introduced in the Senate.[1]

By the time Congress adjourned on July 17, 1862, the Republican party had fired a salvo of emancipatory measures designed to smash the cornerstone of the Confederacy. Both houses approved a joint resolution offering financial aid to slave states that would adopt gradual emancipation. Bondsmen in the District of Columbia and the territories were declared free. The use of military power to return fugitive slaves to their masters was prohibited; and a militia act liberated Union slave soldiers and their families owned by rebels. Climaxing this program was the Confiscation Act of July 17, 1862, which provided that slaves owned by persons supporting the rebellion should be forever free.[2] If enforced, this law would have freed practically every slave in the Confederacy.

The drive toward emancipation met with intractable resistance from the loyal slave states, from conservative Republicans, and from northern Democrats. Among its most implacable foes were the Democrats of the Midwest. Even though they were outnumbered in 1862 by over two to one in the House of Representatives by their Republican counterparts, held only two Senate seats, and did not con-

13

trol a governorship, they were too powerful to be ignored, for their party had captured about forty-three per cent of the popular vote in the Middle West in the presidential election of 1860.[3]

Disconcerted and demoralized by the departure of the southern branch of their party, and by the defection of War Democrats into the Republican-Unionist coalition, the great majority of midwestern Democrats had closed ranks behind the war effort, but with one reservation: they would not fight a war for abolition. Although they admitted no love for slavery, most of them considered federal emancipation to be unconstitutional and inexpedient. As champions of state rights and strict construction, they usually opposed congressional action against slavery on the grounds that it would violate the Constitution, consolidate power in the national government, build a centralized despotism, abridge property rights, and pervert a lawful struggle for the Union into an unlawful war for liberation and the Negro. Any concession to the abolitionists would frighten the wavering slave states into the arms of the Confederacy, other Democrats argued; it would destroy the latent Unionism in the South, and it would shatter all hope of peacefully restoring the Union.[4]

Midwestern Democrats also continued to cherish an array of racial objections to freeing the slaves. Led in Congress by Representatives Samuel S. "Sunset" Cox of Ohio and William A. Richardson of Illinois, and in the Middle West by powerful organs such as the Chicago *Times,* the Detroit *Free Press,* the Cleveland *Plain Dealer,* the Cincinnati *Enquirer,* the Columbus *Crisis,* the Indianapolis *Sentinel,* and the Dubuque *Herald,* Democrats turned the hostility and contempt for the black race against emancipation. Most of them did not defend slavery as a positive good; instead they held that it was a lesser evil than would be an increase of free Negroes in the Midwest. Their attitude was that expressed by the editor of the Dubuque *Herald,* Dennis A. Mahony, who opposed "Slavery *per se,*" but who was confident that the slaves would not benefit from freedom, and said "there can be little doubt of the demoralizing effect it will have upon the white race, in the North . . . to have these emancipated blacks introduced among them." "Sunset" Cox, whose fine education, broad intellectual interests, and earnest religious convictions were unable to purge him of unrelenting Negrophobia, was more pointed as he informed the House: "If slavery is bad, the condition of . . . Ohio, with an unrestrained black population, only double what we now have, partly subservient, partly slothful, partly criminal, and all disadvantageous, will be far worse."[5]

With skill and guile Democrats branded every proposal to confiscate or emancipate the slaves a menace to the Midwest. Bills calling for federal compensation to slave states which would adopt emancipation were condemned as projects for taxing the whites to build black communities in the North.[6] Congressmen and editors recited the familiar hardships of "free negroism" and "Africanization": colored freedmen would invade the Middle West,[7] fill the jails and poorhouses,[8] compete with white labor,[9] and degrade society.[10] Democratic newspapers hammered these old arguments home by predicting where the Negroes would settle: 110,000 in Michigan; at least 15,000 in Detroit; from 200,000 to 300,000 in Ohio; and about 600 colored persons in Cairo alone.[11]

Professing to believe that Republicans longed to "equalize" the races, midwestern Democrats raised the specter of racial equality. Because the Negro was incapable of rising to the level of the white man, they warned that equality for the black race would contaminate society and politics and debase the American people.[12] A Republican bill in Congress recognizing Haiti and Liberia drew a stream of abuse from alarmed Democrats who suspected that the recognition of the black republics and reception of Negro diplomats were instruments for forcing equality. Cox objected to receiving colored ministers in Washington, he said, because history taught that the states "and this Union were made for white men; that this Government is a Government of white men; that the men who made it never intended by anything they did to place the black race upon an equality with the white." To Congressman Richardson of Illinois, long a trusted lieutenant of the late Stephen A. Douglas and a leading midwestern Democrat in his own right, the Republicans seemed to be mocking the Almighty. "God made the white man superior to the black," he cried, "and no legislation will undo or change the decrees of Heaven . . . and unlike the abolition equalizationists I find no fault and utter no complaint against the wisdom of our Creator."[13]

While Democrats waged their struggle against emancipation and the Negro, Republicans slowly pushed their antislavery program to fruition. Though most Republicans detested slavery, they differed widely on why, when, and how to end it. A great gulf separated the radicals, who eagerly sought to convert the war into an antislavery vehicle, from the moderates and conservatives, most of whom harbored serious doubts about the wisdom of freeing the slaves. Despite this rift in the party and even though they disagreed over tactics, radical Republicans deftly forged the passions of war into a weapon of abolition.

The architects of freedom deliberately aimed their blows at slavery from a patriotic rather than a humanitarian position. Senator Charles Sumner of Massachusetts had pointed out this subtle path to emancipation. The cause of liberation, Sumner said in November of 1861, "is to be . . . presented strictly as a measure of military necessity and the argument is to be thus supported rather than on grounds of philanthropy." Later this strategy was largely followed in Congress. On December 21, 1861, Senator Timothy O. Howe, Republican of Wisconsin, declared that the emancipationists were blaming slavery for the listless prosecution of the war. "For every wrong that is done, for every right that is *not* done," he wrote, "the ready explanation is found in the existence of slavery."[14] Radical midwestern Republicans presented an appealing case for emancipation, declaring that slave confiscation and liberation would cripple or crush the Confederate war effort, save the Union, punish the South, and insure future national unity. While some of them also denounced slavery as a sin against God, humanity, morality, and natural rights, they carefully explained that these were subordinate issues, that their chief concern was the restoration of the sacred Union. Even Representative Owen Lovejoy of Illinois, a plain-spoken pietist whose preachments on slavery rang with the fiery Calvinism of his Puritan forebears, hastened to reassure the lower house that he did "not wish the inference to be drawn . . . that we are for making a war directly upon slavery."[15]

There were many reasons for this approach to emancipation. Public opinion and the realities of politics demanded that "Union," and not "Emancipation," be the Republican war cry. To most Republicans in 1862, the war was indeed being fought to restore the Union, and not to abolish slavery. Few Republicans would object if slavery should die a natural death during the rebellion, but many conservative and moderate Republicans held that overt federal emancipation would violate their past pledges of non-interference with the institution in the states. Some of them also shared, with the Democrats, fears that such a policy would consolidate inordinate power in the central government, deprive citizens of their constitutional property

Emancipation, Race, and Politics

rights, alienate the loyal slave states and southern unionists, and aggravate the race problem.[16]

These feelings were also embraced by the great mass of the northern people. The Republican press warned of the pitfalls of radicalism. A leading administration paper, the Columbus *Ohio State Journal,* advised the "super-zealous advocates of emancipation" that the Midwest would consider a radical antislavery movement "as a shock upon her loyalty." James G. Blaine later recalled that had President Lincoln attempted in late 1861 to persuade northern laborers that slavery should be abolished, he would have seriously damaged the popularity of his administration. "The laborer of the North," wrote Blaine, "was disposed to regard a general emancipation of the slaves as tending to reduce his own wages, and as subjecting him to the disadvantage of an odious contest for precedence of race."[17] At this early stage of the war, excessive emphasis on the humanitarian goals of emancipation would have lent truth to Democratic charges that the war was being fought not to save the Union, but to liberate the Negro. Midwestern Republicans were unwilling to bear this stigma, for they knew that their section would not shed blood solely to free the black race.

The strategy of the emancipationists eventually bore fruit. During 1862 most moderate Republicans advanced haltingly to the belief that the confiscation of bondsmen in the Confederacy would sap the strength of the rebellion. But pleas of national necessity did not bring instant unity to the Republican party, nor did they calm the widespread anxieties about the wisdom of antislavery proposals. Rather, as slavery came under increasing fire in Congress, a wave of Negrophobia swept over much of the North. Throughout most of the Middle West, Pennsylvania, and New Jersey, insistent voices demanded positive action to shield the North from a Negro invasion. In December of 1861 and in the early months of 1862, between 30,000 and 40,000 citizens flooded the Ohio state legislature with petitions praying for laws to forbid further Negro settlement in that state.[18] In Illinois, where the state constitution and a legislative statute already barred black immigrants, a constitutional convention controlled by Democrats voted in March of 1862 to submit a new Negro exclusion section to the electorate. In a June referendum, Illinois voters refused to ratify the new constitution, but they endorsed exclusion by a vote of over 2 to 1.[19]

More drastic steps to repel incoming blacks were taken in parts of the Midwest. In some areas of Illinois and Indiana the exclusion laws and the Fugitive Slave Law were enforced. In June of 1862 a former Whig and United States senator, Thomas Ewing of Lancaster, Ohio, reported that the influx of black refugees "has already produced one mob on a small scale in our quiet town and is causing much disaffection among the laboring portion of our people."[20] Discontent with antislavery radicalism erupted into violence at Cincinnati. At a lecture there in March of 1862, a crowd giving "groans for 'nigger Phillips'" pelted the eloquent abolitionist orator, Wendell Phillips, with eggs and stones. Phillips was forced to retire when some of the audience rushed the stage threatening to lynch and tar and feather him.[21]

These events and the furor over a Negro influx gravely disturbed the Republicans. Although they realized that Democrats were leading the clamor, they also understood that the majority of midwestern voters opposed having large numbers of Negroes come into their communities. Senator John Sherman of Ohio and Thomas Ewing privately agreed that the passage of a general abolition bill "would have made Southern Ohio uninhabitable or driven us to the enactment of harsh and cruel [exclusion] laws." When the radical Senator Jacob M. Howard of Michigan was notified by a colleague that, if the slaves were freed and distributed among the various states in proportion to the white population, Michigan would have about 123,000 blacks instead of the 6,800 it then had, Howard retorted, "Canada is very near us, and affords a fine market for 'wool.'" Senator Lyman Trumbull of Illinois candidly told the Senate, "There is a very great aversion in the West—I know it to be so in my State—against having free negroes come among us. Our people want nothing to do with the negro."[22] Time and time again Republicans voiced these sentiments.[23] Some party leaders arraigned the region for its anti-Negro attitudes, but no one questioned the prevalence or intensity of this feeling.

Beneath the fears about the destination of the freedmen lay the broader problem of assimilating a dependent, largely untutored slave population into free white society. The threat of a Negro inundation sharpened the Midwest's awareness of the vexing complexities that would be involved in such an adjustment wherever it might take place. This in turn caused many midwesterners to approach emancipation with caution and trepidation. In 1862 antislavery spokesmen freely admitted that anxieties about these two closely related issues— racial adjustment and Negro immigration—slowed and imperiled the passage of slave confiscation and emancipation measures. They were the major obstacles to the confiscation bill, according to Senator Trumbull, who emerged early as a leading antislavery radical and who strove diligently to gild the congressional assault on slavery with constitutionalism. The people of the Midwest, he said, were asking: " 'What will you do with them [slaves]; we do not want them set free to come in among us; we know it is wrong that the rebels should have the benefit of their services to fight us; but what do you propose to do with them?' " William P. Cutler, an Ohio congressman, put it more bluntly as he cried, "The nation . . . has been led astray quite long enough with the miserable partisan war cry that emancipation means 'to turn the niggers loose.' " Representative Samuel B. Blair of Pennsylvania charged that Negrophobia, camouflaged as constitutional scruples, was stalling confiscation. "We cannot get an effectual confiscation of property," he complained, ". . . out of fear lest the black population of the North may be increased; and so, after all, it is but this prejudice that is the battery of our adversaries, masked behind the brush-work of legal quillets."[24]

Beset with this dilemma, the friends of emancipation sought answers to the historic question: What can be done with the freed slaves? Some conservative and moderate Republicans believed that the solution could be found in gradual rather than immediate abolition. Such a policy, they hoped, would enable the bondsmen to make an orderly transition to freedmen and thereby avert the economic chaos and racial strife that had accompanied emancipation in the Caribbean.

Some, more radical Republicans, had no such qualms. Owen Lovejoy confidently maintained that he would free the slaves and "let them alone to take care of themselves and they are abundantly able to do it."[25] This prescription was immensely popular with some of the more earnest antislavery champions in the Middle West, for it ignored the subject of race. Perhaps their intense concentration on the evils of slavery had led these men to believe that liberation was the miracle cure for such problems, for there were those who admitted the existence of prejudice against the Negro, but felt that it would vanish under the benign influence of freedom. More likely, most midwestern radicals recognized the difficulties of racial adjustment and declined to discuss them at this time for fear of jeopardizing emancipation.

At any rate, both suggestions were plainly inadequate. Gradual emancipation ignored the need for immediate slave confiscation, and Lovejoy's proposal ignored reality and public opinion. Moreover, they said nothing about where the slaves would go after they were freed, and to the citizens of the Midwest this was a crucial point. With masterly skill, numerous Republicans supplied this deficiency. Going right to the heart of the matter, they emphasized that northern worries about a Negro inflow and racial adjustment were groundless because the freedmen were going to remain in the South. According to this idea, slavery was a national sin and disgrace but the problems of freedom and race were to be worked out in the South. Following a familiar pattern, antislavery politicians and editors of every rank and persuasion cried that emancipation would staunch the flow of colored immigrants from the South; that it was bondage rather than freedom that was driving them into the North. Free the slaves, they said, and a warm climate, a sentimental attachment to their native land, and northern race prejudice would induce them to stay on southern soil.[26]

Many went even further, predicting that the same forces would send all or most of the northern Negroes rushing southward. Two optimistic radicals, Congressmen George W. Julian of Indiana and Albert G. Riddle of Ohio, expected that freedom in the South would drain the North and Canada of their colored populations.[27] They were joined in this soothing refrain by their colleagues from Pennsylvania including the leading radical Republican in the House, Thaddeus Stevens.[28]

Slave-state representatives who accordingly complained that emancipationists intended for the South to shoulder the entire burden of racial adjustment were either reminded that this was only fair or they were ignored. In reply to a Missouri congressman's accusation that Indiana would not receive Negro immigrants, Representative Albert G. Porter of Indiana retorted that black labor was not needed in his state; that Hoosiers had "elected in favor of the white race by prohibiting slavery"; that Missouri had chosen slavery and thereby agreed to accept its disadvantages; and that if any "inconveniences" should follow emancipation "the duty to be just to the freedmen is yours, and you cannot fairly shift either the burden or the duty to us."

Albert G. Riddle was equally forthright as he scoffed at southern fears of Africanization. The slave states, he said, "outraged heaven and insulted the earth to get [the Negroes]; and it is because they have them that the war came. Where should the especial consequences fall, if not on them?"[29]

Statements that the South was destined to become the permanent home of American Negroes were far more than Machiavellian utterances fashioned to deceive the North. While there may have been those who used such arguments without sincerity, most Americans of all sections were convinced that Negroes could not flourish in the cold North primarily because of their biological make-up. The conviction that the Negro was a creature of the tropics, or at least of the warm climates, had long been an integral part of the stereotype of the black race.

Physicians, sociologists, statisticians, divines, and intellectuals accepted and promoted this popular axiom. Science, religion, political tradition, experience, and, ironically, the proslavery argument sustained it. Leading scientists, including Josiah Nott, the noted anthropologist and medical researcher, and Louis Aggasiz, the eminent naturalist, strongly upheld the doctrine of climatic determinism, claiming essentially that the law of climate determined the geographical location of the races; that the temperate zones were set aside for Caucasians and the tropics and semitropics for Negroes. The idea that man was governed by the laws of nature was quite congenial to a people nurtured on the natural rights philosophy and orthodox Christianity, both of which stressed the belief that God had created a well-ordered universe and ruled it according to immutable principles. Furthermore, the scarcity and slow increase of the colored population of the North and the comparatively high mortality and low birth rates of northern Negroes seemed to indicate that they would indeed eventually disappear from the section if their numbers were not swelled by fugitives from slavery. One of the major defenses of slavery led implicitly to the same conclusion; proslavery men had often justified the institution as an economic necessity because black men alone were acclimated to the hot, humid areas of the South.[30]

Even the private correspondence of antislavery men in the Midwest reflected a sincere belief that the Negro race would work out its destiny in the South. In a letter to his congressman, an irate midwestern Republican described as "fallacious" the Democratic claim that the freedmen would invade the North. David Noggle, a state judge who boasted of his radicalism, censured Senator James R. Doolittle of Wisconsin for espousing foreign colonization for the freed slaves. "With all due deference to your wild notions of colonization I think you can't but believe that [by] abolishing Slavery in the Southern States the Northern States would be speedily cleared of their present free colored population." Expressing a similar view as he called for military emancipation in the deep South was Secretary of the Treasury Salmon P. Chase of Ohio, a man of considerable talent, humane impulses, sublime vanity, and soaring ambition. In a letter to Major-General Benjamin F. Butler, then the Union commander of the Department of the Gulf, Chase admitted, "Many honest men really think they [Negroes] are not to be permitted to reside permanently in the Northern States." While he said he had no objection to the presence of colored people in his state, Chase felt they would prefer the southern clime. "Let, therefore, the South be opened to negro emigration by emancipation along the Gulf, and it is easy to see that the blacks of the North will slide southward, and leave no question to quarrel about as far as they are concerned."[31]

But faith in the laws of nature did not assuage the racial worries of the northern people in late 1861 and 1862. With Negro immigrants entering the North and the outcome of the war in serious doubt, Republican assurances that the blacks would gravitate southward when slavery was abolished had a ring of sham. To insure that the freedmen would remain in the South, some midwestern Republicans proposed the use of federal power. They suggested that the blacks be colonized in Florida, or placed in the Indian territories of the southwest, or apprenticed on confiscated plantations, or restrained and employed in the South by the government.[32]

Yet after listening to these ideas and propositions, the Republican party finally adopted voluntary Negro colonization as its official policy. The blacks that were to be freed and who consented to leave were to be sent outside the United States. For a long time, many Americans had favored such a plan. Before the Civil War there had been active, if ineffective, colonization societies in Ohio, Indiana, and Illinois. War revived the nation's flagging interest in the scheme. In his message to Congress in December of 1861, President Lincoln recommended that slaves seized under a confiscation act passed in August of 1861 and those who might be freed by state action be removed to "some place, or places, in a climate congenial to them," and asked the lawmakers to consider also including free Negroes who were willing to depart.[33] A deportation movement now got under way in earnest with a vanguard of prominent midwestern Republicans: Senators Lyman Trumbull, John Sherman, James R. Doolittle, Orville H. Browning of Illinois, Henry S. Lane of Indiana, and Secretary of the Interior Caleb B. Smith of Indiana.

The philosophy of colonization was an amalgam of racism and humanitarianism with its roots deep in the American heritage. Most of the true friends of deportation were convinced by the nation's past that inherent racial differences—mainly that of color rather than slavery—lay at the core of the race problem. Senator Doolittle, leading advocate of colonization in the Senate, explained, "the *question of race* is a more troublesome one than the question of condition [slavery] in the truth." In August of 1862, President Lincoln reminded a group of colored men that the broad "physical difference" between the two races is "a great disadvantage to us both, as I think your race suffer very greatly, many of them by living among us, while ours suffer from your presence." They were just as sure that anti-Negro prejudice was a national characteristic which would not be dispelled by universal emancipation, as some abolitionists thought it would. A House committee, headed by Albert S. White, an Indiana Republican, endorsed emancipation and colonization, and reported that a belief in the inferiority of the Negro was "indelibly fixed upon the public mind. . . . There are irreconcilable differences between the two races which separate them, as with a wall of fire. . . . [The] Anglo-American never will give his consent that the negro, no matter how free, shall be elevated to such equality."[34] Genuine concern for the welfare of the Negroes, as well as racial antipathy, nourished the deportation movement. Republican colonizationists knew well that all men aspired to equality, and they truly sympathized with the condition of the Negro, free or slave. They urged— since history and the evidence on every hand indicated that white Americans would not admit black men to full equality—that emancipation be accomplished by the voluntary resettlement of the freedmen in foreign lands where they could enjoy equal rights and govern themselves. Such a course would benefit both races, they said. The whites would profit from the departure of an alien people; the blacks would escape from domination and oppression.[35]

23

Using these pleas and presenting their proposals as humane and equitable, the supporters of colonization sought to include voluntary deportation provisions in the major emancipation bills before Congress in 1862. Those who professed these statesmanlike and philanthropic goals were doubtless sincere; but political exigencies also turned the Republican party to colonization. Many Republican strategists, including Lincoln, hoped that the enactment of such legislation would placate the loyal slave states and persuade them to move toward emancipation. More important, it was a key part of the program to make slave confiscation and liberation more palatable to the northern states by blunting the threat of a Negro ingress. As he waged his fight for colonization, Senator Doolittle wrote that it "would save the country as well as save the Republican party. . . . [If] our Republicans are such fools as to allow the Democrats to raise the cry of *emancipation & colonization* as the rallying cry against *native abolition* as the war cry of the Republicans, the Republican party is at once reduced to a mere handful and its power forever gone." And, as an antislavery constituent of Senator Trumbull pointed out, it would take the sting from the taunts of the Democrats. "When it is made evident," he stated, "that we prefer a separation of the races . . . much will have been done toward allaying their continual hue & cry of negro worshipers & c."[36]

Republicans, in fact, openly avowed in Congress that deportation was designed partly to keep the freedmen out of the North. When Lyman Trumbull placed a confiscation measure before the Senate, he claimed that the colonization section in the bill would answer those midwesterners who wanted the slaves freed but objected to having them·brought into their section. Senator John C. Ten Eyck of New Jersey announced that the committee which considered the bill thought colonization to be "of the utmost importance" because the North's opposition to being overrun by Negroes called for a declaration of the government's intentions. Speaking in favor of coupling deportation with slave confiscation, Representative Porter of Indiana said that his state desired a separation of the races. Even stronger advice came from Senator Joseph A. Wright, an Indiana War Democrat who had befriended the Lincoln administration. In the debates on the bill to free the slaves in the District of Columbia, Wright sternly counseled, "We [Indiana, Illinois, Ohio] tell you that the black population shall not mingle with the white population in our States. We tell you that in your zeal for emancipation you must ingraft colonization upon your measure."[37]

Colonization was at first bitterly criticized by many Republicans, particularly by radicals who protested that it was inhumane, impractical, uneconomical, and unchristian.[38] Nevertheless, the combined forces of racism, humanitarianism, and political necessity gradually converted the party. In April, congressmen from the Middle West, the middle states, and the loyal slave states overrode stiff resistance and included a deportation provision in the District of Columbia Emancipation Act.[39]

As the session dragged on, more and more reluctant Republicans, mainly heeding the compelling argument of political expediency and the spring election returns which showed Democratic gains, advanced to the support of colonization or lapsed into silence. In June of 1862, Joseph Medill, the radical associate editor of the Chicago *Tribune* and formerly a foe of deportation, decided that a colonization clause should be included in the confiscation bill because it would help maintain party unity. For the time being, the Chicago *Tribune* took a new tack and favored a plan to place the freedmen in Haiti.[40] In June, Republicans passed a direct tax bill containing an unspecified appropriation for aiding colonization. On July 14, 1862, the House, with the votes of leading midwestern radicals—John A. Bingham and James M. Ashley of Ohio, Owen Lovejoy, and George W. Julian—appropriated $500,000 to finance the removal of the slaves freed in the District of Columbia and "those to be made free by the probable passage of a confiscation bill." The Confiscation Act, finally approved later that month, also provided for the voluntary removal of confiscated slaves.[41]

As Congress inched toward emancipation and colonization, the Republican party took steps to improve the lives of free Negroes. With the support of midwestern Republicans, Congress recognized the black republics, Haiti and Liberia, established separate schools for colored children in the District of Columbia, made blacks and whites at the capital subject to the same legal code, prohibited the exclusion of witnesses on account of color in judicial proceedings in the district, and omitted from a new militia law the traditional restriction limiting service to white men.[42] All of these actions recognized the humanity of the black man, and the legislation on the legal code in the district probably indicated a desire to extend equal protection of the law to all men.

And yet throughout the congressional discussion of these and other measures relating to the Negro, it was apparent that the Republicans from the Middle West were not advocating racial equality. If there were any egalitarians among them, they pondered their principles in silence; those who discussed their motives for attempting to better the lot of Negroes disclaimed any yearnings for racial equality. Instead, they agreed that political and social rights were outside the province of federal law; only the states could confer political privileges, and each individual could regulate his social relations.[43] Representative John A. Bingham, a forceful champion of emancipation and personal liberty, defined the irreducible rights of man. The people could not curtail the rights of a "natural-born citizen" to move at will in the United States, he said. Nor could they "deprive him of his right to live there, to work there, and to enjoy the fruits of his own toil; but I do recognize the right of the majority . . . to limit and restrain the exercise of political privileges, among which is the right of suffrage."[44] To go beyond this point in 1862, was to court political disaster, a risk which even the most advanced midwestern Republicans refused to assume.

Charity and humanity, not equality, were the Republican watchwords in Congress. Sympathy for the victims of slavery, a spirit of *noblesse oblige,* and an urge to do justice to the oppressed inspired their benevolence. "These measures have no relation to political or social equality," testified Representative John Hutchins of Ohio. "Because we are willing to do justice to the humblest in society, does it follow that we are bound to extend to them the same social and political privileges which we enjoy?" According to Senator James Harlan of Iowa, a radical Republican who scoffed at the notion that the slaves could not survive under freedom, civilized society was obligated to protect the Negroes, "another feeble people," but their liberation would neither bring nor require equality with the whites.[45]

Meanwhile, Republicans at home in the Middle West displayed much the same attitude. In one way or another the Republican press opposed the exclusion crusade; the conservative papers usually ignored it, and some of the most radical journals roundly denounced it. In Ohio, Republicans in the state legislature withstood the demand for Negro exclusion legislation. Outnumbered Republican delegates to the Illinois constitutional convention fought but failed to keep an exclusion article out of the proposed constitution.[46] On the other hand, even the most outspoken newspapers showed no signs of desiring political equality for the Negro. In Iowa and Ohio, Republican-dominated legislatures met and adjourned without molesting the anti-Negro laws on their statute books. The heavily Republican Iowa legislature amended its militia law, but continued to limit the enrolment to white males. In February the Iowa House of Representatives overwhelmingly defeated an attempt to strike the word "white" from a Senate resolution to extend the privileges of citizenship to all white persons in federal military service.[47]

Behind this mask of apparent unanimity there were midwesterners, including some Republican politicians, who wished to grant equal political rights to Negroes, yet they were too few and too weak to commend their goal to the Republican party. The referendum on a new state constitution for Illinois indicated the size of this minority in that state. In a direct vote on the franchise, the people of Illinois, by a majority of over 5 to 1, chose to continue their ban on Negro suffrage and office holding.[48] In such an atmosphere no political party, and few, if any, individual politicians could admit egalitarian principles and survive.

As they talked in Congress and at home, many stalwart midwestern Republicans spoke the language of white supremacy. William Dennison, a founder of the Republican party in Ohio and a former governor of the state, referred to the "superior [white] race." Because of the Negro's "kindly and affectionate" nature, remarked the radical Chicago *Tribune,* he is "rarely agitated by the profound passions which belong to his superiors."[49] Republican Senators John Sherman, Orville H. Browning, James R. Doolittle, and James Harlan were certain that a higher law transcended man-made rules and governed race relations. They stressed that natural instincts implanted by the Creator forbade equality of the races. God and nature, not prejudice, accounted for racial antipathy, and what God had decreed they did not propose to deny. The law of caste, asserted Sherman, was the unchangeable "law of God. . . . The whites and the blacks will always be separate, or where they are brought together, one will be inferior to the other." Doolittle stated that "in the temperate zone, the Caucasian race has always been dominant, and always will be. In the torrid zone the colored man dominates and will forever. . . . The Creator has written it upon the earth and upon the race."[50] Responding to a query about the possibility of interracial marriages, Senator Harlan asked, "Has the hand of nature fixed no barrier to such loathsome associations?"[51]

Thus the attack on slavery in 1862 wrought no fundamental change in the racial attitudes of the Middle West. The blend of antislavery idealism and racism manifested by the region's leading Republicans mirrored clearly the views of their followers. Most midwesterners were frequently torn among their dislike of slavery, their pity for the slaves, and their aversion for the Negro. Senator Sherman struck this note when he announced, "The great mass of this country are opposed to slavery—morally, socially, politically." But he added that Ohio did not like Negroes; that the people of the Midwest were "opposed to having many negroes among them"; and that colored people were "spurned and hated all over the country North and South. . . ." In a like vein, Senator Doolittle, whose detestation of slavery was matched by his fears about the consequences of emancipation, forecast the reaction of whites in the free states should the slaves be freed and distributed among them. "Their humanity would rejoice at their freedom," he said, "but their instincts would shrink back at their apportionment."[52]

This theme resounded throughout the Midwest. An unabashed expression of this feeling appeared in a leading Republican organ, the Springfield *Illinois State Journal*:

> The truth is, the nigger is an unpopular institution in the free States. Even those who are unwilling to rob them of all the rights of humanity, and are willing to let them have a spot on earth on which to live and to labor and to enjoy the fruits of their toil, do not care to be brought into close contact with them. . . . Now we confess that we have, in common with nineteen twentieths of our people a prejudice against the nigger, but we do not hold on that account we are bound to vote the Democratic ticket, nor spend three or four hours of each day of our life in devising schemes to rob the black man of all the rights of human nature, and herein we differ from modern Democracy.

In Ohio, a committee of the legislature reported against exclusion, but it confidently hoped that the federal government would colonize the freedmen if it should emancipate many slaves. Even though a Republican editor in the Western Reserve strenuously objected to exclusion as being immoral, he confessed, "We have no special affection for negroes. We neither desire their companionship or their society. . . . We would be glad if there was not one in the State or one in the United States."[53]

When Congress adjourned in mid-summer, 1862, the emancipationists could point with pride to the blows they had dealt slavery. During the seven months Congress was in session, they had done more to destroy the institution than had been done since the founding of the Republic. They owed their success mainly to their ability to convince a majority of Republican congressmen that the Union could be saved only by depriving the Confederacy of its chief sustenance—slave labor. Whether the Republican party could persuade the people of the Middle West that such action was indeed necessary and that emancipation and white supremacy were compatible remained to be seen.

Notes

1. Edward McPherson, *The Political History of the United States, during the Great Rebellion* (2d ed.; Washington: Philip and Solomons, 1865), p. 287; *Congressional Globe*, 37 Cong., 2 sess., pp. 5, 6, 18–19.

2. David Donald and James G. Randall, *The Civil War and Reconstruction* (2d ed.; Boston: Heath, 1961), pp. 372–75.

3. In the second session of the Thirty-seventh Congress, which met from December 2, 1861, to July 17, 1862, there were 34 Republicans and 15 Democrats from the Midwest in the House of Representatives. See *Biographical Directory of the American Congress, 1774–1961* (Washington, D.C.: Government Printing Office, 1961), pp. 173–77. Statistics for the election of 1860 are based on returns in *The Tribune Almanac and Political Register for 1861* (New York: New York Tribune, 1868), p. 64.

4. Representative James A. Cravens of Indiana to Abraham Lincoln, January 5, 1862, Robert Todd Lincoln Collection (Manuscript Division, Library of Congress); Representative William S. Holman of Indiana to Allen Hamilton, March 2, 1862, October 9, 1863, and February 28, 1864,

Allen Hamilton Papers (Indiana Division, Indiana State Historical Library, Indianapolis); *Congressional Globe,* 37 Cong., 2 sess., pp. 907–8.

5. *Herald* (Dubuque), April 13, 29, 1862; *Congressional Globe,* 37 Cong., 2 sess., Appendix, pp. 244–45. See also *Times* (Chicago), March 18, 1862; David Lindsey, *"Sunset" Cox: Irrepressible Democrat* (Detroit: Wayne State University, 1959), pp. 90–95.

6. *Congressional Globe,* 37 Cong., 2 sess., p. 1647; *Herald* (Dubuque), April 29, 1862, June 1, 1862; *News* (Milwaukee) quoted in *Herald* (Dubuque), April 20, 1862.

7. *Gazette* (Cairo), April 3, 1862; *Times* (Chicago), April 18, 1862; *Crisis* (Columbus), January 29, 1862; *Times* (Portsmouth, Ohio) quoted in *Crisis* (Columbus), May 7, 1862; *Enquirer* (Cincinnati) quoted in *Herald* (Dubuque), June 26, 1862; *Sentinel* (Indianapolis), April 29, 1862, quoted in Emma Lou Thornbrough, *The Negro in Indiana: A Study of a Minority* (Indianapolis: Indiana Historical Bureau, 1957), p. 189; *Herald* (Dubuque), April 16, 19, 1862; *Congressional Globe,* 37 Cong., 2 sess., p. 1468, and Appendix, pp. 120, 140, 243–48.

8. *Free Press* (Detroit), December 10, 1861, April 13, 1862; *Gazette* (Cairo), April 19, 1862; *Times* (Chicago), May 22, 1862; *Congressional Globe,* 37 Cong., 2 sess., Appendix, p. 248.

9. *Enquirer* (Cincinnati) quoted in *Herald* (Dubuque), June 26, 1862; *Times* (Chicago), April 8, June 28, 1862; *Crisis* (Columbus), January 29, 1862; *Free Press* (Detroit), June 15, 1862; *Herald* (Dubuque), June 13, 22, 1862; *Sentinel* (Indianapolis), April 29, 1862, quoted in Thornbrough, *The Negro in Indiana,* p. 189; *Congressional Globe,* 37 Cong., 2 sess., Appendix, pp. 120, 248, 285.

10. *Herald* (Dubuque), June 1, 1862; *Congressional Globe,* 37 Cong., 2 sess., p. 573.

11. *Free Press* (Detroit), April 13, 1862; *Enquirer* (Cincinnati) quoted in *Herald* (Dubuque), June 26, 1862; *Gazette* (Cairo), April 19, 1862.

12. *Congressional Globe,* 37 Cong., 2 sess., Appendix, p. 245; *Free Press* (Detroit), June 14, 1862; *Gazette* (Cairo), April 3, 1862.

13. *Crisis* (Columbus), May 7, 1862; *Congressional Globe,* 37 Cong., 2 sess., pp. 60, 2207, 2502.

14. Sumner to John Jay, November 10, 1861, in Edward L. Pierce, *Memoir and Letters of Charles Sumner* (4 vols.; Boston: Roberts Bros., 1887–93), IV, 49; Howe to his niece, Grace, December 13, 1861, Timothy O. Howe Papers (Wisconsin State Historical Society, Madison).

15. *Congressional Globe,* 37 Cong., 2 sess., pp. 76, 194–95, 327–32, 348–49, 858–59, 1816.

16. Caleb B. Smith, December 16, 1861, to Warner Bateman, Warner Bateman Papers (Western Reserve Historical Society, Cleveland); Senator

James R. Doolittle to Mary Doolittle, March 9, 17, 1862, James R. Doolittle Papers (Wisconsin State Historical Society, Madison); *Ohio State Journal* (Columbus), December 8, 9, 11, 1861, January 31, 1862.

17. *Ohio State Journal* (Columbus), December 8, 9, 11, 1861, January 31, 1862; *Congressional Globe,* 37 Cong., 2 sess., p. 197; James G. Blaine, *Twenty Years of Congress: From Lincoln to Garfield* (2 vols.; Norwich: Henry Bill Publishing Co., 1884), I, 353.

18. George H. Porter, *Ohio Politics during the Civil War Period* (New York: Columbia University, 1911), pp. 96–97; *Crisis* (Columbus), December 26, 1861, January 16, 29, February 4, 12, 26, March 19, April 30, 1862.

19. Arthur Charles Cole, *The Era of the Civil War, 1848–1870* (Springfield: Illinois Centennial Commission, 1919), p. 271; *Illinois State Journal* (Springfield), August 5, 16, 1862; *Tribune* (Chicago), March 6, 1862.

20. Thornbrough, *The Negro in Indiana,* pp. 184–85; *Congressional Globe,* 37 Cong., 2 sess., p. 2803; *Register* (Springfield) quoted in *Tribune* (Chicago), March 11, 1862; Thomas Ewing to John Sherman, June 2, 1862, William Tecumseh Sherman Papers (Manuscript Division, Library of Congress).

21. *Crisis* (Columbus), March 26, 1862; Charles R. Wilson, "Cincinnati's Reputation during the Civil War," *Journal of Southern History,* II (November, 1936), 476–77.

22. Thomas Ewing to John Sherman, June 2, 1862, W. T. Sherman Papers; John Sherman to Thomas Ewing, June 5, 1862, Thomas Ewing Papers (Manuscript Division, Library of Congress); *Congressional Globe,* 37 Cong., 2 sess., pp. 944, 1780.

23. *Congressional Globe,* 37 Cong., 2 sess., pp. 1357, 1491, 1606, 2243, 2923, and Appendix, pp. 84, 297; J. M. Burgess to John Fox Potter, April 16, 1862, John Fox Potter Papers (Wisconsin State Historical Society, Madison); M. M. Meight to Trumbull, July 7, 1862, Lyman Trumbull Papers (Manuscript Division, Library of Congress).

24. *Congressional Globe,* 37 Cong., 2 sess., pp. 944, 2301, and Appendix, p. 118.

25. *Congressional Globe,* 37 Cong., 2 sess., p. 1368.

26. *Sentinel* (Milwaukee), December 11, 1861, June 28, 1862; *Illinois State Journal* (Springfield), April 26, 1862; *Transcript* (Peoria) quoted in *Tribune* (Chicago), April 22, 1862; *Congressional Globe,* 37 Cong., 2 sess., pp. 332, 2243, and Appendix, pp. 212, 327.

27. *Congressional Globe,* 37 Cong., 2 sess., pp. 441, 1107, 1495, 2301; *Tribune* (Chicago), March 24, April 22, 1862; *Sentinel* (Milwaukee), February 27, May 10, 1862.

28. *Congressional Globe,* 37 Cong., 2 sess., pp. 332, 441, 2243.

29. *Ibid.,* p. 2243, and Appendix, pp. 296–97.

30. Louis Agassiz to Samuel G. Howe, August 9, 1863, in Elizabeth Howe (ed.), *Louis Agassiz: His Life and Correspondence* (2 vols.; Boston: Houghton Mifflin, 1885), II, 596, 600, 609, 611; Samuel G. Howe to Louis Agassiz, August 18, 1863, in *ibid.,* p. 615; Joseph C. G. Kennedy, *Population of the United States in 1860* . . . (Washington, D.C.: Government Printing Office, 1864), pp. xi–xii; Samuel Gridley Howe, *The Refugees from Slavery in Canada West: Report to the Freedmen's Inquiry Commission* (Boston: Wright and Potter, 1864), pp. 21–24, 28–29, 35–36; "Final Report of the American's Freedmen's Inquiry Commission to the Secretary of War," May 15, 1864, in U.S., War Department, *The War of the Rebellion: A Compilation of the Official Records of the Union and Confederate Armies* (128 vols.; Washington, D.C.: Government Printing Office, 1880–1901), 3d ser., IV, 373–75, 377; William Stanton, *The Leopard's Spots: Scientific Attitudes toward Race in America, 1815–59* (Chicago: University of Chicago Press, 1960), p. 71; *Congressional Globe,* 37 Cong., 2 sess., pp. 441, 596, 2243, 2301, and Appendix, p. 83; *Sentinel* (Milwaukee), February 27, 1862.

31. Noggle to Doolittle, May 30, 1862, Doolittle Papers; J. M. Burgess to John Fox Potter, April 16, 1862, Potter Papers; Chase to Butler, July 31, 1862, Jessie Ames Marshall (ed.), *Private and Official Correspondence of General Benjamin F. Butler during the Civil War* (5 vols.; Norwood: privately printed, 1917), II, 132–33. A similar view was expressed by J. T. Worthington, an Ohio unionist of unknown party affiliation, in a letter to Rufus King, June, 1862, Rufus King Papers (Cincinnati Historical Society, Cincinnati).

32. *Congressional Globe,* 37 Cong., 2 sess., p. 35, and Appendix, pp. 212, 234; *Tribune* (Chicago), December 11, 1861, January 2, 1862; *Ohio State Journal* (Columbus), January 7, 1862.

33. *Times* (Chicago), November 25, 1861; *Crisis* (Columbus), November 7, 1861; "Annual Message to Congress," December 3, 1861, in Roy P. Basler (ed.), *The Collected Works of Abraham Lincoln* (9 vols.; New Brunswick, N.J.: Rutgers University Press, 1953), V, 48.

34. Doolittle to Mary Doolittle, April 19, 1862, Doolittle Papers; "Address on Colonization to a Deputation of Negroes," August 14, 1862, in Basler (ed.), *The Collected Works of Abraham Lincoln,* V, 371–72; *Reports of Committees of the House of Representatives, No. 148,* 37 Cong., 2 sess., pp. 13–15. This report was signed by five slave state representatives, one Pennsylvanian, and the chairman, Albert S. White of Indiana.

35. *Congressional Globe,* 37 Cong., 2 sess., pp. 332, 1491–92, 1520, 1604, 2923, and Appendix, pp. 83–84, 297.

36. M. M. Meight to Trumbull, July 7, 1862, Trumbull Papers; Doolittle to Mary Doolittle, April 4, 1862, Doolittle Papers.

37. *Congressional Globe,* 37 Cong., 2 sess., pp. 944–46, 1468, and Appendix, p. 297.

38. *Congressional Globe,* 37 Cong., 2 sess., p. 1605; *Sentinel* (Milwaukee), March 28, 1862; David Noggle to James R. Doolittle, May 30, 1862, Doolittle Papers; J. M. Burgess to John Fox Potter, April 16, 1862, Potter Papers.

39. *Congressional Globe,* 37 Cong., 2 sess., Appendix, p. 348. In a key vote in the Senate, Republicans from the Midwest, New York, Pennsylvania, and New Jersey voted 12 to 3 for colonization while New England's senators voted against it, 6 to 5. *Congressional Globe,* 37 Cong., 2 sess., pp. 1522–23.

40. Medill to Trumbull, June 5, 1862, Trumbull Papers; *Tribune* (Chicago), June 15, 1862. The *Tribune* later reversed its position and again opposed colonization.

41. *Congressional Globe,* 37 Cong., 2 sess., p. 3331, and Appendix, pp. 361–62, 410, 412–13.

42. *Ibid.,* pp. 356–57, 361, 397.

43. *Congressional Globe,* 37 Cong., 2 sess., p. 3131, and Appendix, p. 322. See also *Western Christian Advocate* (Cincinnati), July 16, 1862.

44. *Congressional Globe,* 37 Cong., 2 sess., p. 156.

45. *Ibid.,* pp. 1359, 3131, and Appendix, pp. 118, 322.

46. Porter, *Ohio Politics during the Civil War Period,* pp. 96–97; *Crisis* (Columbus), April 30, 1862; *Tribune* (Chicago), March 6, 1862; *Illinois State Journal* (Springfield), March 6, 27, 1862.

47. *Times* (Chicago), February 13, 1862; *Acts and Resolutions Passed at the Regular Session of the Ninth General Assembly of the State of Iowa* (Des Moines: F. W. Palmer, 1862), p. 231.

48. *Illinois State Journal* (Springfield), August 16, 1862.

49. *Ohio State Journal* (Columbus), January 7, 1862; *Tribune* (Chicago), March 24, 1862.

50. *Congressional Globe,* 37 Cong., 2 sess., pp. 1521, 3199, and Appendix, pp. 83–84.

51. *Ibid.,* p. 321.

52. *Congressional Globe,* 37 Cong., 2 sess., p. 1491, and Appendix, pp. 83–84.

53. *Illinois State Journal* (Springfield), March 22, 1862; Porter, *Ohio Politics during the Civil War Period,* pp. 96–97; *Register* (Sandusky, Ohio) quoted in *Crisis* (Columbus), March 26, 1862.

e⧼3⧽

Toward a Solution

The summer of 1862 was a time of racial turmoil in the Midwest and one of decision for the Union. The adjournment of Congress did not still the clamor over slavery and the Negro; instead, the debate continued without respite as the struggle entered a new and grimmer phase. Even before Congress adjourned, the campaign for the fall elections was in progress and the opposing political parties were bitterly fighting over emancipation and the status of the Negro. Against this background of discontent, Abraham Lincoln quietly and surely drew the outlines of a plan for coping with the problems of slavery and race. The attitudes of the Middle West helped shape the fateful course of its most famous son.

As the political campaigns proceeded, events in the Midwest warned of growing hostility toward the black race. While Union armies drove southward, a stream of fugitive slaves flowed from the war-torn plantations into the free states. Exaggerated press reports of the fugitives' numbers publicized their flight to freedom. Northern laborers were told that low wages were being paid to black workers arriving in the North. According to Democratic newspapers, the daily wages being commanded by Negroes ranged from ten cents in Illinois and Pennsylvania to about eighteen cents in Iowa.[1] In July and August tension over Negro labor competition snapped into violence in Toledo, Chicago, and Cincinnati. After a group of Negroes underbid white workers for a job on the Chicago docks, a general riot ensued. At Toledo, race strife over wages left one man dead, several wounded, and a number of Negro shanties torn down. The worst outbreak erupted on July 10, 1862, at a Cincinnati river landing where about a hundred whites and a number

34

of Negroes battled over wages and employment. Five days later, one thousand whites attacked "Bucktown," a Negro ghetto in Cincinnati, and caused considerable property damage. One month later, another attack was launched on Negro dock laborers in the same city. A friend of the colored people of Cincinnati remarked that anti-Negro sentiment was so fierce in the summer of 1862 that "it was at the hazard of his life that a colored man could walk the streets," and "the courts gave them no redress."[2]

But racial violence was not caused by labor competition alone. With the dread of racial equality haunting the Midwest, the need to remind the Negro of his place in society frequently supplied the spark to set off a bloody riot. After two white men in New Albany, Indiana, were reportedly shot by Negroes, a white mob meted out its punishment; one Negro was killed and another wounded in a thirty-hour riot marked by beatings, shootings, and vandalism in the Negro sector of the town. Afterward, when a number of blacks fled to Louisville, the New Albany *Ledger* wrote with grim irony: "They fly to a slave State to enjoy that liberty and security which is denied them in a free State. . . ." In Chicago, the "Omnibus Riot" flared when a bus driver ejected a Negro from his vehicle crying, "There can't any nigger ride in my bus." The sheriff of Cook County was called out to protect colored people in the vicinity from assaults and threatened mob action. In Peoria, Illinois, a crowd of whites broke into the local jail and beat a Negro prisoner who had slashed a policeman with a razor.[3]

Meanwhile, the Democrats of the Midwest continued to lead the campaign against emancipation and the Negro. They had been, for the most part, a loyal opposition in Congress, voting money and supplies for the war, but they clung tenaciously to their original position: federal emancipation was unconstitutional, impractical, and unwise. Now that most of the Republicans in Congress had slipped into antislavery radicalism, Democrats complained that the true goals of Republicanism were at last unmasked, that the war had in truth become an antislavery crusade, a war for the Negro. Bewailing this change in policy, and taunting their opponents with attempting to Africanize the Midwest, the Democrats dared them to settle the emancipation issue at the polls.

The strategy of state Democratic organizations in the Midwest followed a well-established party line. They claimed to be the conservators of the Constitution, state rights, and white supremacy. Between June 18 and September 11, 1862, militant state conventions drafted resolutions declaring that emancipation and its corollary, Negro immigration, would ruin the Midwest. Conventions in Iowa, Illinois, Indiana, and Ohio denounced compensated emancipation because it would require additional taxation to buy freedom for the slaves. Iowa Democrats resolved that "this is a Government of white men, and was established exclusively for the white race; that the negroes are not entitled to, and ought not to be admitted to political or social equality with the white race." To halt economic competition between the races, the Democrats of Ohio opposed emancipation and demanded a ban on Negro immigration into the Buckeye State.[4] Excoriating slave liberation, the Illinois and Indiana conventions demanded enforcement of their Negro exclusion laws on the grounds that white men alone were suited to the free institutions of their states. Wisconsin's Democrats adopted and published an address asserting that social equality of the races was contrary to the laws of nature: "Nature never placed the races together; when brought together the servitude of the inferior is the best condition for both races."[5]

At the national level, the cleavage between the two parties was apparently sharp and clear. The passage of the Confiscation Act of July 17, 1862, demonstrated that Republican congressmen had grown more radical. In the anger, frustration, and alarm that engulfed the North after the Union army was thrown back from Richmond in the "Seven Days" battles (June 25–July 1, 1862), most of the moderate and conservative Republicans had joined with radicals to vote for the confiscation bill. Despite the continued conservatism of the Lincoln administration, the Republican congressional party was now fully committed to the destruction of slavery in the Confederacy, and it hoped to free the slaves in the border states. In less than a year that party had shifted from a policy of non-interference with slavery in the states to one of total emancipation.

But the unity that was born of desperation was superficial; the rifts in the party were not healed. Elated by success, radical Republicans had driven onward, calling for the enlistment of Negro soldiers and strict enforcement of antislavery enactments. Some urged the President to issue a proclamation of emancipation. Many of the more moderate and conservative Republicans bridled at these demands. They were now a dwindling group in a Congress whose constitutional scruples and concern over the problems of emancipation were gradually being worn away by the success of Confederate arms in Virginia. Though most of them had finally and often grudgingly assented to the confiscation law, they continued to recoil from most of the radical program. They had slowly advanced to the position that slave confiscation would weaken the rebellion, but they had doubts about the constitutionality of the Confiscation Act and the wisdom of or necessity for enrolling Negro troops. They therefore denied the need for a proclamation of emancipation. Enough had been done for the time being, they declared.

Republican congressmen returning home to campaign for the fall elections found the Midwest also deeply divided on slavery. The conservative Senator Orville H. Browning vowed that Republican strength in Illinois was largely a result of Lincoln's conservatism. Senator Joseph A. Wright, War Democrat stumping in Indiana, claimed that the state's Union ticket would gain 20,000 votes if the President would jail abolitionist Wendell Phillips for making "traitorous" speeches. On the other hand, two radical senators, Zachariah Chandler of Michigan and James W. Grimes of Iowa, happily reported that radicalism was rampant in their states.[6] More convincing evidence of growing antislavery feeling came from Senator John Sherman, a wily Republican trimmer keenly sensitive to popular currents. In early August, Sherman wrote his brother, General William Tecumseh Sherman, that the officer who acted on the principle of "Death and Confiscation to the rebels" would "secure general favor. No one cares about the negro except [that] as . . . he is the cause of the war he . . . [should] be made useful in putting an end to it." Later that month he noted that public opinion on emancipation had changed: "I am prepared . . . to meet the broad issue of universal emancipation," he said—strong language for a man who only nine months earlier had opposed federal action on slavery.[7]

State party platforms reflected the bitter divisions within the Republican party. Part of this lack of accord resulted from the fusion of War Democrats and Republicans in some midwestern states. This coalition, usually referred to as the Union party, was reluctant to tamper with slavery partly because most War Democrats and conservative Republicans continued to oppose a war on the institution. Although Republicans made up the bulk of the Union party, the conservatives—Democrat and Republican—probably held the balance of political power in Indiana, Ohio, Illinois, and Wisconsin. In these states the Union party usually moved cautiously. The Union platform in Ohio, for example, ignored the slavery issue and denied that the war was being fought to overthrow state institutions. The Unionists of Indiana called for the restoration of the Union with all the rights of the states unimpaired. In Iowa where the Republicans refused to forsake the traditional party label because of their dominance in state politics, their organization was more opposed to slavery. The Iowa Republican convention endorsed the antislavery legislation passed by Congress and added, "If, as a last measure for the preservation of the Republic, it shall become necessary to blot out the institution of slavery from the soil of every State, we shall say Amen!"[8]

In the middle of this tug of war over slavery stood Abraham Lincoln, now the central figure in the struggle. Lincoln's hatred of the slave system probably matched the moral fervor of the abolitionists. Yet his antislavery zeal was tempered by his respect for private property, by his constitutionalism, by his fear of losing the support of the loyal slave states, by his keen realization of the problem of two free races coexisting within the same society, and by his recognition and understanding of northern attitudes toward the Negro. Lincoln's policy toward slavery followed a tortuous path filled with indecision and doubt, but it always contained the elements of morality, practicality, statesmanship, and political expediency.

In the summer months of 1862 Lincoln was slowly converted to an active antislavery position. His conversion is notable because it paralleled the course taken by some conservative and most moderate midwestern Republicans at about the same time. During the first year of the war, Lincoln had epitomized the conservative Republican attitude toward slavery. A strong constitutionalist, he viewed slavery as a state institution, one that was beyond the legitimate authority of the national government. His reverence for the Constitution and for the principle of federalism made him reluctant to lay hands on an institution which he had repeatedly stated could be abolished only by voluntary state action. On July 1, 1862, the President summarized his early views of slavery and the war as he told Senator Browning that Congress possessed no power over slavery in the states "and so much of it as remains after the war is over will be in precisely the same condition that it was before the war and must be left to the exclusive control of the states where it may exist."[9]

Somehow, Lincoln believed, slavery should be put on the road to extinction without stretching the powers of the central government beyond the Constitution. In a message to Congress in December, 1861, he had set forth his views on achieving this goal. The President urged the states to move voluntarily toward gradual emancipation with compensation for those owners whose slaves were freed; he asked Congress to give financial aid to states adopting such a plan; and finally, he requested that Congress provide some means of colonizing abroad the freed Negroes, including those who were already free, who consented to leave. These two features—voluntary state emancipation with compensation and colonization—became the guideposts of Lincoln's antislavery program.[10] His intent was clear. Voluntary state action would preserve state rights, appease the loyal slave states, and ultimately destroy slavery. Gradual liberation and deportation would cushion the social and economic shocks of emancipation and bring a lasting solution to the race problem.

As his insistence upon gradual emancipation and colonization suggests, the President's constitutionalism and his concern for the border slave states were equaled by his profound concern over the social and economic consequences of emancipation. This was best revealed by his words and actions following the passage of the law freeing the slaves in the District of Columbia. After the passage of this bill in April of 1862, Lincoln praised Congress for including the principles of compensation and deportation in the measure. Senator Doolittle privately said that the bill would have been vetoed had it not provided for colonization. However this may have been, Lincoln certainly had serious objections to the measure, even though he signed it. He confided his dissatisfaction to Browning, complaining that the act called for immediate rather than gradual freedom—"that now families would at once be deprived of cooks, stable boys & c. and they of their protectors without any provision for them." He continued, "in the strictest confidence," that he would delay signing the bill for two days while a Kentucky congressman removed from Washington "two family servants who were sickly, and who would not be benefitted by freedom." He did so delay.[11] Perhaps a number of healthier slaves also were removed from Washington while Lincoln waited.

Throughout the winter and spring of 1862 the radicals assailed Lincoln for being soft on slavery, charging that he had no plan for reaching it in the rebellious states. It was true that the President was chiefly concerned with reunion, not slavery. His program based on moral and financial suasion and state action was not geared to the situation in the rebel states, since they showed no enthusiasm about embracing emancipation or rejoining the Union. And yet, despite his silence on the subject, Lincoln had a realistic policy for dealing with slavery in the Confederacy. He believed that war itself would be the most effective emancipator. A thorough-going fatalist, Lincoln preferred to let the confusion and chaos of battle uproot slavery, if it were so willed by God, without specific congressional or executive action.[12] In this way, the *federal* nature of the Union would be preserved intact and centralization of power averted. The idea that war alone would abolish slavery, if it lasted long enough, was popular among conservative and moderate Republicans and among some Democrats during the early stages of the war. In July, 1862, Lincoln explained this theory, warning congressmen from the loyal slave states that the "mere friction and abrasion" of armed conflict would extinguish slavery in their states. The same reasoning would have had even greater application to the Confederate states.[13]

But even as he uttered these words, Lincoln's conservatism was being eroded by the want of military success, by the reluctance of the border slave states to accept his plan of emancipation, and by the mounting radicalism of Congress. Under heavy pressure from radical Republicans who were by then obviously strong enough to pass the stringent confiscation bill, Lincoln was already groping for a bolder, more positive approach to slavery in the Confederacy. Shortly after McClellan's retreat from Richmond, the President mused that he would issue an edict of emancipation "if I were not afraid that half the officers would fling down their arms and three more states would rise [rebel]." Even this reservation was weakening. On July 13, 1862, he disclosed to Secretary of State William Seward and Secretary of the Navy Gideon Welles that he had almost decided that an emancipation proclamation was a "military necessity." "He had," Welles recorded in his diary, "given it much thought and had about come to the conclusion that ... we must free the slaves or be ourselves subdued." Nine days later Lincoln made known to his cabinet his intention of proclaiming the freedom of all slaves in the states that were still in rebellion on January 1, 1863 [14]

Lincoln then turned to the chore of preparing the North for the emancipation proclamation. This was a towering challenge. With the Midwest, and perhaps most of the nation as well, overwhelmingly opposed to fighting a war primarily to free the slaves, he knew that popular acceptance of such a decree would hinge partially upon his ability to convince the people that it was a military necessity and thus essential to the salvation of the Union. Nor was this all. With unrest over the race question steadily rising, he also knew that public approval of slave liberation would depend to a great extent upon his ability to put forth suitable solutions to two great, closely-related problems confronting the administration: providing for the Negroes being freed by the war and the long-range task of racial adjustment.

The first of these problems had long perplexed the commander-in-chief. For some time, Lincoln had been aware of the military difficulties involved in feeding, clothing, controlling, and protecting the slaves seeking refuge in Union lines. In fact, part of his reluctance to issue an emancipation proclamation seems to have stemmed from his awareness of the burdensome consequences that would probably follow a heavy influx of Negroes into the Union military lines.[15] Lincoln had established no uniform policy governing the army's disposition of southern slaves. Army commanders in the field were usually allowed to deal with the slaves as they chose. A variety of different policies had resulted. Some generals refused to allow runaway slaves to enter their lines; others enticed bondsmen away from their masters; a few made attempts, usually abortive, to arm the fugitives; and still others employed them as laborers.[16]

By the time Lincoln decided upon his emancipation proclamation, the vagrant slaves had become a major political issue as well as a troublesome military problem. Pressures for a statement of administration policy increased throughout the summer of 1862. Many Republicans demanded that Negroes be mustered into the military service and armed. At the opposite pole, many Democrats and Republicans opposed the enrolment of Negroes; numerous Democrats even complained that the government was wasting time and money in caring for black refugees who were impeding troop movements and the war effort. The situation in the field was equally pressing, with Union generals appealing to Washington for guidance as more and more slaves entered their lines.[17] The number of blacks who were already congregating around federal camps was expected to multiply under the terms of the Confiscation Act of July, 1862.

In spite of this pressure, it was only after he had decided to proclaim freedom that Lincoln suddenly gave instructions for handling southern slaves. As late as July 3, 1862, he had refused to commit himself. Yet on July 21, 1862, only eight days after he informed Seward and Welles of his decision to proclaim emancipation, he advised his cabinet that he had prepared a directive granting the military arm the authority to use Negroes as laborers.[18] After resisting such a pronouncement for more than a year, it was no coincidence that Lincoln acted when he did. Instead, his action was triggered by the need to adjust military policy to the Confiscation Act and to the forthcoming emancipation proclamation, which he anticipated would draw a great increase of slaves into the federal lines, and also by the desire to justify liberation as a positive asset.[19] Previously, it had been hard to demonstrate that emancipation would be a source of strength to the Union. Although the hope of freedom had withdrawn black laborers from the rebels, this had proven to be a dubious blessing. Many of the refugees remained with the army, relied on the federal commissary for support, and hampered rather than helped military operations. Some wandered aimlessly from place to place suffering from want and disease. Still others had moved into the North. A new approach was plainly required.

It was in response to these conditions that Lincoln made public his new policy. On August 4, 1862, he divulged that he "would employ all colored men offered as laborers, but would not promise to make soldiers of them." Arming the Negro, he argued, "would turn 50,000 bayonets from the loyal Border States against us." He took this occasion to reassure his radical critics that he would vigorously prosecute the war and carry out the confiscation laws. Less than two weeks later, Secretary of War Edwin M. Stanton ordered military and naval commanders to employ as many southern Negroes as laborers as they could advantageously use. Then came a puzzling order from the Department of War. On August 25, 1862, the Secretary of War authorized General Rufus Saxton, operating in South Carolina, to arm and equip not more than 5,000 men of color.[20] Whether this order signified a new departure on Lincoln's part is unknown. He did not countermand it or publicly comment upon it, and in view of the President's well-known previous opposition to activating Negroes as soldiers, it is difficult to believe that Stanton would have issued such an order without the approval or knowledge of his chief. It seems likely that this directive was a trial balloon sent up by Stanton, closely watched by Lincoln, to test the popular reaction to the government's enlistment of Negro soldiers, and at the same time to conciliate the radicals.[21]

Despite the apparent confusion, the administration's plan for providing for southern slaves was finally on record. It skilfully combined political and military expediency. Although it did not give beleagured commanders instructions for caring for those refugees who were unable to work, it potentially supplied them with a massive supply of labor and established a policy of utilizing some of the Negroes for military purposes. From a political standpoint, it was masterful: it offered something to almost everyone. While Lincoln's public opposition to arming the slaves pleased northern conservatives, his promise to enforce confiscation and his order to use the blacks as military laborers heartened the radicals. They were even more encouraged by Stanton's authorization to recruit Negro troops and by Lincoln's ensuing silence. At the very least, this strongly implied that the President was becoming more receptive to the idea of recruiting black soldiers. Of equal political importance, the call for the employment of Negroes provided the North with an imperfect but partial answer to the question of dealing with the freedmen and fugitive slaves. This solution, based on the extensive use of southern blacks on their native soil, would offer a military justification for emancipation, and it would help to assuage fears that a northward exodus of freedmen from the South would follow liberation.

On the same day that Lincoln announced his intention of using freedmen as laborers, he once again turned to colonization—his favorite answer to the race problem. On July 21, 1862, the President advised the cabinet that he was considering an executive order on colonization; but he changed his mind the next day and apparently dropped the plan. Later that same month, Assistant Secretary of the Interior John P. Usher of Indiana revived a movement to get the President's approval of a scheme to transport the Negroes to the Chiriqui land grant in Central America. In a letter to a fellow Indiana colonizationist, Usher begged Colonel Richard W. Thompson, a friend of Lincoln's, to come to Washington to lobby for the project. Thompson, he said, should ask Senator Wright, who was highly esteemed by the President, to write a letter to the Secretary of the Interior "urging . . . an immediate arrangement for the colonization of the blacks, as that will enable our friends to show that there will be no danger of an influx of that population among us. . . . *The colonization is to be done with the rebels' money.* I think much can be made of it upon the stump."[22]

Whether Thompson saw Wright is not known, but it is known that the Senator supported colonization in a letter written to Lincoln on August 18, 1862. While he campaigned for the Union party in Indiana and Illinois, Wright gave the President some advice on political tactics. The administration should confiscate rebel property, he maintained, and then it "must meet these *Rebel* Democrats with the statement, that we intend to colonize every slave of the Rebels made free by the sale of his master's property. Then faith is strong we shall succeed." In the meantime, Usher himself had pressed the matter. On August 2, 1862, he urged Lincoln to accept a proposition for colonizing the freedmen in Chiriqui, because it would allay apprehensions that the North was going to be overrun by free Negroes.[23]

Twelve days later the President publicly reaffirmed his stand on colonization. At a widely publicized conference with a group of colored men, he said that hopes for freedom would be greatly enhanced if some free Negroes would agree to be colonized. "There is an unwillingness on the part of our people, harsh as it may be, for you free colored people to remain with us," he said. "Now if you could give a start to the white people, you would open a wide door for many to be made free."[24] Shortly afterward Lincoln moved to set the languishing program into action. He apparently hoped, if possible, to begin the resettlement movement before issuing the emancipation proclamation. In late August a supporter of the Chiriqui proposal, Senator S. C. Pomeroy of Kansas, asserted that Lincoln would issue the proclamation as soon as he was assured that the deportation project would succeed. Under the watchful eye of the President, the Secretary of the Interior signed a contract on September 12, 1862, with the promoter of the Chiriqui scheme.[25]

Lincoln was then and is now criticized for espousing colonization. In 1862 deportation was often condemned as an inhumane and impractical illusion. One of the most determined foes of the movement,

Secretary of the Treasury Salmon P. Chase, complained in his diary about Lincoln's urging the freedmen to accept resettlement abroad. "How much better," he wrote piously, "would be a manly protest against prejudice against color!—and a wise effort to give homes in America!" Ironically, only fifteen days had elapsed since Chase had advised General Butler to decree emancipation along the Gulf partly in order to remove the Negroes from the North.[26]

Modern critics who denounce the program as unrealistic and illusory[27] have underestimated Lincoln, for colonization was not only an attempt at racial harmony; it was also a political weapon. Although he was a sincere believer in deportation, Lincoln undoubtedly knew that he had little to lose and much to gain by supporting the removal of the Negro race, whether the plan succeeded or failed. This strategic position had long been evident to midwestern Republicans. Before the war began, an Ohio Republican congratulated Senator Benjamin F. Wade for advocating colonization. "I believe practically it is a d-n humbug [.] But it will take with the people," he wrote. "If we are to have no more slave states what the devil are we to do with the surplus niggers? Your plan will help us out on this point. But practically I have not much faith in it [.] You could not raise twenty five cents from a Yankee to transport a Nigger to South America." In 1862 a keen observer of Wisconsin politics made the point a little differently in a letter to Senator Doolittle. While all men did not agree that colonization was practical or necessary, he doubted "whether there is one who will oppose you on that score. On the other hand there are many who have great faith in it, and who if not before friendly would be apt to support you for that reason."[28]

The urgent attention given colonization, after Lincoln decided upon his proclamation, and the timing of both his interview with the Negroes and of the signing of the contract all indicate that the President was, in fact, acting to calm northern fears of wholesale Negro migration from the South as well as to promote his pet project. These activities, duly reported in the press, were partly designed to smooth the way for the emancipation proclamation. Moreover, the race for the fall elections was under way and the Democrats were capitalizing on the Negro immigration issue. By committing his administration to deportation, the President hoped to convince the voters that the Republican party held the answer to the race problem—an answer which would reconcile freedom for the slaves and white supremacy.

Finally, Lincoln prepared the people for emancipation by waging a skilful campaign of education in the press, openly suggesting that sterner measures might have to be taken to save the nation. But in sounding this note he made it plain that he would be guided solely by the needs of the Union. Horace Greeley, editor of the New York *Tribune* and an oracle of the abolitionist press, supplied an ideal opportunity for the President to convey this message. When Greeley, in his "Prayer of Twenty Millions," lectured Lincoln for being too easy on slavery, the President countered on August 22, 1862, with a pithy statement of his views. He would save the Union "the shortest way under the Constitution," with or without slavery, he said; patriotism and military necessity rather than politics, moral judgments, or his personal wishes would determine his course. He closed his rebuttal with his *"personal* wish that all men could be free."[29]

While this open letter to Greeley did not expose Lincoln's purpose of proclaiming emancipation, it marked a new tack for him. For the first time he had publicly admitted that he felt that he possessed the constitutional power to hit harder at slavery, and that he would do so if the welfare of the Union required it. Later, he went even further. On September 13, 1862, in a discussion with two Chicago ministers who presented memorials calling for national emancipation, Lincoln candidly refined his views. In weighing the advantages and disadvantages of freeing the slaves, he declared that he had the legal right to proclaim liberty; that he viewed it as a "practical war measure"; that he had the matter under consideration; that he would do whatever appeared to be God's bidding; and that slavery was the "root of the rebellion or at least its *sine qua non.*"[30]

Before this interview was published, the Army of the Potomac forced Lee's Confederate army out of Maryland, and Lincoln seized upon this victory to issue on September 22, 1862, his Preliminary Proclamation of Emancipation. In it, he again pledged to ask Congress to give financial help to states adopting gradual emancipation and that efforts toward colonization would continue. Yet on the whole the proclamation was a dramatic change in direction for the administration. The key sentence declared that slaves in any "state, or designated part of a state" still in rebellion on January 1, 1863, would be considered free.[31] While this ultimatum did not go beyond the Confiscation Act of 1862, and the final decree was even more limited in scope, this was the first official notice that Lincoln was reversing his stand of non-interference with slavery in the states.

In its wording, the proclamation was the logical extension of Lincoln's insistence that it was purely a military necessity; the document was devoid of humanitarian and moral preachments. The President firmly grounded his action on national expediency by opening with the declaration that the restoration of the Union remained the object of the war. He had, in fact, originally conceived of the emancipation order as a way of depriving the rebels of their black laborers and of forestalling foreign recognition of the Confederacy. Although these motives were still dominant, Lincoln was privately showing the first signs of a growing tendency to interpret both the war's meaning and his own role in it in the language of the abolitionists.

Lincoln's statement in September, 1862, that slavery was the cause or the *sine qua non* of the rebellion was a key article in the abolitionists' creed. Like many of the radical spirits he was also beginning to believe that he was the instrument of a righteous God—a God who was ordering him to destroy slavery. It was, after all, only a short step from the belief that slavery was morally wrong to the conviction that the war was a scourge sent by the Lord to punish a wicked nation for the sin. On September 13, 1862, Lincoln stated that his action regarding slavery would depend on "Whatever shall appear to be God's will." When the President later announced his final decision to issue the preliminary proclamation, Gideon Welles wrote that Lincoln had explained to his cabinet that he had made "a vow, a covenant," that if God made the Union army victorious in Maryland, "he would consider it an indication of Divine will, and that it was his duty to move forward in the cause of emancipation. . . . God had decided the question in favor of the slaves. He was satisfied it was right and confirmed and strengthened in his action by the vow and the results."[32] But if Lincoln the fatalist was becoming the sword of the Lord, Lincoln the supreme pragmatist allowed none of these sentiments to creep into the proclamation because of the fear that the people of the North were not yet ready to occupy such high ground.

With the publication of the Preliminary Emancipation Proclamation, the outlines of a comprehensive plan for dealing with slavery and race were visible. Though some of the lines were vague, Lincoln had finally developed a policy that attacked these problems on a broad front. The principles of his old program remained constant: gradual voluntary emancipation with compensation and colonization were still his avowed goals. Certain new elements were strikingly bold, especially that of proclaiming freedom to the slaves in the Confederacy. With measured and timely words he had attempted to prepare the people for this stroke by basing it on military expediency and by offering some possible answers to the race problem. In the Midwest, the test of his strategy would come in the fall elections.

Notes

1. *Herald* (Dubuque), June 13, 22, 1862; *Enquirer* (Cincinnati) quoted in *Herald* (Dubuque), June 26, 1862; *Times* (Chicago), June 28, 1862.

2. *Times* (Chicago), July 15, 1862; *Tribune* (Chicago), August 10, 1862; *Crisis* (Columbus), July 16, 1862; Charles R. Wilson, "Cincinnati's Reputation During the Civil War," *Journal of Southern History,* II (November, 1936), 478–79; W. M. Dickson to Lew Wallace, January 26, 1864, Wallace Collection (Indiana State Historical Society, Indiana State Historical Library, Indianapolis).

3. *Ledger* (New Albany), August 4, 1862, quoted in Emma Lou Thornbrough, *The Negro in Indiana: A Study of a Minority* (Indianapolis: Indiana Historical Bureau, 1957), pp. 185–87; *Tribune* (Chicago), July 15, 1862; *Times* (Chicago), July 15, 1862; *Union* (Peoria) quoted in *Times* (Chicago), July 24, 1862.

4. *Herald* (Dubuque), July 22, 1862; *Crisis* (Columbus), July 9, 1862.

5. *Illinois State Journal* (Springfield), September 11, 1862; *Journal* (Indianapolis), July 31, 1862; *Address to the People by the Democracy of Wisconsin, Adopted in State Convention at Milwaukee, Sept. 3d, 1862* ([Madison, 1862]), p. 3, pamphlet in Moses M. Strong Papers (Wisconsin State Historical Society, Madison).

6. Browning to Abraham Lincoln, August 11, 25, 1862, Robert Todd Lincoln Collection (Manuscript Division, Library of Congress); Wright to Lincoln, August 18, 1862, Joseph A. Wright Collection (Indiana Division, Indiana State Historical Library, Indianapolis); Chandler to Lincoln, August 8, 1862, R. T. Lincoln Collection; William Salter, *The Life of James W. Grimes* (New York: D. Appleton, 1876), pp. 215–16.

7. John Sherman to W. T. Sherman, August 8, 24, 1862, William Tecumseh Sherman Papers (Manuscript Division, Library of Congress).

8. *Times* (Dubuque), July 27, 1862; *Crisis* (Columbus), August 27,

1862; *American Annual Cyclopaedia and Register of Important Events of the Year, 1862* (New York: D. Appleton, 1872), pp. 519–20, 528.

9. Theodore Calvin Pease and James G. Randall (eds.), *The Diary of Orville Hickman Browning* (2 vols.; Springfield: Illinois State Historical Library, 1927–33), I, 555.

10. "Annual Message to Congress," December 3, 1861, in Roy P. Basler (ed.), *The Collected Works of Abraham Lincoln* (9 vols.; New Brunswick, N.J.: Rutgers University Press, 1953), V, 48; Richard N. Current, *The Lincoln Nobody Knows* (New York: McGraw-Hill, 1958), pp. 221–22.

11. "Message to Congress," April 16, 1862, in Basler (ed.), *The Collected Works of Abraham Lincoln*, V, 192; Doolittle to Mary Doolittle, April 29, 1862, James R. Doolittle Papers (Wisconsin State Historical Society, Madison); Pease and Randall (eds.), *The Diary of Orville Hickman Browning*, I, 541.

12. The influence of fatalism upon Lincoln is examined, though not precisely in this context, in Current, *The Lincoln Nobody Knows*, pp. 71–75, and in James G. Randall and Richard N. Current, *Lincoln the President: Last Full Measure* (4 vols.; New York: Dodd, Mead, 1945–55), IV, 370–72.

13. "Appeal to Border State Representatives To Favor Compensated Emancipation," in Basler (ed.), *The Collected Works of Abraham Lincoln*, V, 317–19.

14. Sumner to John Bright, August 5, 1862, in Edward L. Pierce, *Memoir and Letters of Charles Sumner* (4 vols.; Boston: Roberts Bros., 1887–93), IV, 82–83; Howard K. Beale (ed.), *Diary of Gideon Welles: Secretary of the Navy under Lincoln and Johnson* (3 vols.; New York: W. W. Norton, 1960), I, 70–71; *Diary and Correspondence of Salmon P. Chase* (Washington, D.C.: Government Printing Office, 1903), pp. 48–49.

15. For expressions of Lincoln's concern with the refugee problem, see "Reply to Emancipation Memorial Presented by Chicago Christians of All Denominations," September 13, 1862, in Basler (ed.), *The Collected Works of Abraham Lincoln*, V, 420–21, 423; Pease and Randall (eds.), *The Diary of Orville Hickman Browning*, I, 555.

16. Dudley T. Cornish, *The Sable Arm: Negro Troops in the Union Army, 1861–1865* (New York: Longmans, Green, 1956), pp. 17, 24–25, 58.

17. *Ibid.*, pp. 58–59; Pease and Randall (eds.), *The Diary of Orville Hickman Browning*, I, 555.

18. E. M. Stanton to Butler, July 3, 1862, in Jessie Ames Marshall (ed.), *Private and Official Correspondence of General Benjamin F. Butler*

during the Period of the Civil War (5 vols.; Norwood: privately printed, 1917), II, 41–42; *Diary and Correspondence of Salmon P. Chase,* pp. 45–46.

19. For Lincoln's opinion that emancipation would accelerate the exodus of slaves from the Confederacy, see "Reply to Emancipation Memorial Presented by Chicago Christians of All Denominations," September 13, 1862, in Basler (ed.), *The Collected Works of Abraham Lincoln,* V, 423.

20. "Remarks to Deputation of Western Gentlemen," August 4, 1862, in Basler (ed), *The Collected Works of Abraham Lincoln,* V, 356–57; Cornish, *The Sable Arm,* pp. 80–81; General Order 109, U.S., War Department, August 16, 1862, Adjutant General's Office, Record Group 94 (National Archives, Washington, D.C.).

21. Cornish suggests that Stanton's order of August 25 "may have been designed to conciliate abolitionist sentiment in the North and West." Cornish, *The Sable Arm,* pp. 80–81.

22. David Donald (ed.), *Inside Lincoln's Cabinet: The Civil War Diaries of Salmon P. Chase* (New York: Longmans, Green, 1954), pp. 95, 98–99; Usher to Richard W. Thompson, July 25, 1862, Richard W. Thompson Collection (Indiana Division, Indiana State Historical Library, Indianapolis).

23. Wright to Lincoln, August 18, 1862, Wright Collection; John P. Usher to Lincoln, August 2, 1862, R. T. Lincoln Collection; John P. Usher to Margaret Usher, August 10, 1862, Usher Papers (Kansas State Historical Society, Topeka).

24. "Address on Colonization to a Deputation of Negroes," August 14, 1862, in Basler (ed.), *The Collected Works of Abraham Lincoln,* V, 372.

25. Allan Nevins, *The War for the Union* (2 vols.; New York: Charles Scribner's Sons, 1959–60), II, 233; "Approval of Contract with Ambrose W. Thompson," September 11, 1862, in Basler (ed.), *The Collected Works of Abraham Lincoln,* V, 416.

26. Donald (ed.), *Inside Lincoln's Cabinet,* p. 112.

27. Richard Hofstadter, *The American Political Tradition and the Men Who Made It* (New York: Vintage Books, 1949), p. 130; Nevins, *The War for the Union,* II, 10.

28. Dan Tilden to B. F. Wade, quoted in Robert Franklin Durden, *James Shepherd Pike: Republicanism and the American Negro, 1850–1882* (Durham: Duke University Press, 1957), p. 37; C. L. Scholes to J. R. Doolittle, May 20, 1862, Doolittle Papers.

29. "To Horace Greeley," August 22, 1862, in Basler (ed.), *The Collected Works of Abraham Lincoln,* V, 388–89.

30. "Reply to Emancipation Memorial Presented by Chicago Christians of All Denominations," September 13, 1862, in *ibid.*, pp. 419–25.

31. "Preliminary Emancipation Proclamation," September 22, 1862, in *ibid.*, pp. 433–36.

32. "Reply to Emancipation Memorial Presented by Chicago Christians of All Denominations," September 13, 1862, in *ibid.*, p. 425; Beale (ed.), *Diary of Gideon Welles,* I, 143; *Diary and Correspondence of Salmon P. Chase,* p. 88.

❦ [4] ❧

The Elections of 1862

The Preliminary Emancipation Proclamation added a new dimension to the war. With this stroke of Abraham Lincoln's pen, what had been a battle for national sovereignty began to be exalted also as a struggle for human liberty. But the effort to expand the objectives of the war wrought no quick change in the national purpose; rather, it widened the breach between the two political parties and raised the voices of dissent to a greater pitch.

The proclamation of September, 1862, was fraught with political consequences. The radical faction of the Republican party previously had championed emancipation without presidential sanction or support; now the administration was also openly committed to a stringent antislavery policy if the war should continue. No longer could conservative and moderate Republicans veil the increasingly radical character of their party beneath the mantle of Lincoln's moderation. Nor could most Democrats continue to rally behind the President on the grounds that essentially he shared their conservative views on the relationship of slavery to the war. For the first time emancipation was squarely before the people as a partisan issue.

Postmaster-General Montgomery Blair had anticipated that such a development would be unfortunate; at a cabinet meeting on the night before the emancipation order was to be promulgated, he warned the President that it was inexpedient and untimely. Not only would it carry the loyal slave states into the rebel camp, he said; "there was also a class of partisans in the Free States endeavoring to revive old parties, who would have a club put into their hands . . . to beat the Administration." Lincoln replied that he had considered the "first objection, which was undoubtedly serious, but the objection was certainly as great not to act; as regarded the last, it had not much weight with him."[1]

On its face, this cavalier dismissal of Blair's advice concerning an adverse reaction in the North has a tone of altruistic statesmanship about it. Lincoln sounds as if he had risen above such considerations as public opinion, as if he was willing to risk the unpopular because he knew he was in the right. But this does not quite ring true. Actually the President had high expectations that the North's response to the proclamation would be favorable. After the passage of the Confiscation Act of 1862, many War Democrats had rejoined the Democratic party. Having lost much of his conservative support, Lincoln believed he had little left to lose by proclaiming freedom. In this way he could overtake his increasingly radical party and regain the reins of leadership. Then, too, many emancipationists had been urging for months that a sterner antislavery policy would fire the northern heart, put God in the Union camp, and encourage army enlistments by adding the cause of liberty to that of preserving the nation.[2] Though Lincoln was convinced that these claims were exaggerated, he had decided that the proclamation would indeed do more good than harm. He knew that the northern people were not yet ready for a war of liberation; yet he felt that their desperation and hatred of the South had grown so strong that they would welcome an opportunity to strike down slavery in the name of military necessity and the Union.

In the fateful month of September, 1862, Lincoln himself revealed the extent of his hopes. On September 13 he conceded to a delegation of emancipationists that a proclamation of freedom "would help *somewhat* at the North, though not so much, I fear, as you and those you represent imagine. Still, some additional strength would be added in that way to the war." Six days after issuing the preliminary order, the President confided his disappointment to Vice-President Hannibal Hamlin. "It is known to some that while I hope something from the proclamation, my expectations are not as sanguine as are those of some friends. The time for its effect southward has not come; but northward the effect should be instantaneous." Despite the gratifying reception by press and "distinguished individuals," Lincoln complained, "the stocks have declined, troops come forward more slowly than ever. . . . The North responds to the proclamation sufficiently in breath; but breath alone kills no rebels."[3]

Lincoln was only partly correct. The North was responding vocally to the proclamation, but even this kind of response was by no means entirely favorable. In the Midwest Republicans and Unionists greeted the decree with varying degrees of enthusiasm. The radical press was ecstatic. Moderates and conservatives were usually more restrained; some of them practically ignored it, and others suggested that it was unnecessary and poorly timed. On the other hand, Democrats in the Midwest reacted furiously to the proclamation. Most regular midwestern Democrats hotly opposed Lincoln's course; so did numerous War Democrats whose defections from the Union party now increased markedly.[4] Together, they trained their fire on the presidential proclamation and made it one of the major issues of the fall state and congressional elections.

Sustaining a far-ranging political offensive begun in the summer, midwestern Democrats struck at arbitrary arrests, growing federal power, corruption, the enlistment of Negro troops, and concentrated most of all on the conduct of the war, emancipation, and the proclamation. Although Republicans frequently accused them of disloyalty, they ran as a patriotic opposition dedicated to restoring the Union through a more efficient, judicious, and constitutional prosecution of the war. These Democrats distinguished between support for the measures of the Lincoln administration and loyalty to the Union. Calling for the "Union as it was, and the Constitution as it is," they scorned both presidential and congressional emancipation as unconstitutional and hypocritical, and they hurled a familiar barrage of racial objections against liberation. If the slaves should be freed, they would fly to the North to degrade white society, reduce wages, and contaminate politics. In order to preserve white supremacy and to repel the threat of a black invasion, Democrats chorused, the Republican party should be turned out of power before Lincoln could execute his final emancipation proclamation.[5]

Although much of their campaign was directed at emancipation and Negro immigration, Democrats found time to stress several related themes. They sensed the spirit of equalization lurking within every Republican measure or proposal, and they branded the Republicans as "free negro lovers." Demands that blacks be allowed to fight in the Union armies were spurned not only because such action would force white troops into unnatural and repulsive associations but also because Negroes were incapable of becoming effective soldiers. The Indiana Democratic Convention heard Congressman William A. Richardson of Illinois declare that no man of intelligence could believe that the members of "an inferior race" could compete with whites on the battlefield. "In what estimation can you hold that man who tells you that the liberty, independence, and constitutional government of the country depend upon a few miserable, ignorant, cowardly negroes," he asked rhetorically.[6] Another device used by the Democratic press was the "Negro outrage" story. Readers were regaled with reports, often printed under the heading, "Another Negro Outrage," telling of rapes and assaults on whites allegedly being committed by Negroes in the Midwest. These violent crimes and other incidents of social insubordination were described as the final products of the Republican doctrines of emancipation and racial equality.[7]

Democrats also persisted in the cry that the Republicans had perverted the war for Union into a fight for the Negro at the expense of midwestern whites. A prominent Ohio Democrat opened an address in Ohio with the announcement that "every white man in the North, who does not want to be swapped off for a free Nigger, should vote the Democratic ticket." Congressman Clement L. Vallandigham of Ohio, already gaining notoriety as a peacemonger, solemnly charged that the Republicans were diverting rations, clothing, and medical care intended for Union troops to Negro refugees while white soldiers suffered from exposure and hunger. At their state convention, Iowa's Democrats were told that it was an "abolition war, for the freedom of the negro and for the enslavement of the white race."[8]

In spite of their efforts midwestern Democrats were unable to secure a general debate on the racial and moral aspects of emancipation. Republicans sidestepped these questions as much as possible. While they still regarded emancipation as a military expedient above all else, most Republicans of all faiths probably welcomed it for humane and moral reasons as well. Yet after the first outbursts of joy they seldom uttered the higher justifications for destroying slavery. Republican and Union party organizations usually shunned such motives and followed the well-established argument that slave confiscation and emancipation were constitutional war measures that were vitally needed to put down the rebellion and save the nation. With these tactics they again sought to reassure the voters that the war had not become a crusade against slavery, that the restoration of the Union was their only objective.

Few Republicans in the Middle West strayed from this path. The Union party convention in Illinois and the Republican convention in Michigan adopted resolutions commending the emancipation order as an essential war measure, but they passed over all other justifications.[9] At a Union rally in Ohio four of the five speakers simply called the action a military necessity; the other had the temerity to say that it was morally right. Oliver P. Morton, Republican governor of Indiana, ignored all moral reasons for the proclamation and described it as a "stratagem of war."[10] Except for an occasional claim of national emergency, the antislavery measures were largely forgotten for the duration of the campaign by such Republican newspapers as the Springfield *Illinois State Journal*, Columbus *Ohio State Journal*, Indianapolis *Journal*, Milwaukee *Sentinel*, Dubuque *Times*, and the Terre Haute *Wabash Express*.

Republicans took other steps to de-emphasize the emancipation controversy by attempting to make national loyalty the crucial issue in the elections. The real contest was not between slavery and antislavery, they said, but between national sovereignty and disunion, and only a united front could save the country. Supremely confident that theirs was the only road to a reunion, many of them increasingly tended to view any kind of opposition as dangerously misguided at best, as disloyal at worst. Because they believed or professed to believe that the Lincoln administration and the government were one and the same, a great many Republicans were convinced that critics of federal policy were traitors. The verdict seemed to be confirmed by the Democrats' vehement and intemperate attacks on the President and his works, by the presence of avowed peace advocates within their party, and by rumors of internal plots to overthrow the Union. Directly or indirectly stigmatizing their opponents as "Copperheads," "traitors," and "disunionists," Republicans and Unionists called upon the people of the Midwest to lay aside all political partisanship and to rally behind the Union by voting for the party of Lincoln.[11]

In this fashion Republicans and Unionists strove to submerge the slavery issue in the powerful spirit of American nationalism. They could do so without forsaking their antislavery mission, for a commitment to liberty was implicit in the Republican definition of loyalty to the Union. Now that the Republican administration and Congress were both pledged to emancipation, support for the government would in itself insure eventual freedom for the slaves. One Republican stated the case precisely: "Any man who is for the government in this emergency without any mental reservation or qualification covers the whole republican ground *and more too*—for the republican ground has been only opposition to slavery extension, while devotion to the government now is *death to slavery,* and nothing shorter."[12]

Nevertheless, the attack on Republican racial policies was too sharp and too telling to be ignored. Some Republicans did their best to turn it aside with ridicule, claiming that the Democrats had been stricken with a malady variously diagnosed as Negrophobia or "delirium niggers." The disease "not only hardens and thickens the skull, and makes it impervious to a sensible idea, but in addition softens the brain and ends in political idiocy," gibed an Illinois newspaper editor. Another Republican journalist described the symptoms more vividly. Victims of the "distressing mania" believed that they were going to be devoured by the "voracious negro," he taunted. "In whatever direction they turn, the inevitable 'eloshin' [illusion?] leers at them with horrible menace. If they walk the streets, they see him at every corner lying in wait to gulp them down at a swallow. Even in their sleep, images of woolly heads and ivory teeth haunt them."[13]

For the most part, antislavery men chose to ignore charges of egalitarianism, but a few retorted that such accusations were malicious and unfounded. Stung to the quick by allegations that Republican measures would lead to equality of the races and that "our volunteers are periling their lives to make the niggers the equal of whites," the Indianapolis *Journal* exclaimed, "what a monstrous and villainous lie."[14]

Far more attention was devoted to refuting the claim that emancipation would deluge the Midwest with Negroes. Instead of inviting the slaves to seek their liberty in the free states, they again made it clear that they neither wanted nor expected the Negroes to move into the Midwest. To prove their case, a few Republicans pointed to their plans for colonizing the freedmen abroad. Even though colonization had little warm support and some outright opposition at this time, Republican newspapers frequently printed, usually without comment, stories of the administration's efforts at deportation.[15]

But another prescription continued to serve as the favorite treatment for midwestern racial anxiety. A Republican editor in Ohio privately described the remedy to Salmon P. Chase. "They don't want to come North, and we don't want them, unless their coming will promote the conclusion of the war," he wrote. "Our newspapers ought to advocate this view persistently, and demonstrate that even our free colored population would go South if they were secure from sale into slavery." His encouragement was unnecessary. From the antislavery press, pulpit, and platform came the venerable clichés: only the hope of freedom was attracting the slaves into the Midwest; emancipation in the Confederacy would hold them in the land of their labor and lure most of the northern Negroes to the South. The therapy was old, but it had never been applied so assiduously. Over and over again radical and moderate Republicans and Unionists echoed parts or all of this chorus. Among the leading voices were such radicals as Senators James W. Grimes of Iowa and Lyman Trumbull of Illinois, and the editors of the Chicago *Tribune* and the Cleveland *Leader*.[16]

Midwestern Republicans drew strong support from the East in linking liberation with a Negro exodus from the North. Sounding this theme in the East were political weathervanes such as Daniel S. Dickinson of New York, high priests of abolitionism such as Charles Sumner and Governor John A. Andrew of Massachusetts and Cassius M. Clay of Kentucky, antislavery organs such as Henry Ward Beecher's *Independent,* radical Republican spokesmen such as *Harper's Weekly* and George S. Boutwell of Massachusetts, and highly respected magazines such as the *Atlantic Monthly*.[17]

The actions of Governor Andrew gave midwestern Republicans a persuasive talking point. In September, 1862, Major General John A. Dix, Union commander at Fort Monroe, Virginia, asked the governors of Massachusetts, Rhode Island, and Maine for permission to send to their states, before the coming of winter, about 2,000 uprooted Negro men, women, and children under his care who were burdening his troops. Though the governor of Rhode Island apparently wrote a friendly reply, Andrew declined emphatically, suggesting instead that the refugees should remain in the South and receive military training. It would be inhumane to send a people whose habits and "peculiarities of physical constitution" were accustomed to a warm climate to face possible disease and death in the cold and rigorous North; it would also be unwise and unfair, for a congenial welcome and opportunity would be lacking in the region. "For them to come here for encampment or asylum would be to come as paupers or sufferers into a strange land and a climate trying even to its habitues . . . to a busy community where they would be incapable of self-help—a course certain to demoralize themselves and endanger others. Such an event would be a handle to all traitors and to all persons evilly disposed." The failure of the experiment, he concluded, would lead to false charges that the Negroes were incapable of caring for themselves. Dix considered this reply to be so hostile that he decided to drop the entire matter. The radical Andrew was praised in the Midwest for upholding the Republican doctrine of confining the Negroes to the South.[18]

Most of the great religious denominations of the Middle West gave their support to the cause of freedom and the Republican party. Churchmen in the section often took the lead in prodding the government to attack slavery more forcefully. During 1862, most religious bodies, with the exception of the Episcopal and Catholic churches, adopted resolutions either demanding or approving a policy of emancipation as a moral, political, and national necessity.[19] Yet at least some of the eminent theologians who did their best to awaken their followers to the sins of slavery were either blind to their own race prejudice or else they held a narrow view of the gospel of brotherly love. Lyman Abbott, the great Congregationalist minister and emancipationist, stressed that freedom for the slaves would turn the tide of Negro immigration southward. Calvin Kingsley, long a leading antislavery zealot, delivered a similar text in his Cincinnati *Western Christian Advocate,* one of the most popular Methodist publications.[20]

Abbott and Kingsley also rejected the notion that racial equalitarianism was involved in the emancipation movement. "It is not true that the ignorant and the degraded should be invited to participate in Government," Abbott told his Terre Haute congregation in September, 1862. "I would confine . . . Government always to the moral and intelligent. For generations it is probable that the African must be governed." Kingsley offered a somewhat more complex argument. "Where is this social equality, the fruits of which appear in amalgamation, to be found but among the slaveholders of the South?" he asked. "In the North it is a strange and disgusting sight to see a white man with a colored wife. In the South it can be practically seen everywhere. As to political equality, it has nothing whatever to do with the question of emancipation."[21]

Secretary of War Edwin M. Stanton was not so helpful. In the midst of the political campaign, Stanton committed a blunder that partly undermined the program of antislavery education and grievously hampered Republican candidates in the Midwest. Throughout the summer Union troops operating in the Mississippi Valley had channeled hundreds of Negro refugees and freedmen to the federal commander at Cairo, the southernmost town in Illinois. In September the Cairo *Gazette* found that "the levees yesterday were so dark with negroes that pedestrians found it difficult to peregrinate without lanterns." On September 18, 1862, to alleviate this pressure, Stanton authorized the commanding general at Cairo to turn Negro women and children over to committees which would provide them with employment and support in the North.[22]

This order, which violated the Illinois Negro exclusion law, was greeted with dismay. While the Illinois Central Railroad distributed from one to four carloads of Negroes per day across the state, midwestern Democrats took full advantage of their political windfall. Abusing the black "locusts" from the South and describing them as "the first fruits of emancipation," they portrayed the emancipation proclamation and the colonization of Illinois as parts of a Republican plot to Africanize the entire Middle West. According to the Democrats, only Republicans were welcoming and hiring the freedmen. The Chicago *Times* reported: "The abolitionists welcome these negroes with demonstrations of the greatest delight. They seem to regard the time as come when they can inaugurate their doctrine of negro equality." Voters were begged to put down the black invasion by casting their ballots for the Democratic ticket.[23]

Frightened citizens held mass meetings denouncing Stanton's action and the black inundation. A gathering in Pike County condemned the Secretary of War for sending a "worthless negro population" into the Prairie State to supplant white labor and demoralize society. In Quincy, Illinois, it was resolved that white laborers would resist Negro competition "first, under the law; second, at the polls; and third, if both of these fail we will redress our wrongs in such manner as shall seem to us most expedient and practical."[24] Threats made against colored immigrants and persons employing them sent most of the Negroes at Olney fleeing back to Cairo. The mayor of Chicago turned down the army's request that he appoint a committee to assist the incoming Negroes on the grounds that favorable action on the proposal would violate the state's exclusion law and impose hardship upon the working population. The city council sustained the mayor.[25]

Retreating pell-mell, the Republicans explained that the freedmen would only be in Illinois temporarily and that emancipation offered the best hope for getting the Negroes out of the state. After the slaves were freed and the war was over, they would "skedaddle back to the sunny clime of Dixie." Besides, the Democrats had distorted the situation, they said; labor was scarce and only a few Negroes were actually coming into the state; and the Democrats were the real villains of the drama. "We notice that whenever a Tory can pick up a nigger he does so," the Chicago *Tribune* snorted. "The Republicans will generally have nothing to do with them."[26]

Despite their glib rejoinders, Illinois Republicans were in trouble, and they knew it. Leonard Swett, a personal friend of Lincoln and a Unionist candidate for Congress, hastened to say that he was and always had been opposed to the introduction of free Negroes into Illinois. A supporter of the Union party wrote radical Governor Richard Yates that the "scattering of those black throngs should not be allowed if [it] can be avoided. The view . . . here is that if the country should become full of them they may never be removed and with the confirmed prejudices and opinions of our people against the mingling of the blacks among us we shall always have trouble." On October 13, 1862, Yates wired the President, telling him of the damage being done to their cause in Illinois. The next day David Davis, a close friend of Lincoln, advised the President that it was essential that no more Negroes be brought into the state while the elections were pending. "There is danger in the Election here," he added, "growing out of the large number of Republican voters, who have gone to the war . . . and of the negroes, coming into the State." But Stanton, presumably with Lincoln's approval, had already acted on October 13 by forbidding further shipments of blacks out of Cairo. Republican journals now happily announced that the Democrats had been deprived of their sole issue.[27]

The bitter campaign closed at the polls in October and November of 1862. Republicans and Unionists elected a narrow majority to Congress; but in the Midwest the Democrats swept to victory, carrying Ohio, Illinois, and Indiana, and scoring impressive gains in Michigan, Wisconsin, and Minnesota. Only in Iowa, where the opposition was badly split, did the Republicans increase their overall majority over that of 1860; they also captured all six congressional districts. For the federal House of Representatives, the Democrats elected fourteen out of nineteen members from Ohio, seven of eleven in Indiana, nine of fourteen in Illinois, and three out of six in Wisconsin. In Michigan they captured only one of the six openings in Congress, but the incumbent Republican governor's majority of 20,000 in 1860 was whittled down to a 6,600 vote lead in 1862. The next House of Representatives would contain thirty-four Democrats out of a total of sixty-four midwesterners, a gain of eighteen seats for the resurgent party. Democrats also won control of the legislatures in Indiana and Illinois; as a result, Indiana would soon elect two Democrats to the United States Senate, and Illinois one.[28]

Many factors other than emancipation or race inspired the political revolt against the party of Lincoln in 1862. In the Midwest arbitrary arrests by federal authorities, suspension of the habeas corpus privilege, and a disappointing military situation plagued the nominees of the Republican and Union parties.[29] But the emancipation issue with its many ramifications played a leading role in the substantial Democratic gains. Many midwestern Republicans and Unionists conceded its impact. Senator Browning wrote Lincoln that the proclamations suspending the writ of habeas corpus and decreeing emancipation had defeated their party. Senator Sherman contended that the "ill timed proclamation contributed to the general result." Unionist Thomas Ewing maintained that Lincoln's decrees had ruined the Union party in Ohio. Another Ohio Unionist commented that the emancipation order had been a salient factor in their defeat.[30] That clarion of radical Republicanism, the Cleveland *Leader,* asserted that Ohio and Illinois had cast their ballots against freeing the slaves. After first denying that the people had voted against the administration's antislavery policy, the editor of the Republican Indianapolis *Journal* belatedly acknowledged that the election results had indicated that the public was not prepared for such a radical step.[31]

Numerous Republicans, especially radicals, attributed their losses to causes other than emancipation. They blamed Lincoln's political and military ineptitude, his conservatism, military failures in the field, and disloyal Democrats who had stayed at home to vote while the Republicans had gone to fight.[32] A few Republicans, notably Representative Schuyler Colfax of Indiana and Senator Grimes, credited their own successes to the emancipation issue.[33] Most antislavery champions, including Lincoln, were naturally reluctant to admit or perhaps even to believe at the time that the emancipation proclamation had led to the political setback. After the war they were not so reticent. James G. Blaine, Henry Wilson, John Sherman, and Shelby M. Cullom later cited the election results of 1862 as evidence of popular dissatisfaction with Lincoln's order. Horace Greeley also recalled that, while the Democrats had profited in the 1862 elections from war weariness, their "most general and taking clamor deprecated only 'The perversion of the War for the Union into a War for the Negro.' " If a vote on emancipation had been taken, Greeley conceded, the northern people would have voted against it until July, 1863; Lincoln was "probably ahead of the people in the loyal states in definitely accepting the issue of Emancipation."[34] Lincoln evidently agreed. He was later quoted to have said in 1864 that Montgomery Blair had been right in predicting that the Republicans would lose the 1862 elections if liberation was proclaimed.[35]

This opposition to emancipation in 1862 was chiefly the product of Negrophobia aggravated by the threat of a massive influx of Negroes. H. S. Bundy, an unsuccessful Union aspirant for Congress from Ohio, moaned to Secretary of the Treasury Salmon P. Chase that the proclamation had been delivered just in time to defeat him and many other Union candidates in the Indiana and Ohio elections. "I had thought until this year the cry of 'nigger' & 'abolitionism,' were played out but they never had as much power & effect in this part of the state as at the recent elections." The Dubuque *Times* grumbled about the Democrats' use of the Negro immigration issue, declaring that "The election in Burlington was carried for the secesh ticket by '4,000 niggers.' " The radical Janesville, Wisconsin, *Gazette* and the more moderate Milwaukee *Sentinel* admitted that the fear of a Negro infestation had turned the voters against the Republicans.[36]

The Chicago *Tribune* was more ambivalent. Shortly before election day in Illinois, an editorial had interpreted the political reverses in other midwestern states as a signal for the Republican party to re-emphasize its devotion to the "white race." Republicans ought to justify emancipation in terms of its effect upon "the happiness, the freedom and prosperity of the white men of the North," it cautioned. "We need not go beyond that; if we do we bring the prejudices of caste and races into full play, and by weakening the efforts of the North, impair the good the proclamation promises." After the elections the *Tribune* decided that the proclamation had aided Unionist candidates after all. Yet it later referred to the "thousands who were frightened by the clamor of 'nigger invasion.' "[37]

Elated midwestern Democrats hailed the elections as a repudiation of the abolition heresy. The Dubuque *Herald* announced that the popular verdict was "No Emancipation." A headline in the Indianapolis *State Sentinel* reported, "Abolition Slaughtered," and the Democratic paper in Springfield, Illinois, boasted, "The Home of Lincoln Condemns the Proclamation." To the editor of the Columbus *Crisis,* the elections, a contest of "black vs. white," had affirmed that Ohio would never become the refuge for southern Negroes.[38] The Republicans were defeated "by that unwise, ill-timed and seditious proclamation," Samuel S. Cox exulted, and the voters had handed down some new commandments, including one which stated, "Thou shalt not degrade the white race by such intermixtures as emancipation would bring." "The people," an Illinois Democrat told Congress, are "sick and tired of this eternal talk upon the negro and they have expressed their disgust unmistakably in the recent elections."[39]

In the wake of political defeat, midwestern friends of emancipation began a searching reappraisal of the race problem. Humanitarianism, paternalism, and racism often characterized their efforts. As they analyzed the history of anti-Negro feeling, more Republicans reached the conclusion that color was the taproot of racial antipathy. To General John M. Palmer, a Republican who later was elected governor of Illinois, neither freedom nor continued slavery would solve the racial controversy, for he did not "admit Slavery to be the cause of difference. It is the presence of the negro race: a race which the sentiments of our people doom to a condition of racial and political inferiority beyond the reach of all efforts for their elevation." The editor of the Republican Milwaukee *Sentinel* felt that the assumption that the two races could never live on terms of equality in the United States contained much truth. "Whether it is instinct, reason or prejudice, is scarcely profitable to discuss," he observed. "It exists throughout the whole North and time seems to do little or nothing toward modifying it."[40]

Republicans then again turned to the key question: What could be done with the Negro freedmen? Practically all agreed upon two points: foreign colonization was unfeasible, and Negroes were still barred from the North by their own interests, the will of God, nature, and northern hostility.[41] "The border free states . . . are so completely under the influence of color prejudice as to repel them [Negroes]," plaintively remarked Frederick Douglass, the gifted Negro editor, abolitionist, and orator. In a philanthropic appeal for funds to aid freedmen in the South, a Cincinnati relief commission noted that a northward movement of Negroes was "forbidden by their own interests and wishes, . . . by the laws of climate and their own constitution, and [it] is contrary to the plain indications of the providence of God." An Iowa newspaper editor turned down a suggestion that the blacks be taken to the West to work on the Pacific railroad with the explanation that they would not be a homogeneous element there. They were better off where they were, he said, for "it has long been manifest that there was a far greater prejudice existing against association with the negro at the North than at the South."[42]

Where then could the freed Negroes go? The answer was almost unanimous. They could stay in the South where they were understood, where their labor was needed, and where the climate was suited to them. Many Republicans favored letting the natural forces and freedom bring this about. The Chicago *Tribune* voiced a typical opinion when it averred that once the final emancipation proclamation was issued "every fugacious chattel will shape his bearings and route by the Southern Cross instead of the North Star." Others suggested colonizing the Negroes in the South. Eli Thayer of Massachusetts, who wanted the freedmen colonized in Florida "under the friendly guidance of a race superior to himself," found some support in the Midwest from the antislavery editor of a widely read Methodist women's magazine published in Cincinnati who wrote: "A climate like Florida's is their natural home. . . . Were the Negroes to be colonized here under proper oversight, they could be employed with immense profit to themselves and the entire country."[43] Secretary of War Stanton was thinking along the same lines when he proposed a simple way of keeping the Negroes in the South.

Apparently having learned his bitter lesson in the Illinois immigration dispute, Stanton now suggested that the freedmen should be protected in the South while they provided sustenance for themselves and the army; with this "there will be neither occasion nor temptation to them to emigrate to a northern and less congenial climate. Judging by experience, no colored man will leave his home in the South if protected in that home."[44]

Impressed by the North's persistent aversion to the free Negro, President Lincoln labored anew to soothe the fears of his people. In his annual message to Congress in December, 1862, he strongly recommended the adoption of a constitutional amendment calling for compensated emancipation and the voluntary colonization of the freedmen. Both would benefit the northern whites as well as the nation as a whole, he urged. The claim that liberated Negroes would displace white labor he termed "largely imaginary, if not sometimes malicious." If the freedmen should remain where they were, "they jostle no white laborers; if they leave their old places, they leave them open to white laborers." Emancipation alone would probably improve wages, and the colonization of colored workers would certainly increase the earnings of white men.[45]

Lincoln additionally anatomized the belief "that the freed people will swarm forth, and cover the whole land." "Equally distributed among the whites of the whole country . . . there would be but one colored to seven whites," he asserted. "Could the one, in any way, greatly disturb the seven?" This statement is now sometimes applauded as an appeal for the northern people to accept the Negro in their midst. Historian Allan Nevins, for example, feels that the President was asking his constitutents to lay aside their "mean prejudice against colored settlement in their communities."[46] While this may be true, Lincoln's words following this exhortation supplied another antidote. In the same paragraph, he continued:

> But why should emancipation south, send the free people north? People of any color, seldom run, unless there be something to run from. *Heretofore* colored people, to some extent, have fled north from bondage; and *now,* perhaps, from both bondage and destitution. But if gradual emancipation and deportation be adopted, they will have neither to flee from. Their old masters will give them wages . . . till new homes can be found for

them in congenial climes, and with people of their own blood and race. . . . And, in any event, cannot the north decide for itself, whether to receive them?[47]

Thus under the skilful pen of Lincoln, emancipation, colonization, and exclusion became deterrents to a Negro invasion of the North. The elections of 1862 had laid bare the rift in the midwestern psyche. Moral opposition to slavery had helped to bring on the war, and it had later helped to commit Congress and the President to an antislavery policy; but moral principle had not converted the people of the Midwest either to emancipation or equality for Negroes.

Notes

1. Howard K. Beale (ed.), *Diary of Gideon Welles: Secretary of the Navy under Lincoln and Johnson* (3 vols.; New York: W. W. Norton, 1960), I, 143–44.
2. Theodore Calvin Pease and James G. Randall (eds.), *The Diary of Orville Hickman Browning* (2 vols.; Springfield: Illinois State Historical Library, 1927–33), I, 562; *Times* (Dubuque), August 26, 1862; *Sentinel* (Milwaukee), August 1, 23, 1862.
3. Beale (ed.), *Diary of Gideon Welles,* I, 143–44; "Reply to Emancipation Memorial Presented by Chicago Christians of All Denominations," September 13, 1862, in Roy P. Basler (ed.), *The Collected Works of Abraham Lincoln* (9 vols.; New Brunswick, N.J.: Rutgers University Press, 1953), V, 419–25; "To Hannibal Hamlin," September 28, 1862, in *ibid.,* p. 444.
4. Kenneth M. Stampp, *Indiana Politics during the Civil War* (Indianapolis: Indiana Historical Bureau, 1949), pp. 147–48.
5. For examples, see *Free Press* (Detroit), September 28, October 19, 23, 28, 31, November 2, 1862; *Times* (Chicago), September 23, 25, 27, October 3, 1862; *Gazette* (Cairo), August 21, September 27, October 30, 1862; *Crisis* (Columbus), August 13, 27, September 3, 24, October 15, 1862; *Herald* (Dubuque), September 30, October 3, 7, 8, 10, 11, 12, 14, 1862; *State Sentinel* (Indianapolis), October 13, 1862, quoted in Emma Lou Thornbrough, *The Negro in Indiana: A Study of a Minority* (Indianapolis: Indiana Historical Bureau, 1957), pp. 189–90; *See-Bote* (Mil-

waukee), July 9, 23, 1862; *Times* (Oscaloosa, Iowa) quoted in *Times* (Dubuque), September 3, 1862; *Herald* (Quincy, Ill.) quoted in *Gazette* (Cairo), October 30, 1862; *News* (Milwaukee) quoted in *Herald* (Dubuque), October 18, 1862; *News* (Milwaukee) quoted in *Sentinel* (Milwaukee), October 31, 1862.

6. *Free Press* (Detroit), October 19, 23, 28, 31, November 2, 1862; *Herald* (Dubuque), October 8, 10, November 4, 1862; *Times* (Chicago), July 12, September 27, 1862; *Crisis* (Columbus), August 27, October 29, 1862; *Journal* (Indianapolis), October 6, 1862; *See-Bote* (Milwaukee), July 23, 1862.

7. *Crisis* (Columbus), July 9, 30, October 8, 1862; *Herald* (Dubuque), June 19, 1862; Wood Gray, *The Hidden Civil War: The Story of the Copperheads* (New York: Viking Press, 1942), p. 90.

8. *Herald* (Dubuque), July 20, 1862; *Advertiser* (Chillicothe) cited in *Crisis* (Columbus), October 15, 1862; Olynthus B. Clark, *The Politics of Iowa during the Civil War and Reconstruction* (Iowa City: Clio Press, 1911), p. 148.

9. *Journal* (Battle Creek), October 3, 1862; *Free Press* (Detroit), September 25, 1862; *Tribune* (Chicago), September 25, 1862.

10. *Ohio State Journal* (Columbus), October 8, 1862; Stampp, *Indiana Politics during the Civil War,* p. 148.

11. *Journal* (Indianapolis), July 28, 29, 31, October 11, 1862; *Times* (Dubuque), October 8, 9, 10, 11, 14, 1862; *Ohio State Journal* (Columbus), October 14, 1862; *Wabash Express* (Terre Haute), October 2, 3, 4, 8, 11, 13, 1862; Stampp, *Indiana Politics during the Civil War,* pp. 149–50.

12. C. L. Scholes to James R. Doolittle, September 8, 1862, James R. Doolittle Papers (Wisconsin State Historical Society, Madison).

13. *Ohio State Journal* (Columbus), September 4, 1862; *Republican* (Joliet) quoted in *Tribune* (Chicago), November 1, 1862; *Illinois State Journal* (Springfield), October 15, 17, 18, 1862.

14. *Wabash Express* (Terre Haute), September 16, 1862; *Journal* (Indianapolis), October 6, 1862; *Howard Tribune* (Kokomo), October 9, 1862.

15. *Sentinel* (Milwaukee), August 19, September 19, 1862; *Tribune* (Chicago), August 28, 1862; *Times* (Dubuque), August 20, September 2, 6, 26, 1862; *Wabash Express* (Terre Haute), September 18, 1862; *Ohio State Journal* (Columbus), August 28, October 8, 1862; Joseph A. Wright to Abraham Lincoln, August 18, 1862, Joseph A. Wright Collection (Indiana State Historical Society, Indiana State Historical Library, Indianapolis). For expressions of Republican opposition to colonization, see *Sentinel* (Milwaukee), August 30, 1862; *Tribune* (Chicago), August 22, 1862.

16. William D. Bickham to Chase, October 29, 1862, Salmon P. Chase Papers (Manuscript Division, Library of Congress); *Leader* (Cleveland), August 6, 8, 19, 1862; *Howard Tribune* (Kokomo), August 21, 1862; *Tribune* (Chicago), August 7, September 21, 23, October 8, 19, 1862; *Ohio State Journal* (Columbus), September 4, 1862; *Times* (Dubuque), August 21, September 2, 3, 6, 1862; *Sentinel* (Milwaukee), October 10, 31, November 1, 3, 1862; *Torchlight* (Xenia, Ohio), September 17, 1862, quoted in *Crisis* (Columbus), September 24, 1862; *Sonntags-Zeitung* (Chicago), July 27, 1862; *Herald* (Dubuque), September 28, 1862; *Wabash Express* (Terre Haute), September 16, 1862; Edward Younger, *John A. Kasson: Politics and Diplomacy from Lincoln to McKinley* (Iowa City: State Historical Society of Iowa, 1955), p. 136. A few Republicans argued that Negro immigrants could be used to alleviate the labor shortage in the Midwest, but they too usually predicted an exodus of blacks into Dixie. See *Ohio State Journal* (Columbus), August 26, 1862; *Tribune* (Chicago), September 28, October 8, 1862; *Illinois State Journal* (Springfield), September 27, November 3, 1862.

17. *Herald* (New York), August 7, 1862; "The Proclamation of Emancipation," October 6, 1862, in *Works of Charles Sumner* (15 vols.; Boston: Lee and Shepard, 1874), VII, 226–27; *Harper's Weekly*, August 23, 1862, 530–31; Elias H. Derby, "Resources of the South," *Atlantic Monthly*, X (October, 1862), 502–10; *Illinois State Journal* (Springfield), October 17, 1862; *The Liberator* (Boston), October 24, 1862; *Independent* quoted in *The Liberator*, October 24, 1862.

18. *The American Annual Cyclopaedia and Register of Important Events of the Year, 1862* (New York: D. Appleton, 1872), p. 565; U.S., War Department, *The War of the Rebellion: A Compilation of the Official Records of the Union and Confederate Armies* (128 vols.; Washington, D.C.: Government Printing Office, 1880–1901), 1st ser., XVIII, 391, 395, 461 (hereinafter cited as *Official Records*); *Times* (Dubuque), November 13, 1862; *Illinois State Journal* (Springfield), November 13, 19, 1862.

19. *The American Annual Cyclopaedia . . . , 1862,* pp. 188, 255, 580; *Western Christian Advocate* (Cincinnati), July 2, 16, 1862; Davis W. Clark, "The Editor's Table," *Ladies' Repository,* XXII (March, 1862), 190; *ibid.* (October, 1862), p. 640; *Wabash Express* (Terre Haute), September 16, 1862.

20. *Western Christian Advocate* (Cincinnati), October 1, 1862; *Wabash Express* (Terre Haute), September 16, 1862.

21. *Ibid.*

22. *Gazette* (Cairo) quoted in *Crisis* (Columbus), September 17, 1862; *Official Records,* 3d ser., II, 569.

The Elections of 1862

23. Arthur Charles Cole, *The Era of the Civil War, 1848–1870* (Springfield: Illinois Centennial Commission, 1919), p. 334; *Times* (Chicago), September 23, 27, October 9, 10, 1862; *Herald* (Dubuque), September 23, 25, 27, October 3, 1862; *Journal* (Chicago) quoted in *Illinois State Journal* (Springfield), October 11, 1862; Harry E. Pratt, "The Repudiation of Lincoln's War Policy in 1862—Stuart-Swett Congressional Campaign," *Journal of the Illinois State Historical Society,* XXIV (April, 1931), 137.

24. Similar meetings were also held in Wheatland, Illinois, and in Marion, Logan, and Rock Island counties. *Crisis* (Columbus), October 29, 1862; *Times* (Chicago), October 18, November 3, 1862; *Democrat* (Vandalia) quoted in *Times* (Chicago), October 27, 1862; *Herald* (Quincy) quoted in *Times* (Chicago), October 27, 1862; Cole, *The Era of the Civil War, 1848–1870,* p. 334.

25. A. Kitchell to Richard Yates, October 9, 1862, Richard Yates Papers (Illinois State Historical Society, Springfield); *Tribune* (Chicago), September 23, 1862.

26. *Tribune* (Chicago), September 23, 28, October 4, 8, 9, 11, 15, 1862; *Free Democrat* (Carlinville) quoted in *Illinois State Journal* (Springfield), October 11, 1862; *Illinois State Journal* (Springfield), November 3, 1862.

27. A. Kitchell to Richard Yates, October 9, 1862, Yates Papers; David Davis to Abraham Lincoln, October 14, 1862, Robert Todd Lincoln Collection (Manuscript Division, Library of Congress); *Official Records,* 3d ser., II, 663; *Illinois State Journal* (Springfield), October 15, 1862; *Tribune* (Chicago), October 16, 1862; Pratt, "The Repudiation of Lincoln's War Policy in 1862—Stuart-Swett Congressional Campaign," p. 137.

28. *The Tribune Almanac for the Year 1863* (New York: New York Tribune, 1868), pp. 55–62; Gray, *The Hidden Civil War,* p. 108.

29. The issues and the election of 1862 are also treated in Gray, *The Hidden Civil War,* pp. 97–112; Henry Clyde Hubbart, *The Older Middle West, 1840–1880: Its Social, Economic, and Political Life and Sectional Tendencies before, during, and after the Civil War* (New York: D. Appleton-Century Co., 1936), chap. xi; Emma Lou Thornbrough, "The Race Issue in Indiana Politics," *Indiana Magazine of History,* XLVII (June, 1951), 176–79; George H. Porter, *Ohio Politics during the Civil War Period* (New York: Columbia University, 1911), pp. 296–98, 334–35; Allan Nevins, *The War for the Union* (2 vols.; New York: Charles Scribner's Sons, 1959–60), II, 299–322.

30. Pease and Randall (eds.), *The Diary of Orville Hickman Browning,* I, 588–89, 592; John Sherman to William T. Sherman, November 16, 1862, William Tecumseh Sherman Papers (Manuscript Division, Library of Congress); Ohio State Senator Isaac Welsh to Benjamin F. Wade,

70

January 31, 1863, Benjamin F. Wade Papers (Manuscript Division, Library of Congress).

31. *Leader* (Cleveland), November 10, 1862; *Journal* (Indianapolis), November 14, 1864, quoted in Winfred A. Harbison, "Lincoln and the Indiana Republicans, 1861–1862," *Indiana Magazine of History,* XXXIII (September, 1937), 301–2.

32. Lyman Trumbull to Zachariah Chandler, November 9, 1862, Zachariah Chandler Papers (Manuscript Division, Library of Congress); "To Carl Schurz," November 10, 1862, in Basler (ed.), *The Collected Works of Abraham Lincoln,* V, 493–95; John Sherman to W. T. Sherman, November 16, 1862, W. T. Sherman Papers; John Fox Potter to "Dear Edwards," November 24, 1862, John Fox Potter Papers (Wisconsin State Historical Society, Madison); Joseph Medill to O. M. Hatch, October 13, 1862, O. M. Hatch Papers (Illinois State Historical Society, Springfield); *Ohio State Journal* (Columbus), October 21, 1862; *Journal* (Indianapolis), October 17, 1862.

33. James W. Grimes to Gustavus V. Fox, October 24, 1862, in Robert Means Thompson and Richard Wainwright (eds.), *Confidential Correspondence of Gustavus Vaca Fox, Assistant Secretary of the Navy, 1861–1865* (New York: Naval History Society, 1919–20), p. 411; William Salter, *The Life of James W. Grimes* (New York: D. Appleton, 1876), pp. 217–18; Schuyler Colfax to Abraham Lincoln, October 18, 1862, R. T. Lincoln Collection.

34. John Sherman, *John Sherman's Recollections of Forty Years in the House, Senate and Cabinet: An Autobiography* (2 vols.; Chicago: Werner, 1895), I, 330; Henry W. Wilson, *The Rise and Fall of the Slave Power in America* (3 vols.; Boston: Houghton Mifflin, 1872–77), III, 390; Shelby M. Cullom, *Fifty Years of Public Service: Personal Recollections of Shelby M. Cullom* (Chicago: A. C. McClurg, 1911), p. 96; Horace Greeley, *The American Conflict: A History of the Great Rebellion in the United States of America, 1860–'65* (2 vols.; Hartford: O. D. Case, 1865–66), II, 254–55; James G. Blaine, *Twenty Years of Congress: From Lincoln to Garfield* (2 vols.; Norwich: Henry Bill Publishing Co., 1884), I, 441–42.

35. Francis B. Carpenter, *Six Months at the White House with Abraham Lincoln* (New York: Hurd and Houghton, 1867), pp. 87–88.

36. Bundy to Chase, October 18, 1862, Chase Papers; *Times* (Dubuque), October 22, 1862; *Sentinel* (Milwaukee), December 29, 1862.

37. *Tribune* (Chicago), November 2, 3, 16, 18, 1862.

38. *Herald* (Dubuque), October 17, 18, 1862; *State Sentinel* (Indianapolis), October 5, 1862, and *Illinois State Register* (Springfield), November 5, 1862, quoted in Frank L. Klement, *The Copperheads in the*

Middle West (Chicago: University of Chicago Press, 1960), pp. 16–17; *Crisis* (Columbus), October 22, 29, 1862.

39. *Congressional Globe,* 37 Cong., 3d sess., pp. 95, 637, and Appendix, p. 39.

40. Palmer to Trumbull, December 11, 1862, Lyman Trumbull Papers (Manuscript Division, Library of Congress); *Sentinel* (Milwaukee), December 29, 1862.

41. *Sentinel* (Milwaukee), November 26, December 22, 29, 1862; *Times* (Dubuque), November 5, 25, December 12, 1862; *Harper's Weekly,* November 15, 1862; [Alfred H. Guernsey], "The Editor's Table," *Harper's New Monthly Magazine,* XXV (November, 1862), 846.

42. "What Shall Be Done with the Freed Slaves?" November, 1862, *Douglass' Monthly,* in Philip S. Foner, *Life and Writings of Frederick Douglass* (4 vols.; New York: International Publishers, 1950–55), III, 298–99; *Times* (Dubuque), December 20, 1862; William D. Bickham to Salmon P. Chase, October 29, 1862, Chase Papers (Library of Congress); handbill printed by the Contrabands' Relief Commission of Cincinnati, December 9, 1862, in U.S., War Department, Adjutant General's Office, Record Group 94 (National Archives, Washington, D.C.).

43. *Sentinel* (Milwaukee), December 22, 29, 1862; *Times* (Dubuque), December 12, 20, 1862; *Tribune* (Chicago), December 6, 1862; Davis W. Clark, "The Editor's Table," *Ladies' Repository,* XXII (December, 1862), 757.

44. "Report of the Secretary of War," December 2, 1862, *Congressional Globe,* 37 Cong., 3d sess., Appendix, p. 32.

45. "Annual Message to Congress," December 1, 1862, in Basler (ed.), *The Collected Works of Abraham Lincoln,* V, 533–37.

46. Nevins, *The War for the Union,* II, 338.

47. "Annual Message to Congress," December 1, 1862, in Basler (ed.), *The Collected Works of Abraham Lincoln,* V, 535–36.

5

The Crusade Proclaimed

With the elections out of the way, the nation anxiously watched to ascertain whether the political losses in the Midwest and elsewhere had weakened Abraham Lincoln's resolve to issue a definitive proclamation of emancipation. The sign was not long in coming; apparently he had not been budged by the election returns.

In his message to Congress on December 1, 1862, Lincoln announced that only the adoption of a plan to abolish slavery followed by the restoration of the Union would forestall a final emancipation proclamation. His proposal for ending slavery and the war hinged on the acceptance of two constitutional amendments which he recommended to Congress: one providing for federal aid to states adopting gradual emancipation with compensation and another sanctioning congressional support of voluntary Negro colonization. But the President warned that neither the war "nor proceedings under the proclamation of September 22, 1862, [will] be stayed because of the recommendation of this plan. Its timely *adoption,* I doubt not, would bring restoration and thereby stay both."[1]

There is an unrealistic note in this. Under the prevalent theory that secession was unconstitutional, the adoption of Lincoln's recommendations required the overwhelming support of Congress, the unanimous consent of all the loyal states, and the backing of two rebel states—an illusory hope at best. And as Senator Browning pointed out, "If there was no opposition to it, it would require at least four years to have it adopted as he proposes."[2] Lincoln's reasons for bringing forth this improbable plan are unknown. Perhaps he was simply carrying out his promise, made in the preliminary proclamation, to continue the quest for compensated emancipation and colonization. Whatever his motives may have been, he shrewdly, and with the voice of conciliation and reason, drove home his main point—slavery must die in order to save the Union. He offered no alternative. If Congress and the states did not accept the anti-slavery amendments, he would abolish slavery in the Confederacy by executive action and the sword.

During the month that elapsed between this message to Congress and January 1, 1863, the date set for the final proclamation, Democrats and Republicans alike debated Lincoln's antislavery program. In the lame duck Congress then in session, midwestern Democrats boasted that the people had voted against the Republicans' racial policies; they condemned both compensation for slaveowners and colonization on the grounds that they would be financed by levying taxes on the "overburdened" whites; and they again warned that a Negro inundation of the North would follow emancipation.[3] Though most midwestern Republicans were either indifferent or hostile toward compensated emancipation and deportation, they warmly approved, at least publicly, the rest of the President's stand against slavery. Senator Henry S. Lane of Indiana reported that the elections had gone badly because of the administration's lack of vigor and direction; but that the Preliminary Emancipation Proclamation had remedied this situation by giving the nation a sense of purpose; and that the decree had been "hailed with joy all over [Indiana], as the beginning of a new era." On December 15, 1862, the House gave Lincoln an important vote of confidence by passing, largely along party lines, a resolution praising the September proclamation as a constitutional war measure.[4]

Behind the façade of Republican unity was a divided party. There were those who, fearing adverse public opinion, importuned the President to withhold the final liberation order; there were those who, doubting Lincoln's constancy under popular pressure, urged him to hold fast to his course. On January 1, 1863, Lincoln dispelled all doubts when he proclaimed that slaves within areas still under Confederate control were free. Tennessee and certain parts of Virginia and Louisiana—regions that were inside Union lines—were excluded from the provisions of the order. The Emancipation Proclamation sounded no ringing indictment of slavery. Instead, basing his action on military necessity, Lincoln described it "as a fit and necessary war measure for suppressing [the] rebellion."[5] Both the territorial restrictions and the lack of a righteous condemnation of slavery have brought Lincoln under fire from some historians. One of these critics has concluded that the proclamation contained "all the moral grandeur of a bill of lading"; another has suggested that Lincoln may have been a half-hearted and even reluctant emancipator.[6]

Yet it is often overlooked that Lincoln did assert some moral leadership. Twice in late December, Sumner had begged the President to acknowledge that while the Emancipation Proclamation was an "act of military necessity & self-defense, it was also an act of justice and humanity, which must have the blessings of a benevolent God." Secretary Chase had offered similar advice and, with only minor alterations, the President finally accepted a paragraph submitted by him as the conclusion of his historic order. "And upon this act," he wrote, "sincerely believed to be an act of justice, warranted by the Constitution, upon military necessity, I invoke the considerate judgment of mankind, and the gracious favor of Almighty God."[7] Lincoln, Chase, and Sumner doubtless regarded this statement as a meaningful step toward higher ground.

At any rate, Lincoln can be cleared of charges of callousness or indifference. As he later explained, the territorial exemptions in the proclamation were made because the order "has no constitutional or legal justification, except as a military measure."[8] By the same token, he was, to some extent, merely protecting the legal basis of the decree in refraining from a sweeping ethical justification of emancipation. But his motives went deeper. He cast the order largely in cold legal prose in part because he still feared that the northern people would accept freedom for the slaves only as a military necessity. To go further than he did would have tinged the proclamation with abolitionism. Later in the war Lincoln would more boldly exert moral leadership, often indicting the tyranny of slavery; the time was not now ripe for such action.

In the Midwest, the reasons for Lincoln's strategy were obvious. The people of that section were in an unhappy mood at the time the final proclamation was executed. In October and November they had repudiated the administration at the polls, and the military situation had further deteriorated since then. In December, 1862, General Robert E. Lee soundly whipped General Ambrose Burnside's Union army at Fredericksburg. In early January, 1863, Confederate forces in a battle at Murfreesboro, Tennessee, inflicted 13,000 casualties on Union troops, many of them from the Middle West. Then in May came news of the defeat at Chancellorsville. Despair and defeatism clouded much of the Midwest. In this gloomy atmosphere, the reaction to the Emancipation Proclamation burst swiftly.

If emancipationists believed the plea of military necessity would allay midwestern opposition to freeing the slaves, their hopes were quickly dashed. The proclamation merely intensified the anger of the Democrats. Outspoken Democratic critics of Lincoln—increasingly known as "Copperheads"—now became more numerous and more caustic. Congressman Clement L. Vallandigham of Ohio, Samuel Medary of the Columbus *Crisis,* and Dennis A. Mahony of the Dubuque *Democratic Herald,* long bitter critics of Lincoln and abolitionism, grew more violent and abusive. They were joined by some of the milder opponents of the administration who were apparently driven into Copperheadism by the antislavery policy. Wilbur F. Storey of the Chicago *Times,* Henry N. Walker of the Detroit *Free Press,* Marcus Mills "Brick" Pomeroy of the La Crosse, Wisconsin, *Democrat,* and Charles H. Lanphier of the Springfield *Illinois State Register,* all of whom had always been hostile to federal emancipation but comparatively moderate in their criticism of Lincoln until the Preliminary Emancipation Proclamation, now emerged as full-fledged Copperheads.[9]

Although midwestern Democrats continued to complain of the denial of civil rights, the loss of state rights, and conscription, much of their fire in the early months of 1863 was still focused on the emancipation and race issues. Led in the House by Representatives Samuel S. Cox, George H. Pendleton of Ohio, and Daniel Voorhees of Indiana, and in the Senate by Senators David Turpie of Indiana and William A. Richardson, Democratic congressmen loosed a familiar volley of constitutional and racial objections at emancipation and the presidential proclamation, railed at Negro immigration, accused the Republicans of egalitarianism, and fought bills to enlist colored soldiers.[10] Party spokesmen and meetings in the Midwest followed suit.[11]

Democrats gave special attention to the charge that the Republican party was striving toward racial equality; that the Emancipation Proclamation was a long stride in that direction. The Chicago *Times* described the proclamation as "a wicked, atrocious and revolting deed," which had transformed a constitutional war into a struggle "for the liberation of three million negro barbarians and their enfranchisement as citizens." Calling Lincoln a "half-witted usurper," and "Dictator," Samuel Medary denounced "the monstrous, impudent and heinous Abolition proceeding. . . . It is impudent and insulting to God as to man, for it declares those 'equal' whom God created unequal."[12] Raising the terrible cry of "racial amalgamation," Democratic editors alleged that Republicans were also encouraging social contact between the races and were actively promoting miscegenation, the most dreaded form of equality. If this development were not arrested, Democrats feared for the purity of the Anglo-Saxon race. Asserting that Republicanism and "mongrelism" went hand in hand, an Iowa editor mourned, "The attempt to equalize the black and white races . . . [would destroy] the identity of both and substitute in their stead human mongrels in which the characteristic traits of the white race would be absorbed in the more brutal instincts of the negro."[13]

Newly-elected Democratic legislatures in Indiana and Illinois did their part to embarrass the administration, even though final action on much of their program was blocked by irregular tactics employed by the Republican governors and Unionist minorities in these states. Democratic lawmakers in Indiana introduced resolutions demanding the withdrawal of the Emancipation Proclamation, objecting to compensated emancipation and proposals to arm Negroes, and instructing the state's congressional delegation either to oppose emancipation or resign. A resolution introduced in the Indiana Senate stated that the war was filling the North with a "vagabond and servile race"; that attempts to interfere with the "locality and condition" of Negroes and send them into the North were "flagrant violations of the constitution." Democrats also tried but failed to pass a more stringent exclusion law making it a felony, punishable by imprisonment from two to ten years, for a Negro to remain in Indiana after being convicted of illegally entering the state.[14]

Illinois Democrats also took the offensive. A proposition introduced in the state Senate provided that each Negro unlawfully coming into Illinois "shall receive thirty-nine lashes on the bare back." The lower house passed a bill to make the state's Negro exclusion law more effective. On February 13, 1863, that same body adopted a series of resolutions condemning the Emancipation Proclamation, the unconstitutional prosecution of the war, proposals to tax the whites in order to free and elevate the blacks, and the transportation of Negroes into Illinois.[15]

Some midwestern Democrats adroitly used the emancipation and race issues to rally support for making peace. From the start of the war, some Democrats had insisted that compromise and conciliation rather than coercion would best restore the Union; but their voices had been overwhelmed by hopes of quick victory. Thriving on the pessimism and weariness of early 1863, the peace movement burgeoned and reached its peak in the Midwest. Shedding much of their timidity of the past, the promoters of compromise now demanded that the government take steps toward ending the war. These men were not pro-Confederate; they abhorred secession, and they still wanted peace on the basis of union, but their plans for achieving it were vague and usually visionary. Some claimed that the cessation of hostilities would, in some mysterious way, unite the country; others called for a national convention to settle sectional differences; and a small minority, captained by the messianic Clement L. Vallandigham in the Midwest, pleaded for an armistice, hoping that time would heal the nation's wounds and eventually bring reunion.[16]

Peace Democrats argued that the conversion of the war for Union into an abolition crusade had released the people from their obligation to support the war. In adopting resolutions calling for a national peace convention, Democrats in the lower house of the Illinois legislature resolved that "the further prosecution of the present war cannot result in the restoration of the Union and the preservation of the Constitution as our fathers made it, unless the President's Emancipation Proclamation is withdrawn." On January 14, 1863, as he urged an armistice, Vallandigham declared that the West resented fighting an antislavery war. Drawing on the proslavery argument, he contended that his section believed "in the subordination of the negro race to the white where they both exist together, and that the condition of subordination in the South, is far better in every way for the negro than the hard servitude of poverty, degradation, and crime to which he is subjected in the free States."[17] Peace-minded editors also appealed freely to Negrophobia. Two of the Midwest's most outspoken peace journals, the Columbus *Crisis* and the Dubuque *Democratic Herald,* continually reviled the Negro and emancipation while they promoted opposition to the administration and the war.[18]

On the other hand, the Republican reception of the Emancipation Proclamation was warm and favorable—on the surface. Even such organs as the Columbus *Ohio State Journal* and the Springfield *Illinois State Journal*—newspapers that had usually avoided the emancipation issue during the fall political campaign—now joined with their more advanced colleagues with generous praise for Lincoln's action. Almost without exception, midwestern Republicans again took the position that the proclamation was warranted above all else by the exigencies of war, and some even overlooked or denied that it had any other implications.[19]

Yet the psychological process of raising the moral tone of the Union cause—a process which had begun sluggishly with the September warning order—was accelerated somewhat by Lincoln's final proclamation. Before January 1, 1863, few influential midwestern Republicans had openly urged emancipation except on the grounds of military expediency; but now idealistic justifications for freeing the slaves greatly increased. Those who brought forth such reasons claimed that, while the Emancipation Proclamation was chiefly fashioned to win the war, it was also inspired by other lofty considerations and that it would achieve noble goals. The Republican-controlled Michigan legislature resolved that Lincoln's decree was required by the "necessities of war, as well as by the soundest dictates of humanity." Governor O. P. Morton of Indiana held that it would be important "not only in suppressing the rebellion, but in elevating the character of the nation." To Governor Richard Yates of Illinois, the proclamation was not only a great military measure, it was a humane and Christian act. The editor of the Cleveland *Leader* was enraptured with the decree, avowing that it had drawn the Republic closer to its ultimate utopian state. Although issued "solely as a war-measure," he wrote, "it is [also] . . . a magnificent stride in the march of national progress toward the day of Universal Love and Brotherhood."[20]

Finally, the righteousness of the proclamation was extolled by Republicans who believed that God had ordained emancipation and his prophet, Abraham Lincoln, had done his bidding. An Iowa newspaperman confidently offered the opinion that Lincoln had simply carried out the command of the Lord. The editor of the

Chicago *Tribune* viewed the rebellion as a divine scourge sent to punish the nation for the institution of slavery; the Lord had commanded, " 'Let my people go,' " and Lincoln had responded with the Emancipation Proclamation. After having repeatedly maligned Lincoln for incompetence and stupidity, he cried, "Let us thank God for Abraham Lincoln, and pray that through him the nine other plagues may be averted." The President had uplifted the cause of the Union by relying on the "everlasting Right." No longer was the North basing its efforts to subdue the South "upon the entities of political growth," he wrote, "but upon the eternal verities of God and men, we must succeed." The sanctification of Abraham Lincoln and the exaltation of the war were in the making.[21]

After the first outburst of enthusiasm, however, the glorification of emancipation as a war aim and efforts to infuse the midwestern people with high moral purpose were, for the most part, put aside in the region until after the Union victories at Gettysburg and Vicksburg in July, 1863. With the prospects of final victory dim and with no sign that slave liberation was actually a military asset, most midwesterners were not inclined to embrace any new war aim, however lofty in the abstract, that might prolong the conflict. It was hard for war-weary men whose military fortunes were ebbing to become inspired about embarking on a crusade to free a race whose freedom might pose a threat to their traditional mode of life. And, with the exception of the radical antislavery men who never lost sight of their goal and never doubted their rectitude, it was difficult for a believing people to become imbued with a sense of divine mission as long as the antislavery policy was not being blessed with favorable decisions on the field of battle.

These same forces—the discouraging military situation, anti-Negro feeling, and anxiety over racial adjustment—lay behind the angry reaction to emancipation that reached high tide in the winter and spring of 1863. Rather than leading a great moral offensive against slavery as some had anticipated, Republicans found themselves on the defensive, fearing for their own political survival and for the fate of the Union. To be sure, most of the militant opponents of slavery were delighted with the new course of the war, but some of them were deeply concerned about the state of public opinion. "These are dark hours," Charles Sumner confessed in January. "There are senators full of despair—not I." The situation was so grave that even Joseph Medill, previously an arrogant and implacable critic of Lincoln's slowness, was moved to urge in March of 1863, "Our view is, that we ought to do all we can to strengthen the bonds of the administration until the crisis is past. . . . Let us first get the ship out of the breakers; then court-martial the officers if they deserve it." But if these two radicals were reluctant to identify the cause of dissatisfaction, Senator John P. Hale of New Hampshire was not. Formerly a Free Soil presidential candidate and now a radical Republican, Hale twice admitted in January that his party "had made a great mistake upon the slavery question, and that it would have been better for the cause of the Country, and of emanciaption [if] nothing had been said in regard to the negro since the war commenced."[22]

Moderate Republicans and Unionists not only agreed with Hale; they foresaw disaster. Senator Browning, Senator Doolittle, and Thomas Ewing conferred on January 12, 1863, and, according to Browning, "We all agreed that we were upon the brink of ruin, and could see no hope of an amendment in affairs unless the President would change his policy, and withdraw or greatly modify his proclamation." Earlier in the day, Ewing had met with Secretary of State Seward "who agreed with us in our views of the pernicious influence of the proclamation." David Davis of Illinois, a new associate justice of the United States Supreme Court, was also frightened. On January 18, 1863, he begged the President to alter his policy in order to save the nation, but Lincoln refused, replying that it was a "fixed thing," and that he intended to adhere to it.[23]

Republican alarm grew partly from the notion that the Democratic party, particularly in the Midwest, was either disloyal or that it was trending in that direction. While recent studies seem to show that the majority of Democrats were not traitors or advocates of a peace without reunion, the question of loyalty is unimportant here.[24] What is important is that practically all Midwestern Democrats, with the exception of those who had joined the Union party— whether for peace or for a continuation of the war—exploited antiemancipation and anti-Negro feelings; and that, as the appeals of the Democrats demonstrated and as Republicans admitted, a prime source of popular discontent with liberation and the conduct of the war was the continued hostility toward the Negro. In the opinion of Senator John Sherman, the Democratic leaders were disloyal, but the masses were loyal. "They will fight for the flag & the country," he said, "but they hate niggers, and easily influenced by a party cry, stick to their party while its organization is controlled by the [worst] set of traitors in this country North or South."[25]

Republicans were equally disturbed by the extent of the opposition to emancipation. True enough, Democrats were leading the criticism, but disaffection and unrest plainly cut across partisan lines. One indication of this was found in the Union army. In every election held in the field during the war, midwestern troops voted heavily for the Republican-Union coalition; yet until mid-1863 most Union soldiers were either apathetic or hostile toward emancipation. Bell I. Wiley, historian of the common Civil War soldier, estimates that only about one Union fighting man in ten was primarily interested in freeing the slaves; that a "larger group" wanted no part of a war on slavery. Among the reasons he gives for their antipathy to emancipation were belief that it would lengthen the war, fear that it would free an ignorant and irresponsible race, "unreasoning hatred of people with black skins," and apprehension that "hordes of freedmen" would move into the North "to compete with white laborers and to mix with them on terms of equality."[26]

The Emancipation Proclamation stirred the wrath of such soldiers to its highest point. In January, 1863, Admiral Andrew H. Foote, naval hero of the Tennessee River campaign, stated that the two emancipation proclamations had dampened the zeal of the army and had produced "discontent at the idea of fighting only for the negro."[27] In some cases, resignations and desertions from the army were the result. A disgusted Indiana Unionist claimed that the "proclamation and other things have demoralized this army until it is worthless for any good. . . . Soldiers are deserting every day. . . ." Some Indiana, Ohio, and Illinois army officers resigned their commissions protesting against the proclamation.[28]

On the midwestern home front the reaction to the administration's antislavery stand was essentially of the same character and breadth, but the political implications were far more ominous. At a Republican congressional caucus held in late January, 1863, a "western member" criticized Congress for "passing emancipation and confiscation acts—that these had produced divisions at the North and driven Democrats away from us—that slavery would have died out [without the acts]." Senator Sherman blamed the state of affairs on Lincoln rather than on Congress. "I consider Slavery is doomed by the logic of current military movements," he said, "but the attempt to do it by Presidential proclamation only enables the political enemies of the President to avail themselves of a popular prejudice to overthrow him & his administration." Murat Halstead, moderate Republican editor of the powerful Cincinnati *Commercial* spoke frankly about the effects of radicalism on the Middle West. "There is a change in the current of public sentiment out west—a reaction against the Butlerites," he disclosed. "If Lincoln were not a damned fool, we could get along yet. . . . But what we want is not any more nigger—not any more if you please."[29]

Yet the currents of popular opinion had not gone unnoticed by Lincoln. His firm determination to maintain his antislavery position thinly screened an acute awareness that the Emancipation Proclamation had brought some unhappy repercussions. He conceded this on January 14, 1863, when he asked General John A. Dix if colored troops could occupy two points under Union control in Virginia so that the white garrison could be employed elsewhere. "The proclamation has been issued," he explained to Dix. "We were not succeeding—at best, were progressing too slowly—without it. Now, that we have it, and bear all the disadvantage of it, (as we do bear some in certain quarters) we must also take some benefit from it, if practicable." Apparently, he felt that the "disadvantage" was considerable, for three days later he divulged to Sumner that he feared " 'the fire in the rear'—meaning the Democracy, especially at the Northwest—more than our military chances." Nor were these fleeting worries. George W. Julian later recalled that in March, 1863, Lincoln had complained: "My proclamation was to stir the country; but it has done about as much harm as good."[30]

In such a political climate, most midwestern Republicans naturally were still unwilling to chance a head-on clash at the polls over emancipation. In the quest for local political offices in the spring of 1863, Republican newspapers in Dubuque, Springfield, Cleveland, Milwaukee, and Columbus played down or virtually ignored the Emancipation Proclamation and, for the time being, ignored the moral justifications for freeing the slaves. While the Democrats ran a versatile campaign which included the usual attack on the administration's antislavery and racial policies, Republican journals in these cities usually dodged these questions, and talked instead about the only issue being union or disunion and stressed the seditious leanings and activities of their opponents.[31] In spite of these tactics, election returns in the Midwest generally continued to show a Democratic trend, except in Michigan and Wisconsin. Democrats captured six of eleven city council seats in Cleveland, elected a mayor in Chicago, and won the municipal races in other important cities such as Columbus, Springfield, Milwaukee, St. Paul, and Madison, Wisconsin.[32]

Once the elections were over, some Republicans and Unionists again came sporadically to the defense of emancipation, usually upholding it on military grounds and occasionally for humanitarian reasons. Others stayed in the old groove, following the path taken by the Unionist gubernatorial candidate in Ohio, John Brough, who began an early drive for the fall elections. In May, 1863, John Sherman observed that Brough "takes care not to commit himself to these arbitrary arrests or to the proclamation and will I think get an enormous majority."[33]

But whatever the Midwest's views on the expediency and propriety of the Emancipation Proclamation, an economic, constitutional, and perhaps a social revolution had been ordered in the name of necessity and Union by a Republican President and Congress. Yet the tactics and statements of antislavery men, whether they were shaped by sincere convictions or by political exigency or, what is more likely, by both, demonstrated that the fundamental racial attitudes of most midwesterners had not been transformed by the dynamics of the war.

Although the critics of slavery continued to manifest a more humane and enlightened outlook toward the black race than did the Democrats, and although there undoubtedly were those who hoped for a thorough change in the Negroes' political, legal, and economic status everywhere, those who spoke out did not advocate complete equality of the races. Instead, they made it plain throughout early 1863 that they had not banished the theories of the past; that life in the Midwest would not be essentially changed by the abolition of slavery. Antislavery spokesmen denounced slavery and the mistreatment of colored persons, ridiculed the old Negro exclusion laws and resisted the passage of new ones, praised the conduct and ability of the freedmen, and called for the enlistment of black soldiers. At the same time they opposed miscegenation, intimate contact between the races, and Negro immigration, and continued to profess a belief in the superiority of the Caucasian people. In short, the revolution they urged was to be a limited one, and it was to take place in the South.

A few parts of this old pattern cropped up in Congress even though Republican lawmakers largely steered clear of racial matters. In the Senate, midwestern Republicans voted to forbid the exclusion of persons because of color from the cars of a transit company in the District of Columbia, and they rejected a proposal to prevent Negroes from receiving commissions in the army. Still, in the same session, they approved without debate an act providing for a temporary government for the Idaho Territory that restricted the ballot to white males. For idealistic as well as military reasons, Republican Representatives from the Midwest backed a Negro soldier bill in the House, but they also helped to include in the measure an amendment barring colored officers from commanding white men.[34]

The limitations and the ambivalent character of the antislavery movement were more starkly evident in the Midwest where Republicans and Unionists flatly denied the doctrine of racial equality. In May, 1863, Senator Sherman told an Ohio audience, "I am not in favor of negro equality, but because you and I are a little more favored in intellect and refinement, are we to be the masters of those who are made in the Lord's image?" Describing the war as a struggle for the rights of man and labor, John Wentworth, erstwhile stalwart Democrat and recent convert to the Union party, scoffed in Chicago at the idea "that the negroes would crowd out white labor at the North. The inferior race could never encroach upon the rights of the superior." Not content to remain on the defensive, some Republicans counterattacked, accusing the Democrats of running "their sable favorites" for local offices, of indulging "extensively" in amalgamation, and of opposing the enlistment of colored soldiers out of fear that "a nigger might be hurt." A Republican editor jeered that the Democratic newspaper in Dubuque was anti-Negro because it lacked "confidence in the ability of its supporters to resist the attractions of the darkies, and on that account hates a negro more than it does a 'rattlesnake.' "[35]

In Ohio and Wisconsin, Republican-Unionist legislatures neatly mixed compassion and limited egalitarianism with racism as they turned down proposals to pass exclusion laws and then enacted, in the same session, new militia laws that continued to restrict service to white males. While it had "no desire to offer inducement to freed slaves to come into this State," the Wisconsin Assembly resolved that it would be "unconstitutional and inhumane" to bar any immigrant from Wisconsin. The best way to keep southern Negroes out of the North, it added, was to give them freedom, homes, and employment in the South. As it reported against exclusion the majority of a Wisconsin Senate committee penned a systematic statement of midwestern racial mores. Since all men were created equal, the committee said, Negroes should not be prevented from entering Wisconsin. Nevertheless, it continued, emancipation would hold the freedmen in the South and attract northern Negroes southward because of the climate and because every avenue to opportunity and society was closed to them in the North by public opinion. Besides, free Negro laborers would fare better in the South, the report charitably declared. While the northern employer was an exacting taskmaster, the southern employer "has less repugnance to the black man's shiftless ways. They understand each other better . . . and while the black man keeps the place assigned him he would be treated with more consideration in the South."[36]

Such sentiments were not uttered only by politicians of unknown or dubious antislavery principles. Even the most forthright and resolute advocates of emancipation—men who called for a righteous war, men of unwavering devotion to antislavery—failed to extend the hand of fellowship to the Negro. In his message to the Illinois legislature, Governor Richard Yates, a dauntless radical, hailed the Emancipation Proclamation with moralistic praise, but he went on to say that it was highly improbable that the freedman would seek the North "to face the strong competition of northern skilled free-labor, to encounter the prejudice against his color, and the pauperism and neglect which would meet him on every hand." In fact, he added, freedom in the South would clear the blacks out of the North.[37]

A corresponding cast of thought marked the pronouncements of the most courageous Republican newspapers in the Middle West. Throughout much of the war the Chicago *Tribune* and the Cleveland *Leader* had been in the forefront of the abolition movement, castigating the inhumanity and immorality of slavery, urging the use of black soldiers, manifesting sympathy for Negroes, and condemning northern Negrophobes for their oppressions. Both agreed that the Emancipation Proclamation was one of the great moral acts of history as well as an instrument of war. Nevertheless, long after the proclamation was issued, these newspapers continued to reassure their readers that the Negroes would stay in the South if they were to be liberated. On March 14, 1863, the editor of the *Tribune* vividly limned the bounds of his radicalism in a scathing rebuke to Democratic charges that Republicanism promoted miscegenation. Slavery brought racial amalgamation, he wrote, but the Republican doctrine "is to let the African race alone; neither marry or cohabit with them; to give them freedom, treat them as human beings; pay them for their work; separate the whites from adulterous communication with them; and preserve the purity of the Caucasian blood from African admixture."[38]

Nowhere were praise for the moral efficacy and justice of emancipation and expressions of heartfelt concern for the welfare of the Negro more frequently found than in the statements of philanthropists, churchmen, and reformers in the Middle West. And nowhere were many of the traditional racial attitudes of the section more clearly revealed. At this stage of the war, religious leaders of surpassing radicalism and piety exhibited great interest in Christian charity and compassion and little in the equalitarian implications of the gospel of universal brotherhood. In a discourse on the beneficence of God's emancipation policy, a radical Methodist editor referred to "Sambo and Cuffy." In face of bitter criticism and a rash of cancellations from many subscribers, the Cincinnati *Catholic Telegraph,* official organ of midwestern Catholicism, took a strong stand in 1863 against slavery; yet it also opposed "equality of the races" and black competition with white labor, and even predicted that the Negro would be unable to "compete with the white man. It is not in his blood or muscle."[39] In appealing for freedom, uplift, and fair treatment for Negroes, the government-appointed American Freedmen's Inquiry Commission, headed by Robert Dale Owen, the famous Indiana reformer, joined leading churchmen in predicting that the freedmen would stay in the South, in claiming that most of the northern Negroes would move to the free South, and in warning that the slaves would flee to the North if slavery were not abolished. The Western Freedmen's Aid Commission, organized in Cincinnati with Levi Coffin, a devout friend of the Negro, as General Agent, boldly claimed a radical objective, announcing its intention of preparing the freedmen for citizenship. But the commission then tempered its benevolence with the statement that "this can be most effectively done, not by bringing them North, but by locating them on Southern soil, and organizing their labor there."[40]

There was also plenty of other evidence that the policy of emancipation had not converted the Midwest to interracial amity. During late 1862 and the first half of 1863, the enduring strain of anti-Negro feeling continued unabated in the form of threats, intimidation, and unabashed violence. Such activity was especially prevalent in Illinois and Indiana, but it also existed in Iowa, Minnesota, and Michigan.

Race prejudice was particularly direct and forceful in the Hoosier State. At the 1862 Western Yearly Annual Meeting of Friends, it was reported that some Negroes had left southern Indiana and had moved to Canada and other places in the North "where they may enjoy more privileges in educating their children and avoid the prejudices that prevail against them here."[41] In November of 1862 a regiment of Indiana soldiers prevented a group of fugitives from slavery from crossing the Ohio River into Indiana, shouting that "they would fire upon them; that their object in going to war was not to make Indiana an asylum for negroes." After the Preliminary Emancipation Proclamation was issued, authorities at New Albany stationed guards at the ferry landings on the Ohio River to prevent southern Negroes without passes from entering the state. As a result, a number of slaves were arrested there and returned to bondage. In fact, the pursuit of fugitive slaves continued in parts of southern Indiana until at least February, 1864, with some freedmen and apparently some free Negroes being kidnapped and then sold into slavery in Kentucky. Negrophobia was not confined to the southern part of the state. In November, 1862, after a report that some colored barbers in Fort Wayne had "secreted" a white woman in their barber shop, the Fort Wayne *Sentinel* related, "It was determined that our city would not longer be infested with these black skinned scoundrels, and a crusade was inaugurated against the darkeys." Several Negroes were driven out of town, and the remainder received an "irresistible invitation" to depart.[42]

The opponents of a Negro movement into Illinois often used the state's Black Laws and violence to repel Negro immigrants. Black refugees working in the vicinity of Carbondale and a young Negro woman in Edgar County were fined and imprisoned for illegally entering the state. A Union army lieutenant was tried in Woodford County in May, 1863, for the crime of bringing a Negro into Illinois. The trial ended in a hung jury, and the case was dropped after the officer promised that the black man would go with him when he returned to active duty.[43] In May, 1863, two armed men stopped three fugitive slaves from Missouri, shot one, and ordered the other two back to Missouri. A white man in southern Illinois who had employed several Negroes from the South was warned that his house would be burned if he did not discharge them. When he refused to comply, terrorists destroyed his valuable timber.[44] In April of 1863 a gang of whites hunted down and drove off about forty blacks working on a farm in Union County. Later that year, five Negroes were forced out of Mason County. The Chicago *Tribune* complained in March of 1863 that Copperheads at Ottawa, Illinois, were "maltreating the poor negroes who happen to be stopping in that city. These ruffians combine in squads, and hit every wooly head that presents itself."[45]

Anti-Negro sentiment was neither so blatant nor so fierce in Iowa as in Indiana and Illinois. The only attempt to enforce the state's exclusion law was made in January of 1863, and a district judge immediately ruled the law unconstitutional.[46] Opposition to Negroes was mainly expressed in resolutions passed at Democratic meetings. Resolutions denouncing Negro immigration for racial and economic reasons were adopted at rallies in Poweshick, Linn, Marshall, and Lucas counties. The meeting in Poweshick County pledged to ostracize any person employing or harboring a Negro; to resist all efforts "to fill our schools and domestic circles with the African race"; and to "keep out negroes from this part of God's heritage," preferably by moral suasion, but by force if necessary.[47]

Other outbreaks of Negrophobia occurred in St. Paul and Detroit. In May of 1863 two groups of contraband Negroes came to St. Paul upon the request of the Union army commander who evidently intended to employ them as teamsters. When the first contingent arrived, the police attempted to prevent it from landing, claiming that the immigrants were paupers. The second group, under army guard, was met by "Irish laborers" who tried to frighten them away from St. Paul.[48] The only major race riot in the Midwest in 1863 flared up in Detroit on March 6, when soldiers dispersed a crowd attempting to lynch a Negro being tried for raping a young white girl. Having been thwarted, the mob turned on the city's colored population, beat a large number of Negroes, and burned about thirty-five houses before Union troops quelled the uprising. Many Negroes reportedly fled to Canada to escape the rioters.[49]

As the spring turned into summer in 1863, the road to the popular acceptance of emancipation was still partly blocked in the Midwest by military defeat, pessimism, and racial fears. A revolution had indeed been proclaimed, but its supporters had yet to prove that it would save the Union and not burst out of bounds.

Notes

1. "Annual Message to Congress," December 1, 1862, in Roy P. Basler (ed.), *The Collected Works of Abraham Lincoln* (9 vols.; New Brunswick, N.J.: Rutgers University Press, 1953), V, 518–37.

2. Theodore Calvin Pease and James G. Randall (eds.), *The Diary of Orville Hickman Browning* (2 vols.; Springfield: Illinois State Historical Library, 1927–33), I, 591.

3. *Congressional Globe,* 37 Cong., 3 sess., pp. 16, 95–97, 181–86, and Appendix, pp. 39–41, 43–44.

4. *Congressional Globe,* 37 Cong., 3 sess., pp. 77, 92, 162.

5. "Emancipation Proclamation," January 1, 1863, in Basler (ed.), *The Collected Works of Abraham Lincoln,* V, 28–30.

6. Richard Hofstadter, *The American Political Tradition and the Men Who Made It* (New York: Vintage Books, 1949), p. 132; Richard N. Current, *The Lincoln Nobody Knows* (New York: McGraw-Hill, 1958), pp. 227–29.

7. Charles Sumner to John M. Forbes, December 25, 28, 1862, in Sarah Forbes Hughes (ed.), *Letters and Recollections of John Murray Forbes* (2 vols.; Boston: Houghton Mifflin, 1899), I, 348–49, 352–53; "Preliminary Draft of Final Emancipation Proclamation," [December 30, 1862], in Basler (ed.), *The Collected Works of Abraham Lincoln,* VI, 24–25; "Emancipation Proclamation," January 1, 1863, in *ibid.,* pp. 28–30.

8. "To Salmon P. Chase," September 2, 1863, in Basler (ed.), *The Collected Works of Abraham Lincoln,* VI, 428–29.

9. Frank L. Klement, *The Copperheads in the Middle West* (Chicago:

University of Chicago Press, 1960), pp. 43–48, 85–87. Throughout the war Walker's *Free Press* was much more moderate than the Chicago *Times*.

10. *Congressional Globe,* 37 Cong., 3 sess., pp. 181–82, 637, 654, 710, 783–86, 789, 1231–32, 1385–86, 1405, and Appendix, pp. 43, 44, 56. Richardson left the United States House of Representatives on January 29, 1863, and was sworn into the Senate the following day. Democratic opposition to the enlistment of Negro soldiers will be discussed in chapter vi.

11. Klement, *The Copperheads in the Middle West,* pp. 42–50; *Times* (Chicago), January 3, 1863; *Democratic Herald* (Dubuque), January 3, 6, 10, 1863; *Free Press* (Detroit), January 3, 1863; *Crisis* (Columbus), January 7, 14, May 27, 1863. On November 14, 1862, the Dubuque *Herald* had become the *Democratic Herald*.

12. *Times* (Chicago), January 3, 1863; *Crisis* (Columbus), January 14, 1863; Klement, *The Copperheads in the Middle West,* p. 45.

13. *Crisis* (Columbus), June 3, 1863; *Democratic Herald* (Dubuque), January 9, May 21, 27, 1863; *Free Press* (Detroit), February 20, 21, 1863; *Times* (Chicago), March 27, 1863.

14. William D. Foulke, *Life of Oliver P. Morton, Including His Important Speeches* (2 vols.; Indianapolis: Bowen-Merrill, 1899), I, 230; *Indiana True Republican* (Centreville), February 5, 1863; Emma Lou Thornbrough, *The Negro in Indiana: A Study of a Minority* (Indianapolis: Indiana Historical Bureau, 1957), p. 190. Democratic proposals usually died in the Senate where Republicans obstructed action by bolting crucial sessions. Klement, *The Copperheads in the Middle West,* pp. 52–58.

15. *Tribune* (Chicago), January 16, February 12, 13, 1863; *Times* (Chicago), February 13, 1863; *Crisis* (Columbus), February 18, 1863. Republicans blocked votes in the state Senate by frequently refusing to attend sessions in order to prevent a quorum. Governor Richard Yates finally prorogued the legislature on a technicality. Klement, *The Copperheads in the Middle West,* pp. 64–65.

16. Klement, *The Copperheads in the Middle West,* pp. 107–25; Samuel S. Cox to Manton Marble, March 11, 1863, Manton Marble Papers (Manuscript Division, Library of Congress).

17. Klement, *The Copperheads in the Middle West,* p. 115; *Tribune* (Chicago), February 12, 13, 1863; *Crisis* (Columbus), February 18, 1863; *Congressional Globe,* 37 Cong., 3 sess., Appendix, p. 56.

18. *Democratic Herald* (Dubuque), January 9, February 12, 26, March 3, April 7, 16, May 14, 21, 27, 28, 1863; *Crisis* (Columbus), January 7, 14, February 11, 25, April 15, June 3, 1863.

19. For expressions that the proclamation was primarily or solely based

on military necessity, see Reuben Gold Thwaites (ed.), *Civil War Messages and Proclamations of Wisconsin War Governors* (Madison: Wisconsin History Commission, 1962), pp. 178–79; *Journal* (Indianapolis), January 5, 1863; *Leader* (Cleveland), January 3, 1863; *Times* (Dubuque), April 21, 1863; *Illinois State Journal* (Springfield), January 6, 1863.

20. *Illinois State Journal* (Springfield), January 7, 1863; *The Sumter Anniversary: Opinions of Loyalists . . . Expressed . . . on the 11 of April . . .* (New York: C. S. Wescott, 1863), p. 48; *Leader* (Cleveland), January 3, 1863; *Ohio State Journal* (Columbus), January 3, 1863; *Journal* (Indianapolis), January 5, 1863; *The American Annual Cyclopaedia and Register of Important Events of the Year, 1863* (New York: D. Appleton, 1868), p. 645.

21. *Nonpareil* (Council Bluffs), January 10, 31, 1863; *Tribune* (Chicago), January 1, 3, 1863.

22. Pease and Randall (eds.), *The Diary of Orville Hickman Browning*, I, 610–12; Medill to A. S. Hill, March 20, 1863, quoted in James Ford Rhodes, *History of the United States from the Compromise of 1850* (9 vols.; New York: Harper, 1893–1918), IV, 241; Sumner to Francis Lieber, January 17, 1863, in Edward L. Pierce, *Memoir and Letters of Charles Sumner* (4 vols.; Boston: Roberts Brothers, 1887–93), IV, 114.

23. Pease and Randall (eds.), *Diary of Orville Hickman Browning*, I, 612–13, 616–17.

24. Klement, *The Copperheads in the Middle West*, pp. 114–26; Robert Rutland, "The Copperheads of Iowa: A Re-Examination," *Iowa Journal of History and Politics*, LII (January, 1954), 1–30. For the view that the peace Democrats favored peace at any price in early 1863, see Wood Gray, *The Hidden Civil War: The Story of the Copperheads* (New York: Viking Press, 1942), pp. 118–47.

25. John Sherman to William T. Sherman, May 18, 1863, William Tecumseh Sherman Papers (Manuscript Division, Library of Congress). See also *ibid.*, May 7, 1863.

26. Bell Irvin Wiley, *The Life of Billy Yank: The Common Soldier in the Civil War* (Indianapolis: Bobbs-Merrill, 1952), pp. 40–43. In June, 1862, Illinois soldiers voted over 3 to 1 to include a Negro exclusion article and a ban on Negro suffrage in a proposed state constitution. *Tribune* (Chicago), August 20, 1862; *Illinois State Journal* (Springfield), August 16, 1862.

27. Wiley, *The Life of Billy Yank*, p. 42; Pease and Randall (eds.), *The Diary of Orville Hickman Browning*, I, 610–11.

28. Quoted in Klement, *The Copperheads in the Middle West*, p. 51. See also *ibid.*, pp. 51–52; W. H. Terrell, *Indiana in the War of the Rebel-*

tion: A Report of the Adjutant General (reprint [1960] of Vol. I of eight vol. report; Indianapolis: Indiana Historical Bureau, 1866–69), I, 98–99.

29. Julia Perkins Cutler, *Life and Times of Ephraim Cutler . . . with Biographical Sketches of . . . William Parker Cutler* (Cincinnati: Robert Clarke, 1890), pp. 301–2; John Sherman to W. T. Sherman, May 18, 1863, W. T. Sherman Papers; Halstead to John Sherman, February 6, 1863, John Sherman Papers (Manuscript Division, Library of Congress). See also John Olney to Lyman Trumbull, January 6, 1863, Lyman Trumbull Papers (Manuscript Division, Library of Congress).

30. "To John A. Dix," January 14, 1863, in Basler (ed.), *The Collected Works of Abraham Lincoln,* VI, 56; Charles Sumner to Francis Lieber, January 17, 1863, in Pierce, *Memoir and Letters of Charles Sumner,* IV, 114; George W. Julian, "Lincoln and the Proclamation of Emancipation," in Allen Thorndike Rice (ed.), *Reminiscences of Abraham Lincoln by Distinguished Men of His Times* (rev. ed.; New York: Harper, 1909), pp. 235–36.

31. See March and early April files of the *Leader* (Cleveland), *Times* (Dubuque), *Illinois State Journal* (Springfield), *Sentinel* (Milwaukee), and *Ohio State Journal* (Columbus).

32. *Tribune* (Chicago), April 9, 1863; *Leader* (Cleveland), April 6, 1863; Klement, *The Copperheads in the Middle West,* pp. 104–5. In Michigan and Wisconsin the Democratic tide had apparently been checked, but not substantially reversed. See *The American Annual Cyclopaedia, 1863,* p. 646; *The Tribune Almanac for the Year 1864* (New York: New York Tribune, 1868), p. 60.

33. John Sherman to W. T. Sherman, May 18, 1863, W. T. Sherman Papers.

34. *Congressional Globe,* 37 Cong., 3 sess., pp. 599, 600, 604, 1328, 1446–47, and Appendix, p. 234. Republican views on arming Negro soldiers will be discussed in chapter vi.

35. *Ohio State Journal* (Columbus), March 16, April 14, June 1, 1863; *Tribune* (Chicago), April 12, 21, 1863; *Nonpareil* (Council Bluffs), January 23, 1863; *Times* (Dubuque), April 21, May 6, 1863.

36. *Acts of . . . the Legislature of Wisconsin, at the Extra Session, in the Year 1862, and at the Annual Session in the Year 1863 . . .* (Madison: n.p., 1863), p. 367; *Journal of the Assembly of . . . Wisconsin, Annual Session, A.D. 1863* (Madison: S. D. Carpenter, 1863), pp. 313, 442–43; *Journal of the Senate, Annual Session, A.D. 1863* (Madison: Atwood and Rublee, 1863), pp. 357, 404, 462, 635–36; *General and Local Laws and Joint Resolutions Passed by the Fifty-fifth General Assembly of the State of Ohio, at Its Second Session . . .* (Columbus: Richard Nevins, 1863), p. 97.

37. *Illinois State Journal* (Springfield), January 7, 1863.

38. *Tribune* (Chicago), January 1, 3, 7, 25, 31, February 5, March 14, 1863; *Leader* (Cleveland), January 3, 31, February 4, June 22, 1863.

39. *Western Christian Advocate* (Cincinnati), June 24, 1863; *Catholic Telegraph* (Cincinnati), January 7, April 15, 1863.

40. *Western Christian Advocate* (Cincinnati), February 4, 18, May 6, 1863; *Indiana True Republican* (Centreville), April 23, 1863; "Preliminary Report of the American Freedmen's Inquiry Commission," June 30, 1863, in U.S., War Department, *The War of the Rebellion: a Compilation of the Official Records of the Union and Confederate Armies* (128 vols.; Washington, D.C.: Government Printing Office, 1880–1901), 3d ser., III, 436–37 (hereinafter cited as *Official Records*); Davis W. Clark, "The Editor's Table—Development of Treason at the North," *Ladies' Repository*, XXIII (March, 1863), 192; D. Burt, "Popular Government and Slavery," *Congregational Quarterly*, V (January, 1863), 46–52.

41. *Minutes of the Western Yearly Meeting of Friends, 1862*, p. 24, quoted in Thornbrough, *The Negro in Indiana*, p. 187.

42. *Journal* (Evansville), August 8, 1863, quoted in *Tribune* (New York), August 13, 1863; *Indiana True Republican* (Centreville), April 28, 1863; *Journal* (Indianapolis), December 2, 1862; *Journal* (New Albany) quoted in *Pioneer* (St. Paul), November 13, 1862; *Sentinel* (Fort Wayne) quoted in *Democratic Herald* (Dubuque), November 29, 1862; Thornbrough, *The Negro in Indiana*, pp. 187–89.

43. *Tribune* (Chicago), December 11, 1862, May 18, 1863; *Illinois State Journal* (Springfield), May 15, 1863.

44. James L. [Gagr?] January 13, 1863, to Salmon P. Chase, Edwin M. Stanton Papers (Manuscript Division, Library of Congress); *Courier* (Hannibal, Mo.), May 30, 1863, quoted in *Times* (Dubuque), June 16, 1863.

45. *Official Records*, 2d ser., V, 521; *Tribune* (New York), April 4, 1863; *Tribune* (Chicago), March 31, 1863.

46. *Tribune* (Chicago), January 21, 27, February 3, 1863.

47. *Times* (Chicago), January 23, February 13, 26, 1863; *Democratic Herald* (Dubuque), February 14, March 4, 1863.

48. Earl Spangler, *The Negro in Minnesota* (Minneapolis: T. S. Denison, 1961), pp. 50–52; *Tribune* (Chicago), May 14, 1863.

49. *Free Press* (Detroit), March 7, 1863; *Tribune* (Chicago), March 9, 10, 1863; *Official Records*, 3d ser., III, 488; *The American Annual Cyclopaedia, 1863*, p. 646.

❧ 6 ❧

A Solution

With the battle over emancipation at full force in the winter of 1862–63, antislavery men everywhere continued their search for ways to provide for the freedmen. Other than military victory, this was the most haunting and pressing need of the Republican party and the Lincoln administration. After a conversation with the President in November of 1862, a friend reported that Lincoln believed he could convince the people that the Emancipation Proclamation did not transcend his legitimate powers but what "most troubles him is to provide for the blacks." Even such an enthusiastic radical as Charles Sumner was constrained to admit in early January of 1863 that the nation was faced "with the great question what to do for the new-made freedmen, that their emancipation may be a blessing to them and to our country. It is a vast problem."[1] No section had done more to make this clear than the Midwest.

The Republicans' sense of urgency about the freedmen did not stem solely from humanitarianism but from political and military considerations as well. The results of the fall elections of 1862, the stormy reaction to the emancipation proclamations, and unrest in the Middle West drove home anew at least three lessons. However long and impassioned the list of grievances against slavery might be, something more must be done to prove that emancipation was a military asset, that the government could deal effectively and justly with the freed Negroes, and that some satisfactory system of racial accommodation could be worked out.

By late 1862 the administration's program for accomplishing these objectives lay in fragments. The colonization design had apparently failed with the collapse of the Chiriqui project in the fall. The other plan—that of utilizing some of the former slaves in the South—was fundamentally sound in concept, but it had proven to be inadequate in scope and faulty in execution. With the exception of the directive of August, 1862, ordering Union commanders to employ for military purposes as many colored laborers as they could advantageously use, the government had not instituted an overall policy regulating the disposition of the freed Negroes. The shortcomings were glaring. Because of their infirmity or age or because of a lack of demand for their services, only a small minority of the freedmen could be employed as military laborers. Either on their own initiative or upon the advice of the War Department, most army commanders had attempted to care for the remainder in various ways, feeding and clothing them, and sometimes setting them to work on abandoned plantations or hiring them out to planters. Either through their churches or through the auspices of humanitarian organizations such as the Contrabands' Relief Commission, Western Freedmen's Aid Commission, Northwestern Freedmen's Aid Commission, and Indiana Freedmen's Aid Commission, many midwestern civilians assisted in this cause by giving generously of their time and money to provide aid and education for southern Negroes.

None of these measures was adequate. As federal forces struck into the heart of the South, increasing numbers of destitute Negroes rushed into the Union lines, congregated around Union camps, hampered military operations, and frequently lived in privation and disease.[2] In desperation some generals beseeched Washington for instructions. In early 1863, General Ulysses S. Grant described the situation in west Tennessee and northern Mississippi as "serious" and "troublesome." Lincoln, in response to a query from a harassed general, later called the Negro refugee problem "a difficult subject—the most difficult with which we have to deal."[3]

Under these circumstances it was quite difficult to show that emancipation was a blessing either to the slaves or to the Union military effort, particularly with the war going badly. It was harder still to demonstrate that slaves could make the transition from slavery to freedom, or to claim that the race problem was being solved or, for that matter, was even solvable. Then, too, as long as the freedmen remained in their present limbo, the threat of a Negro inundation of the North was always present. After all, the War Department had temporarily attempted to relieve the pressure of the Negroes upon the army by transporting them into Illinois in the fall of 1862, and there was no guaranty that this experiment would not be repeated on a wider scale.

Such were the conditions emancipationists faced in late 1862 and early 1863 as they attacked the race question. A plethora of suggestions were bandied about by men grown desperate in adversity, but the ordeal of final decision rested uneasily on the President. By late 1862, Lincoln had evidently arrived at the conclusion—already reached by most of his party—that the fate of the Negro race was to be settled largely in the South. After discussing emancipation and politics with the chief executive in November, T. J. Barnett confided to a friend, "He thinks the foundations of slavery have been cracked by the war, by the Rebels; and that the masonry of the machine is in their hands—that they have held its fate and can't complain." A few days later Lincoln made these views public when he argued in his message to Congress that the freed Negroes would prefer to stay in the South, and suggested that the North could exclude them.[4] Yet, to his credit, time and war had not dimmed his piercing vision of the agonizing facets of the race problem. Nor had criticism and disappointment blunted his original conviction that the government should strive to ease the friction and stresses of emancipation. In addition to sounding the call in December of 1862 for constitutional amendments to provide for Negro colonization and for compensation for emancipation, he privately continued to wish and urge that the slave states would adopt gradual liberation and apprenticeship systems.[5]

Characteristically, Lincoln also breathed new life into the colonization movement. Twice before, out of principle and policy, he had accompanied his most crucial decisions on emancipation with flurries of activity about deporting the slaves. In December of 1862 with the Emancipation Proclamation about to be promulgated, Lincoln repeated this ritual. On December 26, Eli Thayer's proposition to settle the Negroes in Florida was briefly discussed in a cabinet meeting. Apparently this scheme was discarded, for five days later the President signed a contract with a promoter, Bernard Kock, requiring the resettlement of five thousand Negroes on a Haitian island, the Isle à Vache. A few months later over 400 colonists were taken there, but the undertaking was a fiasco. The 368 survivors of this abortive expedition were returned to the United States in 1864. Even before the colonists had departed for Haiti, Lincoln had grown suspicious of Kock and had cancelled the government's agreement with him.[6]

Though he continued to muse darkly about future race relations and to dream fondly of colonization, Lincoln did not stop there. Not only would deportation scarcely scratch the surface of the Negro problem; the movement's political value was also fading in the deepening gloom of its barren history and bleak prospects. Something more was needed—something quicker, something workable, and above all something convincing and acceptable to the northern people. With this in mind Lincoln and his administration slowly constructed such a device during the first half of 1863.

In essence the system they developed provided for massive employment and care of the freed Negroes in the South. It therefore conformed in theory to the ambitious but flawed plan outlined in August of 1862; but it was far more comprehensive and better executed. One of the major differences was the decision, announced in the Emancipation Proclamation, to accept freedmen in the armed services. Until that time—although Negro soldiers were already being recruited in Kansas and Louisiana without the official sanction of the War Department and in South Carolina with Secretary of War Stanton's authorization—the President was on record as being opposed to arming the Negroes.[7] His change of mind cleared the path for the widespread enlistment of colored men. Though such a step would seem to have been an obvious corollary of emancipation, it was, in fact, a momentous verdict slowly and painfully reached by him.

From the first there had been agitation, usually by radical antislavery men in the early months of the war, for arming the Negroes. Republican pressure for such a measure mounted steadily, and in July of 1862 Congress responded when it gave the President discretionary authority to employ Negroes in the armed forces. Lincoln subsequently ordered the employment of Negroes as military laborers, but he refused to accept them as soldiers, generally taking the position that such action would cost the Union support in the border slave states.[8] While this was doubtless true, his reluctance was greatly strengthened by another somber reality—midwestern race prejudice.

Throughout 1862 and early 1863 much of the outspoken opposition to recruiting Negro soldiers came from midwestern Democrats. Such a course, some contended, would invite servile insurrection and inflict the horrors of Santo Domingo on the South. Expressing genuine doubts that blacks possessed either the ability and intelligence to be disciplined or the courage and will to fight, many argued that the rebels would slaughter them in battle. At the same time they stressed that it was "a white man's war" and cautioned that the presence of colored men in the ranks would degrade white soldiers, cause them to desert, and discourage others from volunteering.[9]

Democrats most frequently charged that the use of Negro soldiers was a secret weapon to force racial equality at home and in the army. If the blacks were to be armed, they would be used after the war to rule southern whites and to subdue northern opponents of the Republican administration. Moreover, they warned, Republicans would first place colored soldiers on the same plane with white troops, and later demand social and political equality for them, saying that they had earned it by fighting for the Union. Representative Chilton A. White of Ohio best summarized the anxieties of his fellow Democrats: "The question is one of political and social equality with the negro everywhere. If you make him the instrument by which your battles are fought, the means by which your victories are won, you must treat him as a victor is entitled to be treated, with all decent and becoming respect."[10]

In one way or another many midwestern Republicans and Unionists agreed with much of what the Democrats said. The editor of the Dubuque *Times* charged that only "craven cowards" advocated arming the blacks; if the intelligent and brave whites could not save the nation, "the poor, subservient, ignorant negro slave never can. The idea of calling on *him* . . . to fight our battles . . . is not only a confession of our own weakness and cowardice . . . but it is the last outcropping of a local insanity." In 1862, David Tod, Unionist Governor of Ohio, rejected a Negro's request to raise a colored regiment in the state. "Do you not know," he reproached, "that this is a *white man's* government; that white men are able to defend and protect it, and that to enlist a negro soldier would be to drive every white man out of the service?" In September of 1862, Lincoln disclosed that he too held a low estimate of the capacity of colored soldiers: "I am not so sure we could do much with the blacks. If we were to arm them, I fear that in a few weeks the arms would be in the hands of the rebels."[11]

Before 1863 most Republicans were apparently certain that the majority of midwesterners were opposed to the enlistment of Negroes. At least the radical Thaddeus Stevens thought so. Two years after the bill had passed he admitted that his party had purposely couched in cautious and ambiguous language an 1862 act authorizing the President to use Negroes for military purposes. "We did it very gingerly. We had to wrap it up in such a way that the gentleman from Indiana [a Democrat] could not use it before his constituents," boasted Stevens. "We authorized the Executive to employ them in and about the Army in such a way as he might deem best. . . . That was not making soldiers of them [but] we intended that [he should]." From the other end of the spectrum a conservative Republican, Senator Browning, confirmed his testimony. As he campaigned in Illinois in August of 1862, Browning counseled Lincoln, "I have heard many say 'If he will accept one black Regiment he will lose twenty white Regiments by it.' The time *may* come for arming the negroes. It is not yet."[12]

Until at least mid-1863 strong resentment toward recruiting Negro troops also prevailed in the army. In July of 1862, Lincoln believed that permitting Negroes to bear arms "would produce dangerous & fatal dissatisfaction in our army, and do more harm than good." Senator James H. Lane of Kansas, one of the earliest organizers of Negro troops, stated in 1864 that the white soldiers would have mutinied if Lincoln had ordered blacks into the service earlier than he did, "for not till thousands of them [whites] had been slain, and other thousands wounded and maimed, did they give a reluctant assent to receive the aid of a black auxiliary."[13] Meanwhile, doubts about the fighting ability of Negroes, belief that putting colored men into uniform was unnecessary, and fear that such a move would threaten white supremacy provoked their opposition.[14]

Midwestern soldiers shared wholeheartedly in these feelings. It is hardly surprising that men who despised the idea of fighting a war to free the Negro would also loathe the possibility of fighting alongside him. General Richard J. Oglesby, a Republican who was to be elected Unionist governor of Illinois in 1864, reported in November of 1862 that he had never encountered twenty Union soldiers who favored placing black men into the ranks. General Lorenzo Thomas, chief recruiter of Negro troops in the Mississippi Valley where most of the Union forces were of midwestern origin, wrote that prejudice in the army "against colored soldiers was quite general, and it required all my efforts to counteract it." Even after Negro regiments were assiduously being raised, General W. T. Sherman of Ohio hoped they would "be used for some side purposes and not be brigaded with our white men. . . . The Companies prefer now to be rid of Negroes—they desert the moment danger threatens. . . . I won't trust niggers to fight yet."[15]

As the situation in the army suggests, the Midwest was not the only part of the North which harbored racial objections to the use of Negro troops. Far from it. A similar pattern of attitudes was visible in the East, particularly in the middle states. In view of these things perceptive Republicans drew the conclusion that national rather than sectional prejudice stalled the drive for Negro soldiers. In August of 1862, William D. Bickham, a perceptive Republican editor in Ohio, privately deplored the strength of "our national prejudice against *color*. Fathers will offer their sons, men their brethren as victims on the battle field to preserve the lives of those whom they profess to abhor because they are 'niggers.'" That same month Senator John Sherman lamented in a like vein: "Nothing but our party divisions & our natural prejudices of caste has kept us from using them [Negroes] as allies in war to be used for all purposes in which they can advance the cause of the country." Time and a safe settlement of the issue did not change his mind. Two years later Sherman again confessed that the enlistment of Negroes had been "postponed until the prejudices of our people gave way to the absolute demands for troops to occupy and hold important positions in the South."[16]

But if the Midwest was not the only region in the North that held such views, it was the most dogged in its resistance to enlisting Negroes as soldiers. To overcome this vehement opposition, midwestern Republicans and Unionists touched various chords of idealism, patriotism, religious zeal, and self-interest. Though they usually concealed such motives for the time being, some wanted to arm the Negro in order to speed his integration into American society. While Negroes were being schooled in the rudiments of civilization by military life and battle, they would win acceptance by proving their mettle as men and demonstrating their devotion to their country.[17] They additionally felt that an appeal for aid from the victims of bondage would help the nation atone for its complicity in slavery and find favor with God; that it would insure permanent freedom for

101

the black race; and that it would open the door to more rights for Negroes.[18]

Yet, they principally marched under the banner of military exigency, claiming that the utilization of black troops would bring greater numbers to bear on the Confederates, demoralize the enemy, and spare whites from duty in undesirable places. Negroes could man the forts and occupied territory in the South, thereby freeing white men to engage the enemy, they urged. Because the blacks were accustomed to the southern climate, they could be assigned to the hot, sickly areas along the Gulf, the Mississippi River, and the South Atlantic seaboard so that whites could fight in healthier, cooler regions.[19]

Certain midwesterners coupled such pleas with appeals to the instinct of self-preservation and the powerful spirit of racial solidarity. Negroes should be recruited, they urged, in order to avoid drafting white men. Following such logic to its natural end and imitating a crude dictum of Thaddeus Stevens, some proclaimed that the enlistment of Negroes would save white lives. In September of 1862, radical Senator Grimes, the most powerful Republican in Iowa, told a Dubuque audience that he "would see a negro shot down in battle rather than the son of a Dubuquer." Iowa's radical governor, Samuel J. Kirkwood, wrote General-in-Chief Henry W. Halleck that he would have no regrets if it were found at the end of the war, "that a part of the dead are niggers and that not all are whites." He later offered a less complex argument, declaring publicly that he "would prefer to sacrifice the lives of niggers rather than those of the best and bravest of our white youths."[20] Some men of God did not find this reasoning at odds with their theology. In the course of a moving antislavery discourse a Minnesota Congregationalist cried, "Why should we send our sons and brothers to perish by thousands, when the slave population is ready to aid the government, if we will give permission?" There were soldiers who wondered the same thing. An army captain from Illinois begged for the recruitment of Negroes because it was the nation's duty "to protect the lives of its white citizens. And the Government will be weakened less by the loss of three negroes than it would by the loss of one white man."[21]

Other effective campaigners for colored troops also pled their cause with words of scorn for the Negro. General Lew Wallace of Indiana, fresh from the battle of Shiloh, toured the lower Midwest in the summer of 1862, campaigning for the use of Negro soldiers, but de-

nying all the while that this step would break down the barriers between the races. In Cincinnati he reportedly shouted that he "despised the negro race [and] couldn't help it. . . . I will fight before
the negro is put on an equality with the white man." Senator
Henry S. Lane, perhaps the most accomplished antislavery stump
speaker in the Midwest, said that he was willing for the rebels to be
killed by rattlesnakes, mules, and Negroes if necessary. Speaking before an Indianapolis audience in February of 1863, General Nathan
Kimball emphasized that he "would not consent to fight by the side
of a negro, and the President would never ask him to do it; but he
would take negroes and let them fight negroes."[22]

The Negro soldier policy that finally emerged in 1862 and 1863
bore much the same stamp. Either by act of Congress or by order of
the War Department, or by both, Negroes were shunted into segregated units, were paid less for their services than were their white
counterparts, and with few exceptions were barred from receiving
commissions as officers.[23] These discriminatory practices were pat-
ently shaped to recognize the martial superiority of white men and
to assuage the anxieties of those, in and out of the army, who feared
that the use of Negro soldiers would become an entering wedge to
racial equality.

The House of Representatives made this plain in early 1863 as it
debated a bill calling for the enlistment of 150,000 colored recruits to
be commanded by black or white officers. Although this proposal
was partly designed to enable Negroes to win commissions in colored
units, it made no real effort to break down racial segregation in the
army. In spite of this, some midwestern Republicans sought an explicit guaranty that Negroes would not be admitted to white regiments or be allowed to officer white soldiers. The champions of the
measure rose to its defense with a profusion of explanations and denials. Thaddeus Stevens explained that it was not designed to place
blacks and whites "upon a social and political equality," but rather
to assure equal protection from the government for Negro soldiers.
Another reported that the original author of the proposal, reputedly
Secretary of War Stanton, had said that he intended "to confine the
appointments to be made, under the provisions of this bill, to white
men." The authorization for black officers would be used only in
critical positions under "extraordinary circumstances." Even Owen
Lovejoy, the Illinois radical, hastened to clarify his position: "Why

. . . I do not advocate putting white men under black officers. Nobody else does or ever did." But, he went on, he would rather have a Negro than a slaveholder for an officer.[24]

These assurances evidently failed to win the Republican votes needed to pass the measure over almost solid Democratic opposition, for Stevens subsequently amended it so as to insure that no Negro could "be appointed to rank, or to exercise military or naval authority over white officers, soldiers or men." This move attracted new support. Carey A. Trimble of Ohio, a moderate Republican, observed that he would now vote for the bill, for while he favored the use of Negro soldiers, he lacked "that exalted idea of the bravery, the capacity, and efficiency of the black compared with white men, entertained by some gentlemen. In no respects is he the equal, nor can he in any situation become the equal of the Anglo-Saxon." Two days later, on February 3, 1863, the modified version passed the House with only two midwestern Republicans voting in the negative.[25]

Against this background the long campaign for colored troops had finally borne fruit on January 1, 1863, with the announcement that Negroes would be taken into the armed services. Yet even after Lincoln had apparently settled the matter he proceeded so slowly and in such a piecemeal fashion that only eight additional Negro regiments were authorized before the end of March.[26] The familiar forces—public opinion, prejudice, doubt, and party strife—continued to plot his cautious path. While Lincoln had decided that the use of colored troops was a means of counterbalancing the bad effects of the Emancipation Proclamation, he knew that his ability to take full advantage of it would depend partly on timing. As a result, he moved deliberately while waiting for the uproar over the Emancipation Proclamation to subside somewhat and for the northern people and the Union army to be more fully convinced that black soldiers were sorely needed to win the war.

Lincoln also lingered because of his concept of the mission of Negro troops—a product both of his doubts about their military capabilities and of his fears about the treatment they would receive from Confederates. In his opinion Negro units could be used more judiciously as an army of occupation to hold the Mississippi River and southern ports than as a fighting force. On January 10, 1863, he suggested that Stanton employ them "where they would not be liable to be captured"; that "they could perform garrison duty at Memphis, Columbus and other places and let the [white] soldiers go on more active service." He accordingly remained reluctant to recruit large numbers of Negroes before the Mississippi River was wrested from rebel hands. "We were not fully ripe for it [colored troops] until the river was opened," he told General Grant in August of 1863. "Now I think at least a hundred thousand can, and ought to be rapidly organized along its shores, relieving all the white troops to serve elsewhere."[27]

By late March the time was right. The passage of the Conscription Act (March 3, 1863) indicated that white volunteers were not coming forward in sufficient numbers, and it also brought hope that a draft might not be called if enough colored men entered the ranks. "Since Congress passed the conscription bill, the opposition to the Negro enlistment has subsided," jeered the Cleveland *Leader*. "Before . . . it was a matter of prejudice and hatred toward the black man, and of denying him the rights of citizenship. The Negro as a . . . soldier . . . was a monster. The Negro as a substitute is very acceptable." With Grant's Vicksburg campaign well under way and the reopening of the Mississippi River apparently near, it also seemed that Negro troops could soon be safely and wisely used. Now the administration struck with speed and vigor. On March 26, 1863, Lincoln asked Governor Andrew Johnson of Tennessee to consider seriously the possibility of raising a colored military force. "The bare sight of 50,000 armed and drilled black soldiers on the banks of the Mississippi would end the rebellion at once. And who doubts that we can present that sight, if we but take hold in earnest?" he wrote in a flush of optimism.[28] The day before, Secretary of War Stanton had ordered Adjutant General Lorenzo Thomas to the Mississippi Valley with instructions to organize Negro regiments.

General Thomas' mission was one of the most ambitious and fruitful of the Civil War. The orders he carried outlined three major objectives: he was to muster Negroes into the army; to take all necessary steps to enable the remainder "to support themselves and to furnish useful service in any capacity to the government"; and to make recommendations to the War Department for their disposition. To gain the co-operation of obstinate Union generals and soldiers, Thomas was instructed to explain "the importance attached by the Government to the use of the colored population emancipated by the President's proclamation, and particularly for the organization of their labor and military strength."[29] This, then, was far more than a simple recruiting assignment; rather, in its broadest sense, it was a major effort to deal comprehensively with the entire colored population in the region where the refugee problem was the most acute—the Mississippi Valley. In short, insofar as possible, Thomas was to mobilize the blacks there for war.

Before going into the South, Thomas weighed his task carefully and then unfolded his plans to Stanton. On April 1, 1863, he wrote that he had decided the freed Negroes who were not employed by the army should not be allowed to rely on the military for their subsistence. "It will not do," he said, "to send them in numbers into the free states, for the prejudices of the people of those States are against such a measure, and some of the States have enacted laws against the reception of free negroes. Such prejudice is particularly the case with those of Irish or German descent." Nor should they be taken to the border slave states where they might be re-enslaved. "Therefore these people must, in great measure, continue in the Southern states now in rebellion, . . . and they should be put in positions to make their own living." The men should either be employed as military laborers or be taken into the army by persuasion "or conscripted if necessary . . . and the others with the women and children placed on the abandoned plantations to till the ground," he concluded.[30]

Stripped from their context, these ideas ring with originality; actually Thomas said nothing that was new. In one form or another many of his recommendations were already being used in parts of the occupied South, and in January of 1863, General Nathaniel P. Banks had established a labor system in occupied Louisiana quite similar to that proposed and later implemented by Thomas.[31] The central theme of Thomas' plan—that the Negroes should stay in the South—was also commonly known. Antislavery men had, of course, long preached that the South was surely and rightly intended to be the home of the blacks, and some had even entreated the government to give destiny a helping hand.

It was in this spirit that Congressman Luther Hanchett of Wisconsin had predicted in May of 1862: "The same power which gives efficiency to the mandate of liberation is competent to and doubtless will provide an adequate police and economical establishment for the restraint and employment of the slaves . . . upon that very soil." At the height of the Illinois immigration dispute in the fall of 1862, the Chicago *Tribune* had requested the government to utilize the Negroes in the South. An Iowa editor had recommended that the freedmen should be put to work on confiscated rebel estates "under competent overseers appointed by the Government. . . . Thus the great question will be met . . . giving the negro his freedom, keeping him in the Cotton States, and furnishing him with work and just compensation." The organization of colored regiments would induce "thousands of the Negroes in the Free States to go South with their families . . . and will thus withdraw [them] from our population," he maintained on another occasion. A proposal to give land in the South to Negro soldiers was praised by the New York *Tribune* on the grounds that it would hold the freedmen there during and after the war, thereby eliminating the fear of a Negro invasion of the North. According to Senator Lyman Trumbull, confiscated southern land should be sold either to Union men or to northerners who could hire the blacks; then "they will not want to come to Illinois. They would prefer staying where they are if you would protect them, and we must protect them."[32]

More important, Edwin M. Stanton himself had propounded substantially the same theory that Thomas proposed to apply in the South. In his annual report to the President in December of 1862 the Secretary of War had advocated that the blacks should be fully utilized in the South, to garrison the unhealthy regions and to farm and thus provide sustenance for themselves and the armies. If this should be done, he said, they would remain in the South thereby avoiding "all possibility of competition from negro labor in the North."[33]

Meantime, Stanton partly hewed to these guidelines in the Mississippi Valley—the region that, because of its location, most concerned the Midwest. Learning much from his poignant experience with transporting the blacks into Illinois, Stanton struggled to make certain that if the masses of southern Negroes emigrated from the South they would not do so under the auspices of the army. After he halted the shipment of freedmen into Illinois, Stanton directed General Grant, operating in Tennessee, to employ the Negroes in the military service and to put them to work picking cotton for the government. Though Grant complied, the refugee problem steadily worsened. Finally, on January 6, 1863, Grant asked Halleck what he could do with the "surplus negroes" and informed him that he had authorized an Ohio philanthropist to take all of the colored people at Columbus, Kentucky, to "his State at Government expense. Would like to dispose of more in the same way." "I am directed by the Secretary of War," Halleck replied, "to say that if you have ordered the shipment of negroes from the slave states to Cincinnati, you will countermand the order." Grant was evidently governed accordingly until Thomas arrived, for in March of 1863 he complained, "I am not allowed to send them out of the department and such numbers as we have it is hard to keep them in." One month later he clung to the same course while issuing orders to one of his subordinate generals: "All the negroes you have you will provide for where they are . . . until other disposition is made of them. General L. Thomas is now here, with authority to make ample provision for the negro."[34]

A similar situation prevailed in middle Tennessee, the sector commanded by General William S. Rosecrans. In mid-April, 1863, a war correspondent of the New York *Tribune* reported from Murfreesboro that Rosecrans was greatly disturbed about the Negro women and children who were flocking into his lines and burdening his troops. "In consequence of the heartless bigotry of the people of the Free States," he wrote, "Gen. Rosecrans cannot send them North— even if he could ship them through Kentucky. The selfish demagogues of the Northern States would raise a clamor about a black immigration that nothing short of physical force would subdue."[35] General Thomas had not yet counseled Rosecrans on this subject, and it is not known whether Stanton or Halleck had ordered him not to send the refugees North, or whether he made this decision himself. Whatever the explanation, a pattern of providing for the refugees in the Mississippi Valley and Tennessee, despite the embarrassment to the army, was clearly appearing in early 1863. The single flaw in the emerging blueprint was a procedure whereby military commanders, upon application, supplied Negro laborers to prospective employers in the Midwest; but this did not mar the design, for such traffic was inconsequential.[36]

But if General Thomas was operating on solid and familiar terrain when he submitted his recommendations to the Secretary of War, the rigors of his mission were not lessened. His was the task of converting these exhortations and sporadic examples into a program of meaningful action. Either tacitly or explicitly Stanton quite naturally accepted Thomas' plan, and the general later claimed that it was sanctioned by Lincoln. In fact, according to Thomas, he was the President's emissary. On April 9, 1863, he opened an address to Union troops at Lake Providence, Louisiana, with the declaration that he came "with full authority from the President of the United States" to announce the government's policy. "The question came up in Washington," he continued, "What is best to be done with this unfortunate race?' They are coming in upon us in such numbers that some provision must be made for them. You cannot send them North. You all know the prejudices of the Northern people against receiving large numbers of the colored race." He then furnished the obvious answer. "Look along the river and see the multitude of deserted plantations upon its banks. These are the places for those freedmen where they can be self-sustaining and self-supporting. . . . They are to be encouraged to come to us. They are to be received . . . fed and clothed; THEY ARE TO BE ARMED. This is the policy that has been decided upon."[37]

In the following months Thomas traversed the Mississippi Valley and Tennessee elaborating and implementing his aims in speeches and detailed orders. His avowed goal was to make the entire "colored population self supporting by earning wages." Under his direction Negroes coming within Union lines in the region were either persuaded or forced to join the army, employed as military laborers, encouraged to remain on the plantation and work for wages, hired out to planters, or, as a last resort, placed in refugee camps.[38] While these measures were in themselves great inducements for the Negroes to stay in the South, there is evidence to suggest that Thomas detained them with other barriers which cast additional light on his intentions. In the fall of 1863, the general directed, "Domestic servants in the employ of loyal citizens will, on application of the latter to military commandants, be permitted to proceed to any Northern point"—a plain indication that those Negroes who were not so engaged were to be retained where they were. The officer in charge of the freedmen at Vicksburg reported in mid-1863 that many under his jurisdiction had "applied for passes to go to the North; but we have steadily refused all such, except in case of special order." In January of 1865, Thomas advised a commander in Tennessee that, since the army had withdrawn much of the Negro labor from the state, "it is . . . essential that all others of this race be kept in the State. No passes should, therefore, be given for blacks to go beyond its limits."[39]

This is not to say that Thomas and the army had completely halted Negroes from leaving the South, or that they even attempted to do so. Thousands of colored people continued to emigrate to the Midwest either on their own initiative or to satisfy requests made to persons in charge of refugee camps for their services. In May of 1863, for example, approximately 300 Negroes were sent from St. Louis to St. Paul to fill a requisition by General Henry H. Sibley who apparently intended to use them as military laborers and teamsters.[40] Nevertheless, for the time being, the practice of employing and caring for the blacks in the South had effectually sealed the vast majority of them in the region. Lacking passes, transportation, money, and usually the desire to go North, most of the freedmen remained in the South under the supervision and care of the army.[41] In this way, the threat of a great migration was destroyed.

This does not mean that the decisions to arm, use, and provide for the black race in the South were designed simply to stifle the threat of a northward exodus of Negroes. While some public figures had joined the Secretary of War in arguing that the enlistment of black men in the army would help to hold the freedmen out of the North, the logic of the war and the needs of the military unquestionably propelled the Negro soldier movement to fruition. On the other hand, as the words and actions of Stanton and Thomas demonstrate and as the pleas of antislavery men indicate, the political motive was crucial in the determination to utilize the unemployed Negro men, women, and children in the South. True enough, this was seemingly an eminently practical solution to an old problem; but the administration could have chosen a different course, one that had been considered and tried, one that was probably even more desirable from military and economic points of view. For had the thousands of able-bodied freed people who were not being used by the armed forces been taken into the many parts of the Midwest that were keenly suffering from lack of laborers and were seeking immigrants from abroad, the army would have been relieved of much of an onerous burden that impaired its efficiency and morale, and the labor shortage would have been alleviated. But after the brief and stormy trial in Illinois, this alternative was deliberately shelved in favor of one that was more acceptable to the Midwest. On the whole, the policy activated by the government in 1863 was a brilliant fusion of common sense, military exigency, and political expediency.

Lorenzo Thomas was one of the unsung heroes of the Union. His successful recruiting, combined with the performance of colored soldiers, was encouraging, and a campaign to muster Negroes into the service was pushed forward vigorously in both North and South. By the end of the war, approximately 178,895 men were serving in "the sable arm."[42] Moreover, both Lincoln and Stanton endorsed his system of employing the freed Negroes on abandoned plantations or of caring for them in the South, and it became the official policy of the federal government in the Mississippi Valley and Tennessee. Wherever practicable Union commanders adopted and expanded it, and with some modifications and variations it endured until the Freedmen's Bureau assumed control in 1865.[43]

In the Midwest, Thomas' program won added support for freeing the slaves. This was partly accomplished by the Republican press which closely followed the general on his tour in the South, publishing and acclaiming his speeches and directives as the long-awaited answer to the Negro problem.[44] They rejoiced for several good reasons. In the first place, the administration was able to demonstrate convincingly that emancipation was a source of energy and strength. Previously, it had been of dubious military value, and the freedmen had usually been a costly nuisance. Now liberation was a two-edged sword: while it divested the Confederacy of many of its slaves, it strengthened Union arms by marshalling them into the war effort as soldiers or workers. This arrangement, in turn, supplied a plausible method of racial adjustment. While Negro soldiers could prove their race worthy of freedom by fighting to liberate their people and to preserve the Union, colored civilians could support and prepare themselves for life in a free society as they labored for wages. Above all else, they now had the opportunity to exemplify their capacity to progress and to win the esteem and approval of the American people. The freedman was still the ward of the nation, but not as before —a usually useless encumbrance. He now appeared to be potentially useful and productive, an ally and an asset of the Union.

Finally, the systematic mobilization of the blacks in the South moderated the racial fears of the Midwest in another way. No longer was the administration merely relying on climate and sentiment to hold the Negroes in the South; it had developed a positive means for containing them there. Though the well-publicized pronouncements and orders of General Thomas spoke quite clearly on this point, some Republican newspapers endeavored to make sure that no one misunderstood their significance. The Dubuque *Times* announced in May of 1863 that the delusion about Negroes invading the North had been demolished because the blacks in Iowa were joining the army to fight for homes in the South. In early 1864 a special correspondent to the Chicago *Tribune* candidly wrote that the use of the Negroes in their home land "not only decides the question of deportation, but also evades the prejudices of Northern communities, and also contributes a valuable addition to the resources of the country."[45]

Apparently two members of Lincoln's cabinet, and perhaps the President himself, had already come to the same conclusion. Shortly after General Thomas began his southern tour, they jettisoned the Negro colonization project, long one of their favorite weapons for combating northern opposition to emancipation. On May 18, 1863, Secretary of Interior John P. Usher, who only nine months earlier had championed Negro deportation as a shrewd political device, advised Lincoln that the War Department's new method of dealing with the freedmen "prevents the further emigration from the U.S. of persons of African descent, for the present, and it in my judgment will not be renewed" in any appreciable measure. Two days later Postmaster-General Montgomery Blair, close friend of the President and the most dedicated colonizationist in the cabinet, announced a major change in administration policy. Speaking before a Cleveland audience and claiming that he was outlining the President's past and future course, Blair declared that Lincoln was now firmly committed to mobilizing and using the Negroes in the South, and implied deportation was a dead letter for the time being but that the Negroes would be removed from the country after the rebellion was suppressed.[46] Even though Lincoln probably never abandoned the belief that colonization offered the best road to racial peace, he never again mentioned the scheme in public—mute evidence that he felt that it was no longer politically essential.

After almost two years of evasion and travail, leaders of the Union had at last fashioned a policy for dealing effectively with the most acute problems of emancipation. Born chiefly of political and military necessity and also unmistakably molded by midwestern racism, it was destined to become a major force in the battle for emancipation and equality.

Notes

1. T. J. Barnett to S. L. M. Barlow, November 30, 1862, quoted in Allan Nevins, *The War for the Union* (2 vols.; New York: Charles Scribner's Sons, 1959–60), II, 336–37; Sumner to Duchess of Argyll, January 4, 1863, in Edward L. Pierce, *Memoir and Letters of Charles Sumner* (4 vols.; Boston: Roberts Bros., 1887–93), IV, 114.

2. For a discussion of the problems connected with the freedmen and refugees, see Bell Irvin Wiley, *Southern Negroes, 1861–1865* (2d ed.; New York: Rinehart, 1953), pp. 175 ff.

3. U.S., War Department, *The War of the Rebellion: A Compilation of the Official Records of the Union and Confederate Armies* (128 vols.; Washington, D.C.: Government Printing Office, 1880–1901), 1st ser., XXIV, 105 (hereinafter cited as *Official Records*); *ibid.*, 1st ser., XVII, 470–71, 481; "Draft of a Communication to Stephen A. Hurlburt," [*c.* August 15?] 186[3], in Roy P. Basler (ed.), *The Collected Works of Abraham Lincoln* (9 vols.; New Brunswick, N.J.: Rutgers University Press, 1953), VI, 387–88.

4. Barnett to S. L. M. Barlow, November 30, 1862, quoted in Nevins, *The War for the Union,* II, 336–37; "Annual Message to Congress," December 1, 1862, in Basler (ed.), *The Collected Works of Abraham Lincoln,* V, 535–36.

5. "Annual Message to Congress," December 1, 1862, in Basler (ed.), *The Collected Works of Abraham Lincoln,* V, 518–37; "To General John A. McClernand," January 8, 1863, in *ibid.,* VI, 48–49; "To John M. Schofield," June 22, 1863, in *ibid.,* p. 291.

6. Howard K. Beale (ed.), *Diary of Gideon Welles: Secretary of the Navy under Lincoln and Johnson* (3 vols.; New York: W. W. Norton, 1960), I, 206; "To William H. Seward," January 6, 1863, in Basler (ed.), *The Collected Works of Abraham Lincoln,* VI, 41–42; "Proclamation Cancelling Contract with Bernard Kock," April 16, 1863, in *ibid.,* pp. 178–79; James G. Randall, *Lincoln the President: Springfield to Gettysburg* (4 vols.; New York: Dodd, Mead, 1945), II, 139–40.

7. Dudley Taylor Cornish, *The Sable Arm: Negro Troops in the Union Army, 1861–1865* (New York: Longmans, Green, 1956), p. 95.

8. "Remarks to a Deputation of Western Gentlemen," August 4, 1862, in Basler (ed.), *The Collected Works of Abraham Lincoln,* V, 356–57; "Reply to Emancipation Memorial Presented by Chicago Christians of All Denominations," September 13, 1862, in *ibid.,* p. 423.

9. *Congressional Globe,* 37 Cong., 2 sess., p. 2207; *ibid.,* 37 Cong., 3 sess., pp. 636, 653–54, 709–10, 1232, 1442, and Appendix, pp. 85, 91, 93;

Emma Lou Thornbrough, *The Negro in Indiana: A Study of a Minority* (Indianapolis: Indiana Historical Bureau, 1957), pp. 193–94; *Times* (Chicago), July 12, 1862, May 13, 1863; *See-Bote* (Milwaukee), July 23, 1862; *Free Press* (Detroit), February 24, April 16, May 8, 1863; *Crisis* (Columbus), August 13, 27, 1862, February 11, 25, 1863; *Democratic Herald* (Dubuque), March 5, 14, May 31, 1863.

10. Horace Greeley, *The American Conflict: A History of the Great Rebellion in the United States of America, 1860–'65* (Hartford: O. D. Case, 1865–66), II, 526–27; *Congressional Globe*, 37 Cong., 3 sess., pp. 599, 653–54, 709–10, and Appendix, pp. 85, 91, 93; *Ohio Statesman* (Columbus) quoted in *Leader* (Cleveland), March 12, 1863; *Democratic Herald* (Dubuque), May 31, 1863; *Times* (Chicago), June 9, 1863.

11. *Times* (Dubuque), July 12, 1862; John Mercer Langston, *From the Virginia Plantation to the National Capitol; or, The First and Only Negro Representative in Congress from the Old Dominion* (Hartford: American Publishing Company, 1894), p. 206; "Reply to Emancipation Memorial Presented by Chicago Christians of All Denominations," September 13, 1862, in Basler (ed.), *The Collected Works of Abraham Lincoln*, V, 423.

12. Browning to Lincoln, August 11, 1862, Robert Todd Lincoln Collection (Manuscript Division, Library of Congress); *Congressional Globe*, 38 Cong., 1 sess., p. 1896.

13. Theodore Calvin Pease and James G. Randall (eds.), *The Diary of Orville Hickman Browning* (2 vols.; Springfield: Illinois State Historical Library, 1927–33), I, 555; *Tribune* (New York), March 31, 1864.

14. Bell Irvin Wiley, *Life of Billy Yank: The Common Soldier of the Union* (Indianapolis: Bobbs-Merrill, 1952), pp. 119–20.

15. Pease and Randall (eds.), *The Diary of Orville Hickman Browning*, I, 583–84; *Official Records*, 3d ser., V, 118–19; W. T. Sherman to John Sherman, April 26, 1863, William Tecumseh Sherman Papers (Manuscript Division, Library of Congress).

16. William D. Bickham to Salmon P. Chase, August 24, 1862, Chase Papers (Manuscript Division, Library of Congress); John Sherman to W. T. Sherman, August 24, 1862, W. T. Sherman Papers; *Tribune* (New York), July 22, 1864. For examples of eastern opposition to Negro soldiers, see *Congressional Globe*, 37 Cong., 2 sess., pp. 404, 1111, 2250; *ibid.*, 3 sess., pp. 634, 651, 1423.

17. *Western Christian Advocate* (Cincinnati), June 17, 1863; *Leader* (Cleveland), March 18, June 1, 1863; "Preliminary Report of the American Freedmen's Inquiry Commission," June 30, 1863, in *Official Records*, 3d ser., III, 436–37.

18. Julia Perkins Cutler, *Life and Times of Ephraim Cutler . . . with*

Biographical Sketches of . . . William Parker Cutler . . . (Cincinnati: Robert Clarke, 1890), pp. 302–3; *Western Christian Advocate* (Cincinnati), June 24, 1863; *Sentinel* (Milwaukee), June 8, 1863; D. Burt, "Popular Government and Slavery," *Congregational Quarterly,* V (January, 1863), 46–52.

19. *Congressional Globe,* 37 Cong., 2 sess., pp. 1651–52, 2246, 3199, Appendix, p. 319; *ibid.,* 37 Cong., 3 sess., pp. 604–6, and Appendix, p. 77; *Sentinel* (Milwaukee), January 7, 1863; *Times* (Dubuque), February 6, 1863; *Leader* (Cleveland), March 4, 28, 1863.

20. *Tribune* (Chicago), February 17, March 4, 1863; *Leader* (Cleveland), March 12, 1863; *Congressional Globe,* 37 Cong., 2 sess., pp. 1652, 3127; Kirkwood to Henry W. Halleck, August 5, 1862, in U.S., War Department, Adjutant General's Office, Record Group 94 (National Archives, Washington, D.C.); *Herald* (Clinton) quoted in *Times* (Dubuque), August 15, 1862; *Times* (Dubuque), September 28, 1862; Dan Elbert Clark, *Samuel J. Kirkwood* (Iowa City: State Historical Society of Iowa, 1917), p. 294.

21. John Lynch to A. Kitchell [1863], Richard Yates Papers (Illinois State Historical Society, Springfield); Burt, "Popular Government and Slavery," pp. 46–52.

22. *Illinois State Journal* (Springfield), July 18, 1862; *The Liberator* (Boston), August 15, 1862; *Journal* (Indianapolis), August 15, 1862; *Journal* (Indianapolis) quoted in *Times* (Dubuque), March 1, 1863. See also speeches in Wallace Collection (Indiana State Historical Society, Indianapolis).

23. Cornish, *The Sable Arm,* pp. 184–86, 214–17.

24. *Congressional Globe,* 37 Cong., 3 sess., pp. 599, 600, 604.

25. *Ibid.,* pp. 557, 600, 604, 689–90, and Appendix, p. 77. Midwestern Democrats voted fourteen to one against final passage. The Senate let the bill die.

26. Cornish, *The Sable Arm,* p. 99.

27. Beale (ed.), *Diary of Gideon Welles,* I, 218; Charles Sumner to John M. Forbes, December 25, 1862, in Sarah Forbes Hughes (ed.), *Letters and Recollections of John Murray Forbes* (2 vols.; Boston: Houghton Mifflin, 1899), I, 348–49; "To Andrew Johnson," March 26, 1863, in Basler (ed.), *The Collected Works of Abraham Lincoln,* VI, 149–50; "To Ulysses S. Grant," August 9, 1863, in *ibid.,* pp. 374–75; "To John A. Dix," January 14, 1863, in *ibid.,* p. 56; Cutler, *Life . . . of Ephraim Cutler . . . ,* p. 303.

28. *Leader* (Cleveland), March 7, 1863; *Official Records,* 3d ser., III, 103; *Tribune* (Chicago), March 4, 1863.

29. Stanton to Thomas, March 25, 1863, Records of the Secretary of War, Record Group 107 (National Archives, Washington, D.C.).

30. Thomas to Stanton, April 1, 1863, General Thomas' Letters, U.S., War Department, Adjutant General's Office, Record Group 94.

31. Wiley, *Southern Negroes, 1861–1865,* pp. 184, 188–90; Fred Harvey Harrington, *Fighting Politician: Major General N. P. Banks* (Philadelphia: University of Pennsylvania Press, 1948), pp. 105–7.

32. *Congressional Globe,* 37 Cong., 2 sess., Appendix, p. 212; *Tribune* (Chicago), September 26, October 19, 1862; *Times* (Dubuque), September 12, 20, 1862, February 6, 1863; *Tribune* (New York), February 12, 1863.

33. "Report of the Secretary of War," December 2, 1862, *Congressional Globe,* 37 Cong., 3 sess., Appendix, p. 32.

34. *Official Records,* 1st ser., XXIV, 96, 187; *ibid.,* XVII, 470–71, 481; *ibid.,* LII, 323.

35. *Tribune* (New York), April 17, 1863.

36. *Catholic Telegraph* (Cincinnati), March 18, 1863; *Sentinel* (Milwaukee), March 27, 1863; *Official Records,* 2d ser., V, 521.

37. *Tribune* (Chicago), April 17, 23, 1863; *Journal* (Battle Creek), April 24, 1863; *Crisis* (Columbus), April 22, 1863.

38. Special Order No. 45, August 18, 1863, Special Order No. 63, September 29, 1863, General Thomas' Letters, in U.S., War Department, Adjutant General's Office, Record Group 94; Thomas to Edwin M. Stanton, April 12, August 23, October 2, 1863, *ibid.*; *Tribune* (Chicago), April 17, 1862; *Times* (New York), April 26, 1863; *Official Records,* 1st ser., XXX, 375–77.

39. Thomas to John F. Miller, January 16, 1865, General Thomas' Letters, Record Group 94; A. L. Mitchell to John Eaton, May 31, 1864, Joseph Warren (comp.), *Extracts from Reports of Superintendents of Freedmen* (Vicksburg: n.p., 1864), p. 22; *Official Records,* 3d ser., III, 917–18.

40. *Tribune* (Chicago), May 14, 1863; *Democratic Herald* (Dubuque), April 7, 16, 1863; *Press* (St. Paul) quoted in *Times* (Dubuque), May 22, 1863; Earl Spangler, *The Negro in Minnesota* (Minneapolis: T. S. Denison, 1961), pp. 50–52; John Eaton, *Grant, Lincoln and the Freedmen* (London: Longmans, Green, 1907), pp. 37–38.

41. See p. 122.

42. Cornish, *The Sable Arm,* p. 288.

43. Wiley, *Southern Negroes, 1861–1865,* pp. 191–229; *Official Records,* 3d ser., IV, 143; Stanton to Thomas, August 29, 1863, Edwin M. Stanton Papers (Manuscript Division, Library of Congress).

44. Thomas' orders and speeches were printed in the *Tribune* (Chi-

cago), April 17, 23, August 27, September 3, 1863; the *Sentinel* (Milwaukee), April 21, 1863; the *Journal* (Battle Creek), April 24, 1863; and in the *Times* (Dubuque), August 30, October 22, 1863. They were sometimes printed under the caption, "What is to be done with the Freed Slaves."

45. *Tribune* (Chicago), January 5, 1864; *Times* (Dubuque), May 31, August 30, October 4, 1863. See also *Tribune* (New York), April 22, 1863.

46. Usher to Lincoln, May 18, 1863, R. T. Lincoln Collection; *Tribune* (New York), May 29, 1863; *Ohio State Journal* (Columbus), May 23, 1863.

❦ 7 ❧

The Turning Point

At the outset of the summer of 1863 the cause of emancipation seemed to be stalemated in the Midwest. While the legal or formal commitment to freedom as a military necessity had already been made by the President and Congress, this crucial region had shown no clear sign of public approval. Capitalizing on the Republicans' antislavery stance and on the discouraging military situation, Democrats had carried the elections in the fall of 1862 and in the following spring blunted a drive to raise the war into a popular struggle for human liberty. Yet, most midwesterners, often tenuously and frequently for differing reasons, did accept the destruction of slavery as a war goal before the national elections of 1864 when they would vote for the party pledged to abolition.

The turning point came in mid-1863. New York editor Horace Greeley thought so. After the war this strident radical critic of Lincoln's antislavery gait conceded that a majority of Union voters opposed emancipation until July of 1863.[1] Lincoln must have agreed. After the great Union victories at Gettysburg and Vicksburg in early July, he progressively exerted more forthright moral leadership and cast the aims of the war on a higher level. Standing before a happy crowd of serenaders celebrating these two military triumphs, he described the rebellion as an "effort to overthrow the principle that all men were created equal." The importance of this statement did not lie in its sentiment, for Lincoln had long regarded both slavery and the rebellion as attacks on the Declaration of Independence. It was significant instead because of its timing. The President had not talked publicly in such a vein in over two years even though this had once been one of his cherished and most effective themes. In the months that followed, though he clung to the position that the struggle was essentially a battle for national integrity and republican government, he increasingly defended emancipation on ethical grounds and identified it either as one of the wholesome consequences of the war or as one of its objectives.[2] Lincoln's unaccustomed boldness in openly expressing these quietly held but deep convictions was not simply a product of his belief that the Confederacy was collapsing. Ever sensitive to public opinion, he had also gauged the pace of antislavery thought and had clearly decided that the resolution of the northern people was ascending to an even loftier plane.

Lincoln was right. The emancipation movement was gaining fervor and momentum throughout the North. New England was in the forefront as usual, but the Middle West, after several false starts, was also advancing. In that section it was the Union victories at Gettysburg and Vicksburg rather than the Emancipation Proclamation that created the ideal conditions for launching a popular crusade against slavery. While the repulse of the southern invasion at Gettysburg shattered the illusion of Lee's invincibility, Vicksburg was even more meaningful, for it split the Confederacy and reopened to the Gulf the vital artery of mid-America. Together they banished the defeatism that had shrouded the Midwest, kindled hopes that the end of the war was in sight, and inspired renewed confidence in the administration and its works.

In this setting midwesterners increasingly accepted emancipation as a legitimate war aim. For the most part their approval sprang from a conviction that the expediency of the measure had now been proven in battle, that it was actually shortening the war. But the heady influence of military success evoked other subtler emotions that seemed to uplift the purpose of the Middle West. Carried along by the religious and patriotic currents that swept in the wake of Gettysburg and Vicksburg, more and more people viewed the war as a fight for liberty and embraced the idea that the antislavery policy had endowed the Union with moral superiority that would help to conquer the South and also ultimately elevate the national character by purging the country of its sole remaining defect. Finally, to the part of the population that had interpreted the rebellion as a divine chastisement for wrongdoing, the turn for the better in the war appeared to be a sign that the Lord had sanctioned liberation, and that He would lift His curse once slavery was abolished.

Adroit political maneuvers reflected the changing temper and shaped its thrust. Accurately sensing the new mood in the summer of 1863, midwestern Republicans and Unionists struck to consolidate support for their measures. Most of all they dwelled on the theme that freeing the slaves had now been proven to be an indispensable source of military power. But they also spoke more boldly and more frequently about the moral, social, economic, and historic benefits of destroying slavery. Most of what they said was familiar to midwestern hearers. Steeped in the rhetoric of abolition and containing a strain of idealism that had usually been obscured or purposely ignored in the intense emphasis upon military expediency, these arguments had occasionally shown through the appeals of even the most conservative antislavery editors and politicians. But never had they been uttered so often by so many in such high places. While Lincoln spoke in July of the Union battling to vindicate the equality of man, two midwestern radicals, Governor Richard Yates of Illinois and Senator Zachariah Chandler of Michigan, along with the moderate Senator James R. Doolittle of Wisconsin agreed later that God had willed the war to destroy slavery. In Iowa, Colonel William F. Stone, the Republicans' outspoken antislavery candidate for governor, shouted that the North was waging an "abolition war" which should not be ended until every slave was freed. His more cautious Unionist counterpart in Ohio, John Brough, also grew bolder. Before Gettysburg and Vicksburg, Brough had usually dodged the slavery question; in August he declared, "I thought that the proclamation was not dictated by good policy, but had long been convinced that the rebellion could not be crushed until slavery was abolished."[3] Emancipation, it was further argued, would free white men from the degrading competition of slave labor, purify the Republic, rededicate the nation to the democratic and egalitarian ideals of the Founding Fathers, persuade God to end the war, and insure domestic peace.[4]

If the emancipation movement rose chiefly on the wings of military victory in the Middle West, there were other trenchant forces at work there that had smoothed its way and would later help to sustain it through the enervating fall days of inaction on the eastern front and near rout at Chickamauga. The flourishing economy, which had often succored the Lincoln government in the past, became a "rushing flood" in mid-1863 and thus gathered additional backing for the administration and its antislavery activities. As Senator John Sherman pointed out in November of 1863, "The wonderful prosperity of all classes, especially of laborers, has a tendency to secure acquiescence in all measures demanded to carry on the war."[5] In some quarters the excesses of peace extremists and charges that Copperheads were plotting to overthrow the government had much the same effect, for they drove into the Republican-Unionist camp some midwesterners who had no interest in abolishing slavery, but feared that the Democratic party was bent on internal civil war and disunion.

The steadily heightening militancy of the churchmen of the Middle West supplied the crusade against slavery with a source of unflagging energy. By mid-1863, most of the great religious organizations of the region and many of the leading pastors were operating as the spiritual arm of the Republican party. While they preached the antislavery gospel and held forth the vision of a holy war for freedom, they thundered against the Copperheads and disloyalty and canonized the Lincoln administration and its policies.[6] In December of 1863 the Chicago *Times* uttered a common complaint of midwestern Democrats when it grieved, "A fair share of the pulpits are . . . devoted to [the Negroes'] cause; the African and him in bondage being the theme, instead of 'Christ and him crucified'; and in which the elect and the abolitionists, natural depravity and democracy, the devil and Vallandigham, the New Jerusalem and negro equality, are constantly used as synonymous." Undoubtedy this was an inflammatory overstatement, but it contained some truth. Some of those souls who persisted in their Democratic political faith withdrew from their churches in the face of antislavery preaching and harassment. Others were sometimes ridiculed before the congregation by their ministers and in some cases were even read out of the church. With sermons and resolutions midwestern clergymen actively tried to rally support for Republican-Unionist candidates in the fall elections of 1863. Methodist preachers in Cincinnati called on their followers to vote "for the unconditional Union ticket" and accused the Democrats of being hostile to the war and to the "Church of God." In October of 1863 the Cincinnati *Catholic Telegraph,* edited by Reverend Edward Purcell, brother of Archbishop John B. Purcell of Cincinnati, obliquely endorsed the Union party slate. This action climaxed an admittedly rather fruitless campaign waged throughout 1863 to convince Catholics, particularly Irish-Americans, that slavery was injurious to white labor as well as immoral. Finally, Purcell officially renounced the Democratic party in December of 1863, condemning it as a proslavery body.[7]

Other developments also quickened the tempo of antislavery thought in the Midwest. In April the New York *Tribune* happily observed that the fear that the North would be deluged with freed Negroes "is beginning to generally be recognized as such."[8] While this was an exaggeration, by the summer of 1863 fears of large-scale Negro immigration and the attendant problem of race relations were beginning to decline very slowly but persistently. The thriving economy, a dearth of labor, rising wages, and rapid absorption of Negro immigrants into the labor force helped to relax some of these tensions. Faith that the Confederacy and slavery were both dying also revived confidence that the blacks would not be driven North in search of liberty, but would remain in their natural and congenial environment under freedom. Of far greater importance, it was simply becoming more apparent that Negroes were not pushing into the North. In 1864 even the Columbus *Crisis,* long a Democratic prophet of woe, grudgingly admitted that freedmen had been "quietly and slyly introduced into Ohio in small numbers, instead of the avalanche intended."[9] Statistics confirmed this observation. Not only did the state and local censuses compiled during and after the war uphold the Republicans' repeated claims that small numbers of Negroes had made their way into the Midwest; they also revealed that the increase in the ratio of blacks to whites was negligible, and that most of the colored residents were concentrated in a few counties.[10]

Recent federal action seemed to insure that there would be no hegira of blacks from the South. With their broad publicity of General Lorenzo Thomas' program and appropriate comments, Republican editors contrived to make it appear that the government's practice of utilizing the freedmen in the South was holding them there and would continue to do so. The system initiated by Thomas, wrote an Iowa editor in August of 1863, "completely demolishes the Rebel bugbears at the North, by which so many thousands, especially of the Irish voters, have been cheated out of their votes by the Rebel demagogues here."[11] Under such circumstances Democratic warnings that a black invasion was imminent were viewed with growing skepticism as the war progressed. Some of the opposition to emancipation waned accordingly.

A gradually improving attitude toward the Negro also speeded the cause of freedom. This turn for the better became perceptible in the Midwest by the summer of 1863, and it would continue throughout the war. Just as apprehensions of a black invasion had heightened anti-Negro feelings, the decline of these anxieties reduced them to some degree. Just as defeat had intensified racism, victory now suppressed it somewhat. Hope of ultimate triumph and the growing sense of the righteousness of emancipation brought forth increasing toleration and good will for the enslaved race—impulses that had often languished in the pessimism of adversity. In this atmosphere the bloody New York City draft riots (July 13–15, 1863), in which mobs vented much of their wrath upon colored people, other acts of race violence in the North, and reports of Confederate atrocities against black troops aroused compassion for Negroes and thus diminished race prejudice. The American Freedmen's Inquiry Commission explained this irony in its 1864 report. "We have found ourselves called upon to interpose in favor of the outraged and unprotected. But such interposition tends to create, even in minds of ordinary sensibility, good will and sympathy toward the sufferers whom one interposes to protect."[12]

But essentially the changing point of view on the Negro was rooted in the actions of the blacks themselves, and it was nurtured by deft political tactics. The system of employing the freedmen on abandoned southern plantations or as military laborers weighed heavily in the scales, for its success helped to counteract doubts that the slaves were fit for freedom and enabled the friends of the Negro to show that colored people were able to live intelligently and productively as a free people. The performance of Negro soldiers did much more to place the black race in a better light. Their conduct under fire on such fields as Port Hudson (May, 1863), Milliken's Bend (June, 1863), and Fort Wagner (July, 1863) earned the gratitude and respect of many midwesterners who had previously questioned their capabilities and hardened the resolve of those who had never doubted. In a typical commentary after the engagement at Port Hudson a Michigan Republican wrote, "It is daily being proved that the negro can take care of himself; that he ardently desires freedom;

that he knows how to conduct himself as a free man; that he will fight, too. . . . The negro loves freedom, and will fight to obtain it."[13]

Nerved by these accomplishments, Republicans and Unionists strove to win further approval for the recruitment of Negro soldiers and emancipation. With fluent phrases, the party press tirelessly praised colored troops for their proficiency and courage, and the President, Secretary of War, army generals, and leading Republicans frequently cited their services and value to the Union. Black soldiers were essential to victory, they urged; only the promise of freedom would rally them to arms; and justice and humanity required that permanent liberty be their reward.[14] Sometimes they capped these arguments with a biting assault on the Democrats—an attack often designed to abate race prejudice. Black men were fighting for the Union, they cried, but Democrats were either obstructing it by opposing the policies of the government or betraying it by subversive activities. In August of 1863, Lincoln eloquently set the style in a letter to a Union meeting at Springfield, Illinois. "I hope [peace] will come soon, and come to stay," he declared. "And then, there will be some black men who can remember that, with silent tongue, and clenched teeth, and steady eye, and well-poised bayonet, they have helped mankind on to this great consummation; while, I fear, there will be some white ones, unable to forget that, with malignant heart, and deceitful speech, they have strove to hinder it."[15]

In the same spirit, many Republicans with growing vigor and frequency defended Negroes against their detractors and assailants. As in the past these defenses were strongly flavored with paternalism; but with a new audacity they also confidently extolled the virtues and humanity of the freedmen and called for tolerance and fair treatment. Some of these appeals were lofty and noble. The Chicago *Tribune,* for example, admonished in August of 1863 that the fate of the nation depended upon its treatment of the Negro. "Hence, we beg . . . for this race the sympathy and admiration that their conduct may justly demand." Others were crude and pointed. The Republican candidate for governor of Iowa reportedly said in the midst of his campaign that he had rather "*eat* with a nigger, *drink* with a nigger, *live* with a nigger, *sleep* with a nigger, than a copperhead." The leading Republican paper in Iowa took a slightly different reading: "It is true that the Negroes belong to a degraded race; but it is equally true that the devils who malignantly abuse them, and deride the Government, are more degraded by far than the greasiest, dirtiest Ethiopian whose body finds a resting place in the 'Lincum Hotel.' "[16]

Other more tangible evidence also revealed that some of the asperities of racial animosity were softening in the Midwest. Although anti-Negro activities continued to crop up in the form of kidnappings, beatings, intimidations, black law arrests and prosecutions, and fugitive slave hunts, they began to taper off in the last half of 1863.[17] Another symbol of change was the Midwest's mounting acceptance of black men as soldiers. While a great many midwesterners both in and out of the army never relented in their opposition to recruiting Negroes, part of the resistance to this measure was gradually worn down chiefly by military considerations and by the avowed desire to spare white lives. In a significant hyperbole General Lorenzo Thomas reported in April that "prejudices in this army respecting arming the negroes are fast dying out." But the tide of opinion was indeed flowing in that direction.[18] Beginning in June, the midwestern states, one by one, received permission to raise black regiments. To some extent this change of heart was non-partisan since Democrats as well as Republicans sometimes evaded the draft by hiring colored substitutes. In time some counties became so earnest in this work that they employed agents to search for Negro recruits to credit to their quotas.[19] Still, whether their motives were base or enlightened, the willingness to accept colored enlistments meant that most midwesterners had learned by experience that black men possessed the ability and will to fight.

For all the Republicans' growing militancy and all the brightening outlook on the Negro, a majority of midwesterners were not striving for racial equality. Nor were they enlisting in a moralistic crusade for freedom. The political campaigns in the summer and fall of 1863 would tell the story.

Discredited by the army's recent successes, torn by internal strife over the peace issue, damaged by the nomination of the pacifistic Clement Vallandigham for the governorship of Ohio, and writhing under accusations of disloyalty, the Democrats pursued a well-worn road as they canvassed for state and local offices. Once again they asserted their desire for peace and reunion, denounced executive usurpation, the loss of civil liberties, the centralization of power in Washington, the use of colored soldiers, emancipation, conscription, Negro immigration, and maintained their abuse and ridicule of the black race.[20] There was, however, some difference in emphasis. Now that the great barriers to emancipation and complete Republican mastery—popular doubts about the constitutionality and wisdom of freeing the slaves—were beginning to crumble somewhat under the weight of experience, mounting exasperation with the rebels, a favorable military situation, and expectation of final victory, the Democrats exploited the fear of racial equality on an unprecedented scale. They said little that was new, but they said it with surpassing bitterness. Trying desperately to provoke a debate on the Negro, Democrats rasped away at the exposed nerve of race prejudice with cunning invective. Confiscation, colored soldiers, and all other measures affecting Negroes, they chanted anew, were all parts of an insidious equalitarian conspiracy which would plunge the country into political and economic chaos and racial amalgamation. Surely, they reasoned, only the Democratic party could save the nation from complete degradation. On election day the Dubuque *Democratic Herald* exhorted, "No Abolitionism, No Emancipation, No Negro Equality," and "We had rather sleep with Democrats than Niggers." In a commentary on the New York riots which were partly aimed at Negroes, the Chicago *Times* unctuously rebuked such violence but grimly warned that "such scenes will be repeated in every city if the repulsive and abhorrent doctrine of negro equality be continually and insultingly thrust in the face of laboring whites. It is a doctrine which the American people will never accept, and if to crush it the extermination of the colored race in this country be necessary the necessity will be accomplished."[21] Another growing concern of the Democrats was revealed by the editor of the Columbus *Crisis,* Samuel Medary, who accused the Republicans of planning to confer citizenship and the ballot upon Negroes, so that *"they can command a balance of power at the polls."* A new touch was reported at party rallies in Ohio where "young Democratic ladies" bore flags imploring, "Father, save us from Negro Equality."[22]

Many of the midwestern War Democrats who still went by that title and usually voted Unionist were not much further advanced than the regular Democrats. They had crept little beyond reluctantly embracing emancipation and the use of Negro troops as military necessities. A meeting of Wisconsin War Democrats announced in September that it backed the war and the administration; then it went on record as "utterly opposed to the admission of the black population of the South among us." Illinois War Democrats repudiated the peace movement and endorsed slave confiscation at their state convention; then they resolved their opposition to political and social equality of the races and recommended that Negroes be colonized outside the United States. General John A. McClernand, probably the most prominent War Democrat in the state, told why: "We wanted no intermixture of white blood with theirs; we wanted them to be free as men, not as citizens. . . . [We] said this in no spirit of enmity to the negro [; we] wanted to help him not equalize him with the white man and bring him into competition with white labor."²³

The course followed by Republicans and Unionists is harder to fathom for they did not hew a straight line. In states such as Iowa where Republicans were distinctly in the majority they tended to be more radical than they were in closely divided states such as Illinois and Ohio. Although their methods varied from state to state and from place to place, the salient features of their strategy were generally patterned closely after that of the past. Seeing that peace Democrats had badly overplayed their hand and were embarrassing their moderate colleagues, they again made national loyalty their principle issue and cast their nets so as to snare the votes of all but die-hard Democrats. James C. Conkling, the man who was entrusted with reading the only major statement made by Lincoln on slavery during the campaign—the letter to the Union meeting in Springfield—described the Union party's position in Illinois. The object was "to prevent our people from being split up into factions—to have but two parties arrayed against each other—patriots on the one hand and traitors on the other," he wrote the President. "We want loyalty to the government to be recognized as the grand fundamental principle and platform upon which the one shall stand and treason, open or disguised, will be the controlling principle of the other."²⁴

And this was the campaign plan for most of the Midwest. Affecting to eschew political partisanship, Republicans and Unionists simply asked for all loyal men to vote down the rebellion by supporting the Union ticket. To blur the Republican image they discreetly continued to use the Union party label in most of the region, and in the critical states of Ohio and Wisconsin they chose prominent former Democrats as their gubernatorial candidates. Inevitably they linked high praise for the administration's beneficent patriotism with unremitting talk about Copperhead plots and Democratic treason. The Columbus *Ohio State Journal* reduced this formula to its simplest terms when it characterized the opposing forces as "patriotism vs. Vallandigham traitors; Union vs. Disunion."[25]

This was a wise approach, for it dulled the cutting edge of the vexing Negro question. This was precisely what it was supposed to do. It is true that antislavery sentiment was rising and that favorable domestic and military conditions were strengthening the administration, but the party of Lincoln had no intention of allowing the Democrats to make emancipation and race the focal point of the campaign. Perceptive politicians knew well that these were still the most divisive issues in the Midwest. Certainly Lincoln had no illusions on this score. In his Springfield address, which was largely an answer to his hostile critics, Lincoln declared that it was his antislavery policy rather than the urge for peace that was generating most of the opposition to his administration. After denying that peaceful reunion was possible at that time he said, "But, to be plain, you are dissatisfied with me about the negro." As he saw it, doubts about the constitutionality and expediency of the Emancipation Proclamation, objections to arming the Negroes, and resentment over fighting to free the slaves fostered their discontent.[26] As he crusaded against slavery, the editor of the Cincinnati *Catholic Telegraph* similarly found that his paper was losing subscribers in Ohio and Indiana because of his stand on emancipation, and that fears of Negro immigration and labor competition still posed "the great argument . . . against our position." Such feelings were not anathema to Republicans. Artful Matthew Carpenter, a War Democrat who helped to promote a Unionist fusion in Wisconsin, argued persuasively that Republicans could not afford to run under their traditional party name because Democratic votes would be needed to offset the loss of "hundreds of Republicans," who were "alarmed at the influx of niggers [and] are intending to vote the Copperhead ticket; as the only way to prevent the competition of black with white labor."[27]

In such a framework mounting support for emancipation was fixed chiefly, not in moral indignation at slavery, but rather in the belief that it was helping to win the war. No one knew this better than the President. On October 2, 1863, he reiterated his determination to rest his policies on military necessity. In detailing his objections to extending the Emancipation Proclamation to the exempted areas in Louisiana and Virginia, he asked Salmon P. Chase if such a step could have any basis other than "that I think the measure politically expedient and morally right?" Would this not place him in the "boundless field of absolutism," and create alarm that he might do the same in the loyal slave states, or perhaps "even change any law in any state? Would not many of our own friends shrink away appalled? Would it not lose us the elections, and with them the very cause we seek to advance?" he asked.[28] In short, emancipation had to be kept in its proper perspective as a necessary instrument to an overshadowing end—the restoration of the Union.

With these hard facts in mind, Republicans and Unionists veered accordingly. Throughout much of the Midwest, to be sure, they increasingly upheld the efficacy of emancipation and the use of Negro soldiers and credited these measures with the resurgence of the Union cause; but they scrupulously explained that the preservation of the Union was their true goal and these actions chiefly a means to that end. While they talked more than ever before of their noble motives for freeing the slaves, few ventured far into such treacherous political sands. Even the most audacious spirits usually returned quickly to the solid ground of military necessity from whence the cautious never strayed. In some places even the mildest antislavery medicine was too strong. Murat Halstead, of the Cincinnati *Commercial,* confided to Salmon P. Chase in late August that whatever its foundation radicalism was decidedly unpopular in Ohio. "[It] is worth while to say here what we all know that if the vote were taken in Ohio between Vallangdigham and the radical policy of the President, the foolish and hopelessly impracticable proclamation, the election of Vallandigham would be the result," he wrote. "The essential thing is to keep the administration out of sight as much as possible, and talk of the cause of nationality and nothing else."[29] Apparently Halstead was not alone in this opinion since the Unionist platform in Ohio ignored slavery, and most of the party's spokesmen generally either soft-pedaled or overlooked it during the campaign. This brand of conservatism extended well beyond the boundaries of the Buckeye State, for Republican journals in such key cities as Milwaukee, Springfield, and Dubuque were, for the most part, equally timorous.[30]

Democratic efforts to prod their opponents into a quarrel about Negro equality met with much the same fate. Republicans and Unionists realized that the improving attitude toward the Negro had in truth barely scratched the hard shell of midwestern race prejudice, and that it would therefore be impolitic to challenge seriously this feeling with the elections so near at hand. This is not to deny that some of the mainstays of the Republican-Unionist coalition were laboring to uplift the Midwest's view of the freedmen. But not all Unionists by any means took part in the campaign against racism. One of those who did not spoke at a Union rally in Illinois where he exclaimed that the rebellion could be disposed of at once "were it not for the negro; he did not like them [*sic*]—they were black."[31] More important, many of those very men who most eloquently pled the case for the Negro shunned the badge of equality and continued to express traditional midwestern viewpoints on race. Sometimes this sentiment took the form of "Sambo" jokes, disparaging remarks about the physical characteristics of Negroes, references to white racial superiority, and denials of egalitarianism. For example, in the midst of a fervent plea for greater sympathy and tolerance for Negroes, the Chicago *Tribune* spoke of the "white and superior race."[32]

In one way or another antislavery champions also endeavored to prove that the welfare of white men was always uppermost in their thoughts. They forcefully proved their solicitude with their repeated claims that the use of Negro soldiers would reduce the demands on whites. The point was too keen to miss whether it came in Lincoln's gentle reminder that he "thought that whatever negroes can be got to do as soldiers, leaves just so much less for white soldiers to do, in saving the Union," or in the Northwestern Freedmen's Aid Committee's blunt assertion that the "good people of the Northwest . . . [should] provide for the families of colored soldiers, every man of whom saves us a white man." Emancipation was again presented as supreme proof of Republican devotion to the Caucasian race. Speaking before a Dubuque audience, Senator Lyman Trumbull praised liberation and said his party was "a white man's party; we are for free white men, and for making white labor respectable and honorable, which . . . can never be done when negro slave labor is brought into competition with it."[33]

Antislavery editors and politicians, including Salmon P. Chase, wheeled out the old shibboleth: emancipation would preserve the white Midwest by halting the flow of Negro immigrants or by turning it southward. In his assaults on slavery, the editor of the Cincinnati *Catholic Telegraph* melded racism with antislavery zeal. In part, he contended that freedom would clear the Negroes out of the North and end competition between blacks and whites. This was as it should be, he continued.

> We desire to see them far apart; there ought to be no partnership between the two races. We have no desire to see them intermingled, neither working together nor even cultivating adjacent field. The natural superiority of the white race ought to be carefully preserved. This is impossible so long as slavery exists, because the poor white man is just as much, or to a great extent, in the power of the rich planter as the slave.[34]

In October and November of 1863 the voters of the Midwest went to the polls and returned a sweeping verdict for the administration and its supporters. Republican-Union candidates won governorships in Ohio, Wisconsin, Minnesota, and Iowa, picked up seats in every state where there were contests for the legislature, and captured many of the local offices held by Democrats.[35] When similar results were reported throughout the Union, Republicans and Unionists breathed a sigh of relief. For the first time since the promulgation of the Preliminary Emancipation Proclamation, they had evidence that the administration had been endorsed by a majority of the people in the Midwest as well as the nation. In turn, whether they had played down or stressed the slavery issue during the campaign, now that the elections were safely past many of them concluded that the people had spoken for freedom when they chose those candidates who were openly or tacitly pledged to support the President and his policies and had rejected the party that boasted of its intention to abrogate emancipation and return the war to its original footing. If the Emancipation Proclamation "had been submitted to a vote of the people of the loyal states before it was issued, there is little doubt that the voice of a majority would have been against it," observed the Springfield *Illinois State Journal* in a typical opinion. "And yet not a year has passed before it is approved by an overwhelming majority of the people."[36]

The President himself attached this fateful significance to the elections. In his annual message to Congress in December of 1863, he candidly analyzed the profound political consequences of the Emancipation Proclamation and the decision to use Negro soldiers. In it he portrayed the plight of the Union in late 1862: insufficient understanding and support abroad, the Confederate threat to commerce, uneasiness and political divisions at home. Then had come the final proclamation of emancipation and the announcement that Negroes would be received in the military services, policies which he frankly admitted "gave to the future a new aspect, about which hope, and fear, and doubt contended in uncertain conflict." Emancipation in any state was beyond the power of the federal government, Lincoln stated, but it "was all the while deemed possible that the [military] necessity for it might come, and that if it should, the crisis would then be presented. It came, and as was anticipated, it was followed by dark and doubtful days. Eleven months having now passed, we are permitted to take another review."

He then hailed the advance of Union armies, the voluntary efforts to free the slaves in Maryland and Missouri, the improvement in foreign opinion, and the value and performance of Negro soldiers. "At home the same measures have been fully discussed, supported, criticized, and denounced," he said, "and the annual elections following are highly encouraging to those whose official duty it is to bear this country through this great trial. Thus we have the new reckoning. The crisis which threatened to divide the friends of the Union is past."[37]

The President and his party thus proclaimed the elections the dawn of a bright new era as they announced that the people had assented to emancipation. The character and the extent of their acceptance would soon be tested.

Notes

1. Horace Greeley, *The American Conflict: A History of the Great Rebellion in the United States of America, 1860–'65* (2 vols.; Hartford: O. D. Case, 1865–66), II, 254–55.

2. "Response to a Serenade," July 7, 1863, in Roy P. Basler (ed.), *The Collected Works of Abraham Lincoln* (9 vols.; New Brunswick, N.J.: Rutgers University Press, 1953), VI, 319–20. See also "Address Delivered at the Dedication of the Cemetery at Gettysburg," November 19, 1863,

in *ibid.*, VII, 23; "Annual Message to Congress," December 8, 1863, in *ibid.*, p. 53.

3. John Sherman to William T. Sherman, May 18, 1863, William Tecumseh Sherman Papers (Manuscript Division, Library of Congress); *Illinois State Journal* (Springfield), July 13, September 4, 7, 1863; *Sentinel* (Milwaukee), August 18, 1863; *Democratic Herald* (Dubuque), July 12, 1863.

4. *Tribune* (Chicago), August 5, 23, 28, 1863; *Illinois State Journal* (Springfield), July 13, September 4, 21, October 12, 1863; *Catholic Telegraph* (Cincinnati), July 8, 15, August 26, November 11, 18, 1863; *Times* (Dubuque), October 8, 10, 1863; *Ohio State Journal* (Columbus), November 10, 1863; *Tribune* (New York), October 19, 1863; *Western Christian Advocate* (Cincinnati), December 2, 1863.

5. John Sherman to W. T. Sherman, November 14, 1863, in Rachel Sherman Thorndike (ed.), *The Sherman Letters* (New York: Charles Scribner's Sons, 1894), p. 216; Allan Nevins, *The War for the Union* (2 vols.; New York: Charles Scribner's Sons, 1959–60), II, 483–511.

6. Davis W. Clark, "The Editor's Table—Development of Treason in the North," *Ladies' Repository*, XXIII (March, 1863), 192; *Western Christian Advocate* (Cincinnati), January 21, March 4, June 24, December 2, 1863; *Illinois State Journal* (Springfield), October 12, 1863; Frank L. Klement, *The Copperheads in the Middle West* (Chicago: University of Chicago Press, 1960), pp. 221–24; George H. Porter, *Ohio Politics during the Civil War Period* (New York: Columbia University, 1911), p. 189.

7. *Times* (Chicago), October 12, December 31, 1863; *Western Christian Advocate* (Cincinnati), October 7, 1863; *Catholic Telegraph* (Cincinnati), February 18, April 8, 15, 23, May 6, 13, 20, June 10, 24, July 8, 15, August 26, October 7, November 11, 18, December 2, 1863; *Illinois State Journal* (Springfield), October 12, November 7, 1863; Klement, *The Copperheads in the Middle West*, pp. 221–24; Porter, *Ohio Politics during the Civil War*, p. 189.

8. *Tribune* (New York), April 16, 1863.

9. *Crisis* (Columbus), March 23, 1864.

10. In 1860 approximately 65,000 Negroes comprised .8 of 1 per cent of the population of the Middle West, while about 154,000 Negroes made up 1.3 per cent of the section's population in 1870. State censuses taken in Michigan in 1864 and in Iowa, Wisconsin, and Illinois in 1865 suggest strongly that nearly half of the Negroes who moved into these states between 1860 and 1870 entered after the war. *Census and Statistics of . . . Michigan: 1864* (Lansing: John A Kerr, 1865), pp. 605–6; Wisconsin, *Annual Report of the Secretary of State, . . . 1865* ([Madison: n.p., 1865]), pp. 87–133; *Reports Made to the General Assembly of Illinois . . . , 1867*

(Springfield: Baker, Bailhache, 1867), p. 9; *Census Returns of . . . Iowa . . . , 1865* (Des Moines: F. W. Palmer, 1865), pp. 155–56; U.S., Department of Commerce, *Negro Population: 1790–1915* (Washington, D.C.: Government Printing Office, 1918), pp. 44, 51.

11. *Tribune* (Chicago), August 27, September 3, 1863, January 5, 1864; *Times* (Dubuque), August 30, October 4, 22, 1863; *Sentinel* (Milwaukee), September 28, 1863.

12. "Final Report of the American Freedmen's Inquiry Commission to the Secretary of War," May 15, 1864, in U.S., War Department, *The War of the Rebellion: A Compilation of the Official Records of the Union and Confederate Armies* (128 vols.; Washington, D.C.: Government Printing Office, 1880–1901), 3d ser., IV, 374 (hereinafter cited as *Official Records*); *Tribune* (Chicago), August 12, 1863.

13. *Tribune* (Chicago), June 28, 1863; *Ohio State Journal* (Columbus), June 10, 1863; *Journal* (Battle Creek), June 12, 1863; Dudley Taylor Cornish, *The Sable Arm: Negro Troops in the Union Army, 1861–1865* (New York: Longmans, Green, 1956), pp. 143–56; James M. McPherson, *The Struggle for Equality: Abolitionists and the Negro in the Civil War and Reconstruction* (Princeton, N.J.: Princeton University Press, 1964), pp. 211–12.

14. *Tribune* (Chicago), June 28, August 12, 28, 1863; *Journal* (Battle Creek), June 12, 1863; *Sentinel* (Milwaukee), June 8, 1863; *Ohio State Journal* (Columbus), May 28, June 10, 1863; *Leader* (Cleveland), August 8, 25, September 4, 1863; "To James C. Conkling," August 26, 1863, in Basler (ed.), *The Collected Works of Abraham Lincoln,* VI, 406–7; "Report of the Secretary of War," December 5, 1863, *Congressional Globe,* 38 Cong. 1 sess., Appendix, pp. 11–12.

15. "To James C. Conkling," August 26, 1863, in Basler (ed.), *The Collected Works of Abraham Lincoln,* VI, 410; *Tribune* (Chicago), August 12, 28, 1863.

16. *Tribune* (Chicago), August 12, 23, 28, 1863; *Democratic Herald* (Dubuque), July 12, 1863; *Illinois State Journal* (Springfield), August 10, 1863; *Register* (Des Moines), August 5, 1863, quoted in Rutland, "The Copperheads of Iowa: A Re-Examination," *Iowa Journal of History and Politics,* LII (January, 1954), 1–30.

17. *Journal* (Evansville), August 8, 1863, quoted in *Tribune* (New York), August 13, 1863; *Times* (Dubuque), September 30, October 10, 1863; *Democratic Herald* (Dubuque), July 15, 1863; *Illinois State Journal* (Springfield), August 19, 1863; *Tribune* (Chicago), September 22, 1863.

18. Thomas to Edwin M. Stanton, April 12, 22, 1863, General Thomas' Letterbook, in U.S., War Department, Adjutant General's Office, Record

Group 94 (National Archives, Washington, D.C.); Bell Irvin Wiley, *The Life of Billy Yank: The Common Soldier of the Union* (Indianapolis: Bobbs-Merrill, 1952), pp. 120–23; Cornish, *The Sable Arm,* pp. 142–47.

19. J. Gillespie to John M. Palmer, December 28, 1863, John M. Palmer Papers (Illinois State Historical Society, Springfield); *Official Records,* 3d ser., III, 229, 380, 598; *Tribune* (Chicago), October 5, 1863; *Ohio State Journal* (Columbus), May 22, June 23, 1863; *Sentinel* (Milwaukee), August 1, 1864; *Times* (Dubuque), May 31, September 10, 1864; *Illinois State Journal* (Springfield), October 14, 1864; *Tribune* (New York), November 3, 1864.

20. *Illinois State Register* (Springfield) quoted in *Illinois State Journal* (Springfield), July 8, August 4, 1863; *Times* (Chicago), July 27, August 20, October 13, 1863; *Democratic Herald* (Dubuque), August 20, 21, 22, September 9, October 8, 1863; *Free Press* (Detroit), October 1, 1863; *Crisis* (Columbus), July 8, August 19, 26, 1863; *Sentinel* (Milwaukee), June 26, 1863; Wood Gray, *The Hidden Civil War: The Story of the Copperheads* (New York: Viking Press, 1942), p. 150; Klement, *The Copperheads in the Middle West,* pp. 128–30; Porter, *Ohio Politics during the Civil War,* pp. 172–80.

21. *Crisis* (Columbus), August 12, 26, September 2, 16, 23, 1863; *Times* (Chicago), July 17, 22, 23, August 11, October 2, 1863; *Illinois State Register* (Springfield) quoted in *Illinois State Journal* (Springfield), July 24, August 10, 1863; *Democratic Herald* (Dubuque), September 16, 22, October 6, 8, 13, 1863; *Free Press* (Detroit), August 21, 25, October 11, 1863; *Howard Tribune* (Kokomo), September 10, 1863; *Official Records,* 3d ser., III, 697.

22. *Crisis* (Columbus), August 26, September 16, 1863.

23. *Illinois State Journal* (Springfield), October 5, 1863; *Times* (Dubuque), September 24, October 4, 1863.

24. Conkling to Lincoln, September 4, 1863, Robert Todd Lincoln Collection (Manuscript Division, Library of Congress); Murat Halstead to Salmon P. Chase, August 24, 1863, quoted in Porter, *Ohio Politics during the Civil War,* p. 180.

25. For examples of these tactics, see the *Leader* (Cleveland), August 1, 17, 19, September 1, 3, 7, 1863; *Ohio State Journal* (Columbus), July–October 13, 1863; *Sentinel* (Milwaukee), August 21, 1863. See also Gray, *The Hidden Civil War,* p. 150; Porter, *Ohio Politics during the Civil War,* p. 180; Eugene H. Roseboom, *The Civil War Era, 1850–1873* (Columbus: Ohio State Archaeological and Historical Society, 1944), pp. 417–21; Klement, *The Copperheads in the Middle West,* pp. 130–32; Frank L. Klement, *Wisconsin and the Civil War* (Madison: State Historical Society of Wisconsin, 1963), pp. 76–77.

26. "To James C. Conkling," August 26, 1863, in Basler (ed.), *The Collected Works of Abraham Lincoln,* VI, 406–9.

27. Matthew Carpenter to Elisha W. Keyes, August 12, 1863, Elisha W. Keyes Papers (Wisconsin State Historical Society, Madison); *Catholic Telegraph* (Cincinnati), July 8, 26, 1863.

28. "To Salmon P. Chase," September 2, 1863, in Basler (ed.), *The Collected Works of Abraham Lincoln,* VI, 428–29.

29. Murat Halstead to Salmon P. Chase, August 24, 1863, quoted in Porter, *Ohio Politics during the Civil War,* p. 180; *Tribune* (New York), October 19, 1863; *Illinois State Journal* (Springfield), September 4, 7, 21, 1863; *Leader* (Cleveland), June 30, September 5, 1863.

30. Porter, *Ohio Politics during the Civil War,* p. 180; *Crisis* (Columbus), June 24, 1863.

31. *Illinois State Journal* (Springfield), August 10, 1863.

32. *Tribune* (Chicago), August 12, 23, 1863; *Howard Tribune* (Kokomo), September 10, 1863; *Illinois State Journal* (Springfield), July 24, August 10, September 21, 1863; *Nonpareil* (Council Bluffs), August 15, 22, 1863; *Catholic Telegraph* (Cincinnati), July 8, 15, 1863; *Register* (Des Moines), August 5, 1863, quoted in Rutland, "The Copperheads of Iowa: A Re-Examination," p. 19.

33. "To James C. Conkling," August 26, 1863, in Basler (ed.), *The Collected Works of Abraham Lincoln,* VI, 409; *Tribune* (Chicago), November 4, 1863; *Times* (Dubuque), August 28, 1863.

34. *Times* (Dubuque), June 10, August 30, October 4, 1863; *Tribune* (New York), October 19, 1863; *Times* (Dubuque), October 8, 1863; *Howard Tribune* (Kokomo), September 10, 1863; *Leader* (Cleveland), June 22, 1863; *Catholic Telegraph* (Cincinnati), July 8, 15, 1863.

35. *The Tribune Almanac for the Year 1864* (New York: New York Tribune, 1868), pp. 60, 62–67; *Crisis* (Columbus), December 9, 1863; *The American Annual Cyclopaedia and Register of Important Events of the Year 1863* (New York: D. Appleton, 1868), p. 532.

36. *Tribune* (Chicago), October 5, 1863; *Illinois State Journal* (Springfield), December 1, 1863; *Leader* (Cleveland), October 20, 21, 23, 1863.

37. "Annual Message to Congress," December 8, 1863, in Basler (ed.), *The Collected Works of Abraham Lincoln,* VII, 48–50.

⚜8⚜

Victory of a Limited Crusade

The elections of the fall of 1863 were followed by a sharp change in emphasis in the antislavery movement. Confident of public support, encouraged by the capture of Chattanooga in November, and beckoned by the mirage of early triumph, the opponents of slavery moved rapidly to deal the institution a death blow. In December, Lincoln announced that under his method of reconstruction loyal governments which might be established in the rebellious states must agree to support the emancipatory measures of the federal government in order to receive executive recognition. When the Thirty-eighth Congress convened in December of 1863, other Republicans went still further as they swiftly launched an assault to make freedom national and irrevocable. On December 14, Owen Lovejoy filed a bill in the House to free all of the slaves in the United States. Most Republicans, however, agreed that an amendment to the Constitution would be the surest way to abolish slavery in the loyal as well as the rebel states. Congressmen James M. Ashley of Ohio and James F. Wilson of Iowa introduced proposals in December to submit such a measure to the states, and in March of 1864, Lyman Trumbull, chairman of the Senate judiciary committee, reported the joint resolution that eventually became the Thirteenth Amendment.[1] The last great debate over slavery had begun.

With the almost unanimous backing of conservative, moderate, and radical Republicans, and of most staunch Unionists, the antislavery offensive pressed onward throughout 1864 and 1865. Behind the leadership of state and local politicians, United States congressmen, churchmen, and the President, it moved along on a great

137

crusade that grew steadily in size and intensity during the last eighteen months of the war, except for one interruption. In the Midwest many motives propelled this drive, but it received its greatest thrusts from the beliefs that emancipation was a military necessity and that abolition would put a permanent end to sectional strife by removing the cause of the war—the institution of slavery and its political power.[2] These were the reasons most often given in support of the antislavery amendment. They were the bedrock upon which most midwestern Republicans and Unionists could stand with ease.

Above this solid foundation ranged a great many other arguments in favor of abolishing slavery—arguments embracing the sublime, the practical, and the vindictive. Certain now of ultimate victory, antislavery advocates in the Middle West talked freely of their other purposes. National emancipation, some claimed, would win favor abroad, carry out the wishes of the Founding Fathers, reaffirm the teachings of the Declaration of Independence, bestow equal or natural rights on the Negro race, reward the blacks for their aid in the war, destroy the iniquitous southern aristocracy, open the South to northern industry and immigration, ennoble white labor, and conform to the law of inexorable progress.[3]

Appealing to the powerful sense of religiosity, many midwestern religious and political leaders continued to accentuate the fatalistic philosophy that the war was a divine tribulation sent to punish the nation for harboring slavery and that the curse would be lifted when the institution was cast out. No one did more to popularize this idea than Abraham Lincoln. In a letter to a Kentucky newspaper editor in April of 1864, he best expressed his philosophic resignation to the will of a righteous God when he confessed that He alone could claim credit for the condition of the country. "If God now wills the removal of a great wrong, and wills also that we of the North as well as you of the South, shall pay fairly for our complicity in that wrong, impartial history will find therein new cause to attest and revere the justice and goodness of God," he concluded.[4]

But if Lincoln was poignantly resigned to the war, others gloried in it. Representative James F. Wilson of Iowa, for example, captured some of the exuberant optimism and moral urgency of the antislavery movement as he called for abolition. "Providence has opened up the way to that higher civilization and purer Christianity which the Republic is to attain," he pontificated in Congress. "Our Red Sea passage promises to be as propitious as was that of God's chosen people when the waters parted . . . for their escape from the hosts upon whom those waters closed and effected the burial appointed by Him who had declared, 'Let my people go.' " In this spirit many portrayed a grand vision of a Christian people on the march, atoning for their sins by uprooting slavery, scourging the slaveholders, uplifting the enslaved, and vindicating the gospel of the brotherhood of man. They envisioned as the fruits of abolition a divided nation made whole, a land of freedom and plenty, a righteous folk assured of the blessings of God, a utopia on earth. Americans could then fulfil their "holy mission," their "manifest destiny": to provide a haven for the oppressed peoples of Europe, to spread Christianity and republican institutions across the continent and around the world.[5]

According to many midwesterners, the war had become even more than a struggle for God, mankind, liberty, and Union. With a mixture of idealism and vengefulness, innocence and arrogance, expansive nationalism and narrow intolerance, many confident souls described the war as a battle for cultural supremacy and national uniformity, the final confrontation of Puritan and Cavalier. Union victory would rightly destroy the effete culture of the South, they said; yet the destruction would contain the healing promise of regeneration, for it would assure the dominance of northern institutions and folkways. For theirs was a mission of mercy as well as of retribution; they were destined to redeem Dixie from its backwardness by remaking it in the image of the North. The heralds of a new order explained that the peculiar southern vices—the plantation system, aristocracy, poverty, sloth, ignorance, immorality, and petty provincialism—were to be supplanted by northern virtues—industrialism, democracy, equality, prosperity, ingenuity, intelligence, and unselfish nationalism. In that florid prose in which he specialized, Joseph Medill, now chief editor of the Chicago *Tribune,* touched almost all of these bases. Once the Union was restored, he predicted, there would be free schools, a free press, free speech, and skilled labor in the South. Not only would colleges and Christian churches be established in the benighted region, "but railroads shall spring up in fugitive paths, the bay of the bloodhound shall give place to the hum of the manufactory, the bleeding slave to the patent reaper, and the bowie knife and the bludgeon shall disappear before the principle of the equal brotherhood of man by right of the universal fatherhood of

God," he proclaimed. "Southern barbarism, the concomitant of slavery . . . shall yield to Northern freedom, equality and enlightenment." Then there would be "perfect peace" and all the states would "obey with a harmony like the 'music of the spheres'—the central Government."[6]

The bold pronouncements and aggressiveness of the leaders of the movement for freedom clearly demonstrated that the notion that the war for the Union was also a moral crusade against slavery was gaining more public acceptance. Their call to arms had not gone unheeded. Stirred by hopes that the rebellion was drawing to a close and touched by the appeals to God, conscience, nationalism, self-interest, and vengeance, new recruits rallied under the antislavery standard in the Middle West. Easing their way were the trends which had emerged in 1863 and which would prevail throughout the war. Fears that masses of southern Negroes would pour into the North gradually continued to abate, attitudes toward the freedmen maintained a slow turn for the better, and military successes generally vindicated emancipation and the use of colored soldiers.

The mounting opposition to slavery helped to move the Union or Republican party to the left, but it also heightened the dissension within its ranks. As they watched their cause gain popularity, many of the radical antislavery men decided that their day had arrived at last. Viewing the fall elections of 1863 as a mandate for radicalism, they concluded that the moderate Lincoln ought not to run for re-election in 1864. He was judged too gentle and incompetent to steer the ship of state in such times. Someone of finer moral fiber was needed to see the war to its conclusion, someone who would not surround himself with "conservative" advisers such as Secretaries Montgomery Blair and William H. Seward, someone who would protect the freedmen and safeguard the victory through a rigorous policy of reconstruction.

Some who held such views schemed to drive Lincoln from the field in favor of another candidate. In December of 1863 a group of unhappy Republicans began touting for president the ambitious secretary of the treasury, Salmon P. Chase, whose concept of morality was broad enough to encompass abolition and equal rights for the freedmen, but too narrow to prevent him from intriguing for the presidential nomination while still a member of Lincoln's cabinet. In spite of their efforts a combination of Chase's clumsy managers and shrewd maneuver by the President spiked the secretary's boom, and he grudgingly withdrew his name from consideration in early March of 1864. Then in late May a group of abolitionists, radical Germans, and dissident War Democrats met in Cleveland, nominated General John C. Frémont, and called for a constitutional amendment abolishing slavery. Nevertheless, Lincoln maintained a tight grip on the party machinery, and in early June he was renominated on the Union ticket. Following his suggestion, the party platform urged the adoption of an amendment to "terminate and forever prohibit the existence of slavery."[7]

But for all its vitality and enthusiasm the crusade for liberty had some severe limitations. In the first place it lacked bipartisan support. The Democrats of the Midwest and most of their followers never accepted freedom as a war aim; instead they continued to resist all forms of federal emancipation. Shocked by their poor showing in the fall elections of 1863 and embarrassed by the pacifistic Democrats and by the brightening prospects of victory, this powerful and obdurate minority was on the defensive; but its leaders pinned their hopes for a comeback partly on a last-ditch effort to stave off emancipation. The extent of their intransigence is indicated by their votes in Congress on the joint resolution to abolish slavery by constitutional amendment. In April of 1864 the Senate passed this proposal with one midwestern Democrat not voting and the other, Senator Thomas A. Hendricks of Indiana, recorded in the negative. Two months later this proposition fell short of the required two-thirds majority in the House because of the combined opposition of Democratic and slave-state legislators. Only one midwestern Democrat backed the resolution, another was absent, and the remaining thirty-two voted against it. In early 1865 after the Union party had won the fall elections of 1864, the measure was resurrected in the second session of the same Congress and passed by the House. Though the final collapse of the Confederacy was imminent, and though their position had been repudiated at the polls, the overwhelming majority of midwestern Democrats did not relent. In the final tally they voted twenty-seven to three against the resolution with four abstentions.[8]

In the meantime midwestern Democrats assailed the abolition amendment in Congress and at home with their accustomed fury. On the whole their charges were stamped with the same die throughout the last sixteen months of the war, though they took on a more subdued tone after the Union party won the general elections of 1864. While these arguments were threadbare for the most part, they are important because they show just how little the war had changed the Democratic case against emancipation. Once again midwestern Democrats portrayed themselves as the embattled defenders of the Constitution, state rights, and civil liberties. There were the usual claims that a constitutional prohibition of slavery would extinguish all hopes for peaceful reconciliation, encroach on private property rights, and unjustly punish the loyal slave states. There were pleas that slavery was dying, and no further action was needed. Some of the stricter constructionists, such as Representatives Joseph K. Edgerton of Indiana and George H. Pendleton of Ohio, Democratic candidate for vice-president in 1864, declared that the amendment would be unconstitutional, that it would tamper with a domestic institution which had existed prior to the ratification of the Constitution and thus would violate the rights reserved by that document to the states.[9]

Other critics, such as Representatives Samuel S. Cox of Ohio and James A. Cravens and William S. Holman of Indiana, conceded that the people possessed the authority to amend slavery out of existence, but they contended that it would be a tragic mistake to do so. Such a move would upset the delicate federal system, centralize power in the national government, subvert state rights, and finally destroy individual liberty. As Joseph K. Edgerton put it, "Better . . . for our country, better for man, that negro slavery exist a thousand years than that American white men lose their constitutional liberty in the extinction of the constitutional sovereignty of the Federal States of this Union." Holman further attempted to remove this debate over the nature of government from the realm of abstraction with an explanation of the connection between federal emancipation and centralization. While he claimed that he had never uttered a word in behalf of slavery and had "ever deplored its existence," this moderate Indiana Democrat told the Republicans that if they persisted in their antislavery policy and if the emancipated Negroes should prove unable to resist the "superior will of the white man" and should fail to maintain their freedom in the South "by inherent force of character, you must maintain it by a permanent military force, which implies the subjugation of the white race." In this way would be planted "the germs of that system of government in which the African will indeed be made the equal of the white race in the universal prostration of liberty."[10]

Midwestern Democrats also indicted emancipation on familiar practical grounds. Although none upheld slavery as a moral good, and even though many expressed distaste for the institution, they generally agreed that abolition would create more problems than it would solve. At the heart of the matter most Democrats still doubted or denied that Negroes possessed the capacity to profit from freedom. "Regardless of all the lessons of history," complained an Illinois congressman, "four million slaves, an inferior and degraded race, whose educational habits wholly unfit them for self-control, are to be thrown upon society to roam at will throughout the land." Some of those who felt this way moved easily to the conclusion that they were actually the best friends of the Negro and the emancipationists his worst enemies. Representative George Bliss of Ohio scorned the abolitionists' "pretense of a humanitarian motive toward the negroes" as a "display of systematic and intense hypocrisy." "All sensible men," he said, knew well that the "negro slaves, whether held under the new bondage of the so-called freedmen, on confiscated plantations, or scattered in want and undeserved suffering over the North, are the much-abused and unfortunate victims of an unlawful interference with the protection and support of which they were born; and that the best possible disposition of them is to restore them to their primal condition."[11]

Part of this compassion for the slaves, whether it was feigned or sincere, rested upon the conviction that the freedmen would suffer grievously at the hands of the whites. In the opinion of many Democrats two such dissimilar races could not live harmoniously within the same society if both were free. After disclaiming any "attachments" to slavery, Senator Hendricks wondered if the bondsmen would be happier if they were freed. If they should enter the "northern States among a people not accustomed to them, and commence to crowd the free white labor of the North, these unfortunate people will come into contact with a northern prejudice that will be hard upon them and their prosperity," he pointed out. Others predicted that abolition would intensify race friction and violence and finally lead to the extermination of the Negroes. The dimmest view was taken by Samuel S. Cox who intoned that "if slavery be doomed, so alas! is the slave. . . . The irrepressible conflict is not between slavery

143

and freedom, but between black and white; and as De Tocqueville prophesied, the black will perish."[12]

Finally, the Democrats of the Middle West fought the antislavery amendment because of the effect they felt that it would have on the white race. They again recited their fears that the freedmen would swarm northward to compete with white labor and degrade society.[13] Now that Republicans were beginning to unveil some of their plans for reconstructing the Union and elevating the Negroes, Democrats redoubled their efforts to depict abolition as the first instalment in a Republican scheme to grant complete social and political rights to Negroes. Some Democrats apprehended that this program would ruin the South. In December of 1863, James J. Faran, editor of the Cincinnati *Enquirer,* the most influential Democratic voice in the lower Midwest, privately wrote that the party in power intended to abolish slavery and give the ballot to the blacks, and in the process "they will devastate the whole South and destroy its white population."[14]

In sorrowful tones they catalogued other dire results which could be expected to flow from freedom and equality: "a mongrel Government, instead of a white man's Government," Negro bloc voting and control of the balance of political power in the South and in parts of the North, racial strife, and miscegenation. Yet they confidently predicted that the experiment would fail in the end because white men would never accept black men as social and political equals. An ironclad prejudice born of instinct or instilled by God would forever bar the way. Senator Hendricks promised that the two races would never "associate" on "terms of equality. It may be preached for; it may be legislated for; it may be prayed for; but there is that difference between the races that renders it impossible. If they are among us as a free people, they are among us as an inferior people." Nor did he believe that these "differences" could be attributed to slavery or other institutions; "it was the pleasure of God to mark that difference upon the races; a difference in intellect, in tastes, in all the qualities that enable a race to go upward and onward."[15]

In addition to the Democrats' rejection of abolition, there was still another important reservation in the Middle West's dedication to freedom. As Republicans plainly indicated by placing the heaviest stress on the military reasons for liberating the slaves, despite the growing moralistic opposition to slavery and the improving outlook on Negroes, emancipation was still viewed and accepted primarily as a means of winning the war. Although there undoubtedly were some who regarded emancipation as the primary goal of the war, most midwesterners were concerned mainly with preserving the Union. If the Confederate states had asked for reunion with slavery intact at any time before the November elections, the main body of the midwestern populace probably would have been unwilling to continue fighting in order to free the slaves. In early 1864, Frederick Douglass analyzed the expedient character of the national commitment to emancipation as he identified the continuing sources of Democratic strength in the North—expense of the war, desire for peace, "popular dislike" of abolitionists, "absence of any deep moral feeling among the loyal people against slavery itself—their feeling against it being on account of its rebellion against the Government, and not because it is a stupendous crime against human nature." But, he said, "superior to all others, is the national prejudice and hatred toward the colored people of the country, a feeling which has done more to encourage the hopes of the Rebels than all other powers besides."[16]

Douglass understandably may have overestimated the relative importance of anti-Negro prejudice, but his analysis of northern opinion was later largely borne out. Antislavery resolve faltered in late June, July, and August of 1864 as war fatigue and doubt again beset the Union. In these months Sherman's advance in Georgia appeared to be tortuously slow and indecisive; Grant seemed to be in a bloody deadlock in Virginia; and General Jubal Early's Confederates menaced Washington. Underlining the depressing war news was the administration's call for 500,000 volunteers with all shortages on quotas to be filled by a draft in September. As hopes of victory faded, the clamor for peace rose anew, particularly in the Midwest.

To draw off some of this pressure Lincoln authorized two peace feelers in July of 1864, the Jaquess-Gilmore expedition to Richmond and the Horace Greeley mission to Niagara Falls, Canada. Both of these efforts failed, but the Niagara venture was destined to have far-reaching repercussions. Unlike Colonel James Jaquess and J. R. Gilmore, who had the President's consent to proceed to the Confederate capital but with no official standing or instructions, the New York editor was an accredited emissary, and he was armed with a statement specifying Lincoln's requirements for further negotiations.

After the Niagara "conference" fell through, the President made public the terms which he offered there in his famous memorandum, "To Whom it may concern."[17]

> Any proposition which embraces the restoration of peace, the integrity of the whole Union, and the abandonment of slavery, and which comes by and with an authority that can control the armies now at war against the United States will be received and considered by the Executive government of the United States, and will be met by liberal terms on other substantial and collateral points. . . .

The popular response to this declaration imperiled Lincoln's party and gave the Democrats new life in the 1864 political campaign.

To their chagrin and alarm Republicans and Unionists soon discovered that it was one thing to argue in good times that emancipation would shorten the war and help restore the Union, but quite another to declare in a period of gloom that the fighting would not cease under any circumstances until slavery was abolished. Only a few extreme pacifists quarreled with reunion being a condition of peace, but a great many others objected to abolition as a war aim. The Democrats reacted quickly and typically. Never had they doubted that the Union war effort was principally sustained by the insistence upon national supremacy. Shortly after his party suffered defeat in the fall of 1863, William S. Holman, a keen judge of public opinion, had written, "The great mass of the people, Democrats and Republicans, are for war until a restoration can be effected [,] but the moment the war can cease with the integrity of the Union maintained the popular voice will demand peace at once no matter what may be its effects on slavery." Still acting on this assumption, midwestern Democrats of all stripes now added to their political indictment the cry that Lincoln had conclusively proven that the war was being fought to free the Negro. The terms imposed at Niagara, they lamented, would prolong the struggle and exact a further toll of men and treasure for a bootless cause. "Tens of thousands of white men must yet bite the dust to allay the negro mania of the President," wrote the peace-minded editor of the Columbus *Crisis*. "A half million more are called for and millions of debts are yet to be saddled upon the people to carry out this single negro idea, while the negroes themselves will be literally exterminated in the effort to make them equals with the white men."[18]

In late July and August the popularity of the administration plummeted. Crafty Thurlow Weed of New York flatly told Lincoln that he could not be re-elected, and that he had not seen "anyone from other States who authorizes the slightest hope of success." Equally alarmed was Henry J. Raymond, Republican editor of the New York *Times* and chairman of the National Executive Committee of the Union party. After corresponding with politicos in every state, Raymond wrote Lincoln that all agreed that the tide was running against their party. Representative Elihu B. Washburne of Illinois, Governor O. P. Morton, and Schuyler Colfax of Indiana reported dark prospects in their states. "If the Democrats had a particle of patriotism or sense they would beat us easily," Senator John Sherman grumbled. "The conviction is general that Lincoln has not the energy [,] dignity or character to either conduct the war or to make Peace." The gravity of the situation was not lost on Lincoln. On August 23, 1864, the despondent President almost resigned himself to defeat, writing in a private memorandum that "it seems exceedingly probable that this Administration will not be re-elected."[19]

Disappointments in the field and the announcement that peace hinged on the abolition of slavery were the fountainheads of the reaction. Henry J. Raymond blamed popular discontent on "the want of military successes, and the impression in some minds, the fear and suspicion in others, that we are not to have peace *in any event* under this administration until Slavery is abandoned. In some way or other the suspicion is widely diffused that we *can* have peace with Union if we would." The Republican speaker of the federal House of Representatives, Schuyler Colfax, informed Lincoln that Unionists in the Hoosier state were embarrassed by the Niagara terms which were "entirely correct," but the "Copperhead Press perverts the facts by insisting that the War is to be continued solely for the Negro."[20] Joseph Medill must have agreed, for he bitterly denounced the Niagara note in private. After initially claiming that the people would support the President's peace conditions, Medill's Chicago *Tribune* later admitted that they had furnished every "Copperhead spouter and editor" with some "very good electioneering claptrap." Adding to the Republicans' discomfort was the defection of some midwestern War Democrats, such as Charles D. Robinson, editor of the Green Bay *Advocate,* who now bolted the Unionist fold, saying that Lincoln had undermined its position by placing the war on an abolition basis. Little wonder that Samuel S. Cox

147

gloated in Columbus that the Niagara affair "has estranged hundreds in this city and thousands in this state from Lincoln."[21]

Frightened by these signs, some Republican leaders begged Lincoln to make a strategic retreat; others encouraged him to stand his ground. In some quarters antislavery purpose began to melt in the face of expediency, or at least it grew devious. Raymond, Colfax, and others entreated Lincoln to proffer new terms for peace negotiations, calling for the restoration of the Union and obedience to the Constitution, but omitting any explicit reference to slavery. Such action, they said, and the certain rejection of Confederate authorities would shatter the peace bubble, steel the martial spirit, and scotch the outcry that war was being waged for the Negro, and, as Colfax slyly reminded Lincoln, it would not involve any abatement of principle since the acts of Congress had already doomed slavery.[22] Meanwhile, certain outstanding midwestern Republicans took the initiative in trying to escape from their predicament. Speaking at Valparaiso, Colfax denied that Lincoln's announcement was an ultimatum; he had not meant "that no other terms would be considered." Once southerners laid down their arms, returned to their national allegiance, and obeyed the laws and Constitution, the war would end, he promised. The President had not established any new demands for peace, claimed the Chicago *Tribune,* for he had not gone beyond the bounds of the Emancipation Proclamation.[23]

Lincoln's role in this crisis is puzzling. It is hard to tell whether he even intended to require the abolition of slavery as a *sine qua non* of peace. Lincoln himself felt that he had been placed in a "false position" by the Greeley mission and by his own statement, "To Whom it may concern." Before and after the election of 1864 he confided that he had been misrepresented and misunderstood, that he had never meant to make freedom a condition of peace and reunion. In view of the wording of his public memorandum, however, it is difficult to see what other construction could have been placed on it. Perhaps he defined his position more clearly in mid-August in the draft of a letter to Charles D. Robinson. "To me," he wrote, "it seems plain that saying re-union and abandonment of slavery would be considered, if offered, is not saying that nothing *else* or *less* would be considered, if offered." Emancipation, he reiterated, was a military measure which had been needed to save the

Union, partly because it had brought colored soldiers to the aid of the nation. Not only would it be morally wrong to allow the Negroes to be re-enslaved; it would also lose their invaluable services. Yet, he closed, "If Jefferson Davis wishes, for himself or for the benefit of his friends at the North, to know what I would do if he were to offer peace and re-union, saying nothing about slavery, let him try me."[24]

If these were Lincoln's true views, why did he not make them plain in his "To Whom it may concern"? Certainly the master of lucid prose did not lack the ability to make himself understood. The answer probably lies elsewhere. It is possible that Lincoln overestimated the will of the northern people, took his advanced stand on emancipation, and then wished that he had not done so when the storm of criticism broke. Then, too, the fiery conflict within the Republican party may have helped to chart his course. In early July, 1863, radicals had driven through Congress the Wade-Davis bill designed to establish a stern system of reconstruction and guarantee congressional control of the process. When Lincoln pocketed the bill and reasserted his determination to control reconstruction, radicals were outraged. Part of their anger centered on the slavery question; one of the provisions of the Wade-Davis measure ordered constitutional conventions in the seceded states to abolish slavery forever. Even though the presidential plan of reconstruction was similar in this respect, some radicals including Chase and Wade feared that slavery might survive because Lincoln lacked the force of character to carry out such a condition.[25] Lincoln may well have cast his peace terms as he did in order to allay these suspicions and hold his party together for the impending elections.

In any case Lincoln wavered in face of the northern backlash. Throughout August he weighed the political considerations of his position on peace and perhaps wrestled with his conscience. On August 17 he drew up the equivocating letter to Robinson but apparently did not send it. On August 24, the day after he had almost resigned himself to defeat, he followed Raymond's counsel and drafted an authorization for a peace mission to Richmond, stipulating only that "upon the restoration of the Union and the national authority, the war shall cease at once, all remaining questions to be left for adjustment by peaceful modes." Then he put it aside, deciding that the overture would do more harm than good.[26] Still he continued to agonize over the need to alter or clarify his stand. At some time between August 29 and September 2 he showed Frederick Douglass what may have been yet another explanatory letter which he had fashioned. In it he explained that the Confederacy had not asked for peace, and that he lacked the power and perhaps the inclination to commit the nation to a war for abolition. The President did not propose "to take back what he had said in his Niagara letter, but wished to relieve the fears of his peace friends, by making it appear that the thing which they feared could not happen, and was wholly beyond his power." According to Douglass, Lincoln maintained, "Even if I would, I could not carry on the war for the abolition of slavery. The country would not sustain such a war, and I could do nothing without the support of Congress." Douglass advised the President to withhold this statement, and apparently he did so.[27]

Lincoln's anguish and hesitation were easy to understand. If he did not modify his terms, he would probably alienate some of those who were heartsick of war and those who believed the restoration of the Union to be the sole justification for the struggle. On the other hand, quite apart from moral and military considerations there were cogent political reasons for standing firm. For if he should discard his antislavery requirement, he might further antagonize those radicals who had revived their plot in August to derail Lincoln for a presidential candidate more to their liking. Even if their intrigue should fail, he would still be flanked by the Frémont ticket which might attract the votes of enough disgusted radicals to throw the elections to the Democrats.[28]

Secretary of State William H. Seward may well have delivered the message that Lincoln wanted to put before the people. In a major address at Auburn, New York, on September 3, 1864, Seward voiced sentiments akin to those the President had revealed to Douglass. Even though the rebels had made no effort toward peace, "our opponents want a distinct exposition of the President's views on the ultimate solution of the slavery question," he said. While he was "unauthorized to speak for the President upon hypothetical questions," he would attempt to supply an answer. As long as the South continued to wage war, the government's actions affecting slavery would be enforced, but when the Confederates "laid down their arms, the war will instantly cease" and all other questions including those touching on slavery "will, by force of the Constitution, pass over to the arbitrament of courts of law and to the councils of legislation." Seward admitted that he did not expect Confederate leaders to ask for peace with reunion, but "so far as I am concerned, and, I believe, so far as the President is concerned, all such applications will receive just such an answer as it becomes a great, magnanimous, and humane people to grant. . . ."[29] Of course, it is possible that Seward spoke only for himself; yet it is hard to believe that the President's most intimate and trusted advisor would speak so authoritatively on such a vital and explosive subject without the consent of his chief. But whether he did so or not, Lincoln did not see fit to repudiate the words of his secretary of state, and some observers naturally believed that the administration had perhaps watered down its conditions for peace.

With the Republicans torn by discord, the optimistic Democrats opened their national convention at Chicago on August 29. Throughout the summer they had delayed their meeting while the Republicans wrangled among themselves, and the administration sank in public esteem. The moderate Democratic majority was determined to run a military man of unquestionable patriotism for the presidency. General Ulysses S. Grant matched this description, but according to Samuel S. Cox he had been dropped from consideration because of a letter he had written to Elihu Washburne in August of 1863 expressing the belief that there could be no lasting peace unless slavery was abolished.[30] General George B. McClellan, who was not laboring under such a disability, received the presidential nomination, and courtly George H. Pendleton of Ohio became his running mate. The platform did not mention emancipation per se, but it did state that the "aim and object of the Democratic party is to preserve the Federal Union and the rights of States unimpaired," and to anyone familiar with Democratic rhetoric this included slavery. To mollify the peace wing of the party, the delegates adopted the fateful platform of an armistice and a national convention to achieve peace and reunion. In an effort to run as a war leader and to sharpen the differences between parties on slavery and peace, McClellan insisted in his letter of acceptance that reunion must be the foundation of any settlement with the South, but that the "Union is the one condition of peace—we ask no more." Each wayward state, he added, was entitled to its "full constitutional rights" when it returned to the Union.[31] Thus, divided though they were about how best to end the war, most Democrats found common ground in their opposition to federal emancipation. In the Midwest they accordingly geared part of their campaign to this issue.

But the Democrats were fated to disappointment. The North was spared the supreme test of its antislavery convictions; there was no direct confrontation at the polls between the champions of peace and reunion without regard to slavery and those who advocated making abolition a condition of peace. The battle lines that had appeared so starkly drawn in August were blurred by Democrats, Unionists, and Confederates in the months that followed. Although Democrats generally ignored it and McClellan disclaimed it, the peace plank in their platform further exposed the party to charges of treason and enabled its opponents to accuse it falsely of seeking peace at the expense of union. Unionists helped to confuse the matter by unsaying much of what Lincoln had said about peace, and the President wisely refrained from making any more public statements on the subject. The Confederates' adamant refusal to consider any terms short of independence took much of the heat out of the debate, since it now appeared that reunion could be accomplished only by military decision.

Against this background Frederick Douglass shrewdly gauged the antislavery resolution of the North and found it wanting. Almost on the eve of the presidential election, he said that the destiny of slavery rested on southern will to resist reunion, rather than on northern determination to establish freedom. Hopes for abolition hung "not upon the disposition of the Republican party, not upon the disposition of President Lincoln; but upon the slender thread of Rebel power, pride, and persistence." However much Lincoln might want to fight until slavery was abolished his party would not sustain him. This "somewhat gloomy view," he said, was supported by the "well-known sentiment of the country," by repeated attempts of the Republican press "to explain away the natural import of the President's address 'To Whom It May Concern,'" and by Seward's Auburn speech.[32]

Significantly, Douglass made his glum appraisal not in the despairing days of late summer, but in the fall when hope was strong and the star of the Union party was in the ascendant. Early in September the circumstances that had favored the Democrats during the summer had begun to fade. On the heels of the Chicago convention came the news that Sherman had taken Atlanta on September 2, and later that month General Philip Sheridan swept Early's troops out of the Shenandoah Valley. This dramatic upsurge in the war effort seemed to substantiate again the antislavery policies of the administration and brought renewed hope of victory. With the end of the rebellion once more in sight, Lincoln and his party regained prestige and confidence. Dissension in the ranks of the Unionists gave way to party solidarity. Frightened by the Democratic platform and awed by the administration's growing popularity, Lincoln's radical critics abandoned their plot to name another candidate and hastened back to support the President. Bowing to the inevitable, Frémont now withdrew from the field. Carried along mainly by the combined forces of military victory and Democratic ineptitude, the Union party decisively won the fall elections. In the Midwest Lincoln gathered almost 56 per cent of the popular vote, while Republicans or Unionists there won every gubernatorial race, regained control of the Illinois and Indiana legislatures, and elected fifty-eight of sixty-eight congressmen.[33]

It is difficult to evaluate the mandate of the elections of 1864. In the Midwest victory probably turned on the recent Union military successes and the largely spurious issue of Democratic disloyalty, but there was no clear-cut referendum on slavery or any other single issue. It is true that the Union party was pledged to an abolition amendment and that the Democrats squarely opposed it, but they also differed on a wide range of other questions before the people— state rights, civil liberties, the prosecution of the war, racial and fiscal matters, reconstruction, Lincoln's character, and national loyalty.[34] It is, therefore, impossible to determine the relative importance of antislavery sentiment at the polls. The great bulk of midwesterners who voted the Union ticket probably fell roughly into one of three categories: (1) those who objected to fighting to abolish slavery but wanted to reunite the nation above all else and doubted that the Democrats could be trusted with the task; (2) those who regarded the restoration of the Union as their overriding concern and would not prolong the war to free the slaves but accepted emancipation principally as a means of quelling the rebellion and of establishing future peace; and (3) those who believed the destruction of slavery to be the primary or perhaps sole object of the struggle. Beneath

these shadings of opinion most Unionists doubtless agreed with varying enthusiasm that slavery was both a moral evil and the source of
national strife. If there were those who would not wage a war only
to abolish slavery, few would mourn its passing.

Whatever their motives may have been, a majority of midwesterners sealed their commitment to emancipation when they voted for
the party of abolition in the elections of 1864. After the lame duck
Congress reconvened, House Republicans reconsidered and nar-
rowly passed the proposed Thirteenth Amendment on January 31,
1865, with the aid of a small but crucial handful of Democrats who
either abstained or voted "aye." Ratification in the midwestern states
swiftly followed over the opposition of a sizable number of Democratic legislators.[35]

The response of the midwestern press to congressional approval of
the antislavery amendment was divided along partisan lines. The
bitterness and frustration shared by some Democrats reached their
peak in a caustic editorial in the Dubuque *Democratic Herald*:

EXCELSIOR, SAMBO!

At last the abolition millennium is about to dawn. The incubus
of slavery which weighed down our country for over eighty
years, and which was foisted upon us by those slave-driving na-
bobs, Washington, Jefferson, Jackson, and others of their ilk, is
about to be removed, and our disenthralled country, with one
huge bound will spring into the fore rank of civilized progress,
amid the shouts and songs of the freed, the twang of banjo, the
clatter of the "fantastic heel and toe," and a most palpable odor!

But the Republicans celebrated the emergence of a cherished dream
into actuality. The Springfield *Illinois State Journal* praised Congress
for passing the most important measure since the government was
established; it "will send a thrill of joy to the hearts of the friends
of freedom throughout all Christendom." When the Indiana legislature ratified the amendment, the Indianapolis *State Journal* proclaimed that the state "speaks for liberty, and . . . gives a fresh pledge
of her fidelity to the Government and her attachment to the principles of liberty." "This gigantic stride in our progress towards national purity, universal liberty, and a righteous peace will be hailed
with deep exultation and religious gratitude by our liberty-loving

American people," the Chicago *Tribune* declared. "[The congress-
men] have removed, so far as they had the power, the last moral
stain from our national escutcheon—the only disgrace from our
flag."[36]

Notes

1. "Annual Message to Congress," December 8, 1863, in Roy P. Basler
(ed.), *The Collected Works of Abraham Lincoln* (9 vols.; New Brunswick, N.J.: Rutgers University Press, 1953), VII, 51; "Proclamation of
Amnesty and Reconstruction," December 8, 1863, in *ibid.*, pp. 53–56;
Congressional Globe, 38 Cong., 1 sess., pp. 19–21, 1313; John G. Nicolay
and John Hay, *Abraham Lincoln: A History* (10 vols.; New York: Century, 1890), X, 74–76.

2. *Ohio State Journal* (Columbus), February 4, March 22, 1864; *Leader*
(Cleveland), August 22, 1864; *Times* (Dubuque), September 8, 19, 1864;
Illinois State Journal (Springfield), September 13, 1864; *Congressional
Globe,* 38 Cong., 1 sess., p. 1314; *ibid.*, 2 sess., pp. 162, 164.

3. *Congressional Globe,* 38 Cong., 1 sess., pp. 20, 1312, 2955, 2989–90;
ibid., 2 sess., p. 142; *Illinois State Journal* (Springfield), September 23,
October 17, 1864; *Leader* (Cleveland), March 25, April 8, 1864; *Times*
(Dubuque), January 6, 1864; *Sentinel* (Milwaukee), February 2, 1864.

4. "To Albert G. Hodges," April 4, 1864, in Basler (ed.), *The Collected
Works of Abraham Lincoln,* VII, 281–82; "To Eliza P. Gurney," September 4, 1864, in *ibid.*, p. 535; "Second Inaugural Address," March 4, 1865,
in *ibid.*, pp. 332–33; *Congressional Globe,* 38 Cong., 1 sess., pp. 1213–14,
2955; Paul H. Buck, *The Road to Reunion, 1865–1900* (Boston: Little,
Brown, 1937), pp. 10–11; Richard N. Current, *The Lincoln Nobody
Knows* (New York: McGraw-Hill, 1958), pp. 71–75; James G. Randall
and Richard N. Current, *Lincoln the President: Last Full Measure* (4
vols.; New York: Dodd, Mead, 1945–55), IV, 370–72.

5. *Journal* (Indianapolis), February 7, 1865; *Illinois State Journal*
(Springfield), February 1, 1865; *Congressional Globe,* 38 Cong., 1 sess.,
pp. 444, 1203, 2036, 2038, 2955; "Final Report of the American Freed-
men's Inquiry Commission to the Secretary of War," May 15, 1864, in
U.S., War Department, *The War of the Rebellion: A Compilation of the
Official Records of the Union and Confederate Armies* (128 vols.; Wash-

ington, D.C.: Government Printing Office, 1880–1901), 3d ser., IV, 360–61 (hereinafter cited as *Official Records*).

6. *Tribune* (Chicago), September 28, 1864; *Sentinel* (Milwaukee), February 2, 1864; *Journal* (Indianapolis), January 24, 25, 1864; *Times* (Dubuque), January 6, February 4, 1864; *Congressional Globe,* 38 Cong., 1 sess., pp. 507, 1188, 1197, 2831, and Appendix, p. 126.

7. William Frank Zornow, *Lincoln & the Party Divided* (Norman: University of Oklahoma Press, 1954), pp. 7–21, 23–54, 72–104; Randall and Current, *Lincoln the President,* IV, 89–130, 307; T. Harry Williams, *Lincoln and the Radicals* (Madison: University of Wisconsin Press, 1941), pp. 306–17; *The American Annual Cyclopaedia and Register of Important Events of the Year 1864* (New York: D. Appleton, 1869), pp. 786, 788.

8. *Congressional Globe,* 38 Cong., 1 sess., pp. 1490, 2995; *ibid.,* 2 sess., p. 531.

9. *Congressional Globe,* 38 Cong., 1 sess., pp. 2986–88, 2992–94; *ibid.,* 2 sess., p. 527; Randall and Current, *Lincoln the President,* IV, 305.

10. *Congressional Globe,* 38 Cong., 1 sess., pp. 1065–66, 2110–12, 2987–88; *ibid.,* 2 sess., pp. 219–20, 239; Holman to Allen Hamilton, February 28, 1864, Allen Hamilton Papers (Indiana State Historical Library, Indianapolis).

11. *Congressional Globe,* 38 Cong., 1 sess., pp. 863, 1078; *ibid.,* 2 sess., p. 150.

12. *Congressional Globe,* 38 Cong., 1 sess., pp. 709, 1457; *Crisis* (Columbus), August 3, 1864.

13. *Congressional Globe,* 38 Cong., 1 sess., pp. 766, 1306, 1457, 2958; *ibid.,* 2 sess., pp. 150, 216, 219; *Illinois State Register* (Springfield), February 24, 1864, quoted in *Illinois State Journal* (Springfield), February 26, 1864; *Illinois State Journal* (Springfield), August 22, 1864; *Crisis* (Columbus), March 23, April 6, 1864; *Democratic Herald* (Dubuque), November 6, 1864; *Times* (Dubuque), November 8, 1864.

14. Faran to Alexander Long, December 11, 1863, Alexander Long Papers (Cincinnati Historical Society, Cincinnati); *Congressional Globe,* 38 Cong., 1 sess., pp. 1307, 2048; *Tribune* (Chicago), July 22, 1864; *Crisis* (Columbus), January 27, 1864.

15. *Congressional Globe,* 38 Cong., 1 sess., pp. 709, 712, 863, 1078, 1304, 1306, 1457, 2047–48, 2958–59; *ibid.,* pp. 150, 216, 219; *Crisis* (Columbus), January 27, April 6, 13, August 3, 1864; *Inquirer* (Cincinnati), May 28, 1864; *Democratic Herald* (Dubuque), April 14, 1864.

16. *Tribune* (New York), January 14, 1864.

17. "To Horace Greeley," July 9, 1864, in Basler (ed.), *The Collected Works of Abraham Lincoln,* VII, 435; "To Whom It May Concern," July 18, 1864, in *ibid.,* p. 451; Randall and Current, *Lincoln the President,* IV, 156–66.

18. Holman to Allen Hamilton, October 9, 1863, Hamilton Papers; Speech of John Brough delivered at Circleville, Ohio, September 3, 1864, in Robert Todd Lincoln Collection (Manuscript Division, Library of Congress); Schuyler Colfax to Abraham Lincoln, July 25, 1864, in *ibid.*; *Sentinel* (Milwaukee), October 15, 1864; *Democratic Herald* (Dubuque), September 15, 1864; *Crisis* (Columbus), August 3, 1864; *Tribune* (Chicago), August 10, 1864; *The Gubernatorial Canvass: Debate Between Gov. Oliver P. Morton and Hon. Joseph E. McDonald at LaPorte . . . August 10, 1864* (LaPorte, Ind.: n.p., 1864), p. 17; Zornow, *Lincoln & the Party Divided,* pp. 165, 169.

19. Colfax to Lincoln, July 25, 1864, R. T. Lincoln Collection; Raymond to Lincoln, August 22, 1864, in *ibid.*; Weed to William H. Seward, August 22, 1864, Nicolay and Hay, *Abraham Lincoln,* IX, 250; John Sherman to W. T. Sherman, July 24, 1864, in William Tecumseh Sherman Papers (Manuscript Division, Library of Congress); "Memorandum Concerning His Probable Failure of Re-election," August 23, 1864, in Basler (ed.), *The Collected Works of Abraham Lincoln,* VII, 514; Lawanda and John H. Cox, *Politics, Principle, and Prejudice, 1865–1866: Dilemma of Reconstruction America* (New York: Free Press of Glencoe, 1963), pp. 3–4; Zornow, *Lincoln & the Party Divided,* pp. 112–14; Randall and Current, *Lincoln the President,* IV, 214–16.

20. Raymond to Lincoln, August 22, 1864, in R. T. Lincoln Collection; Colfax to Lincoln, July 25, 1864, in *ibid.*; Howard K. Beale (ed.), *Diary of Gideon Welles: Secretary of the Navy under Lincoln and Johnson* (3 vols.; New York: W. W. Norton, 1960), pp. 109–10.

21. Tyler Dennett (ed.), *Lincoln and the Civil War in the Diaries and Letters of John Hay* (New York: Dodd, Mead, 1939), pp. 226–27; Charles D. Robinson to Lincoln, August 7, 1864, in R. T. Lincoln Collection; Cox to Manton Marble, July 25, 1864, in Manton Marble Papers (Manuscript Division, Library of Congress); Matthew Carpenter to Charles D. Robinson [September, 1864], in Charles D. Robinson Papers (Wisconsin State Historical Society, Madison); *Tribune* (Chicago), August 10, 1864.

22. Charles D. Robinson to Lincoln, August 7, 1864, in R. T. Lincoln Collection; Raymond to Lincoln, August 22, 1864, in *ibid.*; Colfax to Lincoln, July 25, 1864, in *ibid.*; Dennett (ed.), *Lincoln and the Civil War in the Diaries and Letters of John Hay,* pp. 225–26.

23. Beale (ed.), *Diary of Gideon Welles,* II, 110; *Tribune* (Chicago), August 10, 15, 1864.

24. Beale (ed.), *Diary of Gideon Welles,* II, 83, 110–11; Theodore Calvin Pease and James G. Randall (eds.), *The Diary of Orville Hickman Browning* (2 vols.; Springfield: Illinois State Historical Library, 1927–33), I, 693–94, 699; "To Charles D. Robinson," August 17, 1864, in Basler (ed.), *The Collected Works of Abraham Lincoln,* VII, 499–501.

25. Hans L. Trefousse, *Benjamin Franklin Wade: Radical Republican from Ohio* (New York: Twayne Publishers, 1963), pp. 219–20, 224; Nicolay and Hay, *Abraham Lincoln*, IX, 103.

26. "To Charles D. Robinson," August 17, 1864, in Basler (ed.), *The Collected Works of Abraham Lincoln*, VII, 499–501; "To Henry J. Raymond," August 24, 1864, in *ibid.*, p. 514; Nicolay and Hay, *Abraham Lincoln*, IX, 215–16, 220–21.

27. This meeting may have taken place on August 19, for it is known that Douglass saw Lincoln on that date. If so, the letter they discussed was probably the unmailed draft of the letter to Charles D. Robinson. My reason for assigning the above date for the interview is that Douglass states that it occurred after McClellan had been nominated (August 29) and before the fall of Atlanta (September 2). Furthermore, his description of the message exhibited by the President does not seem to coincide with the Robinson letter. Douglass to Theodore Tilton, October 15, 1864, in Philip S. Foner, *Life and Writings of Frederick Douglass* (4 vols.; New York: International Publishers, 1950–55), III, 422–24.

28. "To Charles D. Robinson," August 17, 1864, in Basler (ed.), *The Collected Works of Abraham Lincoln*, VII, 499–501; "Interview with Alexander W. Randall and Joseph T. Mills," August 19, 1864, in *ibid.*, pp. 506–8; Frederick Douglass to Theodore Tilton, October 15, 1864, in Foner, *Life and Writings of Frederick Douglass*, III, 422–24; Dennett (ed.), *Lincoln in the Letters and Diaries of John Hay*, pp. 225–26; Randall and Current, *Lincoln the President*, IV, 214–16; Cox and Cox, *Politics, Principle, and Prejudice, 1865–1866*, pp. 3–4.

29. George E. Baker (ed.), *The Works of William H. Seward* (5 vols.; Boston: Houghton Mifflin, 1884–88), V, 502–4; see also Cox and Cox, *Politics, Principle, and Prejuidce, 1865–1866*, p. 4.

30. William S. Holman to Allen Hamilton, October 9, 1863, Hamilton Papers; Grant to Elihu Washburne, August 30, 1863, in Grant-Washburne Collection (Illinois State Historical Society, Springfield); Dennett (ed.), *Lincoln and the Civil War in the Diaries and Letters of John Hay*, p. 143; Zornow, *Lincoln & the Party Divided*, pp. 123–24.

31. Edward McPherson, *The Political History of the United States of America, during the Great Rebellion* (rev. ed.; Washington: Philip and Solomons, 1865), pp. 419–21; Zornow, *Lincoln & the Party Divided*, pp. 123–24, 131–33, 135–36.

32. "Address of the Colored National Convention to the People of the United States, October 4–7, 1864," in Foner, *Life and Writings of Frederick Douglass*, III, 414–15.

33. Zornow, *Lincoln & the Party Divided*, pp. 141–48. These returns are

based on figures in *The Tribune Almanac for the Year 1865* (New York: New York Tribune, 1868), pp. 56–64, 67.

34. A comprehensive discussion of these issues is in Zornow, *Lincoln & the Party Divided,* pp. 141–221. See also Emma Lou Thornbrough, *Indiana in the Civil War Era, 1850–1880* (Indianapolis: Indiana Historical Bureau, 1965), pp. 211–23; Kenneth M. Stampp, *Indiana Politics during the Civil War* (Indianapolis: Indiana Historical Bureau, 1949), pp. 217–54; Frank L. Klement, *Wisconsin and the Civil War* (Madison: State Historical Society of Wisconsin, 1963), pp. 99–105; Arthur Charles Cole, *The Era of the Civil War, 1848–1870* (Springfield: Illinois Centennial Commission, 1919), pp. 313–29.

35. *Congressional Globe,* 38 Cong., 2 sess., p. 53; George H. Porter, *Ohio Politics during the Civil War Period* (New York: Columbia University, 1911), p. 202; Emma Lou Thornbrough, *The Negro in Indiana: A Study of a Minority* (Indianapolis: Indiana Historical Bureau, 1957), p. 204; *Journal* (Indianapolis), February 13, 14, 1865. The votes in the state legislatures were Illinois House 48–28, Senate 19–6; Indiana House 56–36, Senate 26–24; Ohio House 57–10, Senate 26–4; Michigan House 75–15, Senate 25–2; Minnesota House 33–5, Senate 16–5; Wisconsin House 77–21, Senate 27–6. McPherson, *The Political History of . . . the Great Rebellion,* pp. 598–99.

36. *Democratic Herald* (Dubuque), February 2, 1865; *Ohio State Journal* (Columbus), February 3, 4, 1865; *Tribune* (Chicago), February 1, 1865; *Illinois State Journal* (Springfield), February 1, 1865; *Journal* (Indianapolis), February 7, 14, 1865.

⚛{9}⚛

The Equalitarian Paradox

At the very moment when slavery was on the road to extinction, the underlying problem of race was growing swiftly in complexity and urgency. With the southern system of racial accommodation about to collapse, critical questions—some old, some new—about the future of the Negro were begging for answers. After the slaves were freed, what should be the status of the Negroes in state and nation? How were the freedmen to adjust to their new condition and become responsible members of a democratic society? Did the federal government have an obligation to assist the newly-freed people, to shield them from exploitation, and to insure their liberty and equality? If so, how was it to perform its duty?

By late 1863 one thing at least was clear: these questions had not been answered. Since midwestern Democrats were not reconciled to the abolition of slavery, they had simply contented themselves with warning of the dire problems which would be created by emancipation and with criticizing Republican efforts to deal with them. On the other hand, the Republicans had failed to develop an acceptable and workable plan of racial adjustment. Proposals that the freedmen be colonized abroad, apprenticed in the South, or just left alone, had failed to pass the tests of practicability and popularity.

The rest of the Republican program had largely been a patchwork of expediency, designed mainly to meet the demands of the moment. Military necessity and humanitarianism were its basic ingredients. By presidential and congressional action Republicans and Unionists had approved the enlistment of Negro soldiers, had attempted to provide relief, care, and employment for the freedmen, and had tried to secure equal treatment for colored soldiers captured

160

by Confederates. These pragmatic and humane measures were leavened with a strain of egalitarianism. In a series of steps that obviously went beyond immediate needs, Congress and the administration had inched gingerly in the direction of greater equality for Negroes. While Congress had pushed slowly forward, with occasional halts and even retreats, toward removing some instances of racial discrimination from federal law and policy, Attorney General Edward Bates had delivered an opinion in 1862 that, contrary to the Dred Scott decision, free Negroes born in the United States were citizens.[1] Though these measures met many of the exigencies of war, they fell far short of providing a long-range means of racial coexistence.

Convinced by their victories in the state elections held in the fall of 1863 that the antislavery crusade was irresistible, Republicans redoubled their search for more acceptable and enduring answers to the race problem. The stopgap measures of the past gave way to a movement to construct a new and better place for Negroes in American society and law. As far as the Midwest was concerned, this was in many ways a new departure. Although most Republicans from the Middle West had voted for congressional laws to aid the Negro and to improve his legal standing, they had usually denied or evaded charges of desiring to alter the existing racial order beyond abolishing slavery. And politicians at home in the Midwest had generally lagged behind Congress on this score. Before the war, it is true, there had been some agitation for the removal of legal disabilities from midwestern Negroes, but since Fort Sumter, most of the batteries of equality had been silenced by the barrage of racial anxiety, and the Republicans had spent most of their time staving off demands for harsher Black Laws.

The mood was quite different in 1864 and 1865. Timothy O. Howe best expressed it when he declared in the Senate that he had twice voted for Negro suffrage in Wisconsin "before the negro was much in fashion. I did it when black was not the popular style, and having done it then, I beg leave to have the advantage of the fashion, now that it has come into vogue."[2] The siren call of politics and patriotism undoubtedly contributed to this feeling. Conviction was strong among Republicans that national security, social progress, and economic prosperity would be safe only in their hands, and some felt that the freedmen should be enfranchised by the federal government to protect these interests. Thus the task of redefining the status of the Negro was entangled with the problem of restoring the South to the Union. But while it is impossible to sort out and weigh precisely the various motives that propelled the drive toward racial reforms, it is plain that these efforts were far more than purely political devices fashioned to convert the freedmen into instruments of Republican supremacy. If most Republicans could see an absolute need for creating a loyal party in the rebel states and were frankly determined to prevent the "slave power" from reasserting itself, they failed to agree on how to accomplish these goals, particularly after Lincoln vetoed the Wade-Davis bill in the summer of 1864. Doubts about the constitutionality and prudence of the proposals for reconstruction, quarrels over strategy, and profound disagreements over what role the Negro should play after the war frayed their hopes for unity.

Instead, an increasing number of midwestern Republicans, churchmen, humanitarians, and reformers joined with their eastern brethren demanding various measures of justice, advancement, and equality for Negroes. Some of these men spoke in unaccustomed tones, but there is still no reason to doubt their sincerity. The obvious decline of the Confederacy, the performance of colored troops, the continuing mistreatment of Negroes, and the religious and nationalistic fervor of the antislavery crusade—with its emphasis upon Christian repentance, responsibility, and brotherhood, with its rhetoric of freedom, with its assurances of moral superiority, with its promise of a regenerated Republic and a new enlightened South—all inspired men to grasp for goals that went beyond the abolition of slavery.

The nation had a dream of equality built into its past, and the Midwest had shared in the vision. The time now seemed ripe to include Negroes in the cast. An exuberant Representative Isaac N. Arnold of Illinois prophesied that a "new nation is to be born from the agony through which the people are now passing. This new nation is to be wholly free. Liberty, *equality before the law* is to be the great cornerstone." The radical Senator Jacob M. Howard of Michigan, who in 1862 had crudely referred to Negroes as "wool" to be sent into Canada, now spoke of his devotion to "elementary principles of human right. I hold that no man ever was born to be a slave; that all men were created equal before their Maker, and that they ought to be treated as equals before the law."[3]

No longer was it enough simply to free the slaves, implored the engineers of a new racial settlement. It would take more than this for Americans to atone for slavery, improve the moral character of the nation, fulfil the ideals of the Founding Fathers, and defeat the rebels. In calling for the repeal of the "infamous Black Laws of Illinois," the Chicago *Tribune* claimed, "The safety of the white race lies in doing justice to the blacks, for God has declared against their oppressors." To win God's blessing and thus the war, Salmon P. Chase wrote in May of 1864, that Lincoln must "let the black loyalists have a fair chance—that is let them come into the army on a perfectly equal footing as to pay, chances of promotion, and right to vote on the soil which they help recover from rebellion." The editor of the Cincinnati *Western Christian Advocate* applied this theory to the North as well. After describing the conflict as "God's warfare for man," he warned, "[We] shall be used as His instruments to scourge the oppressor and to open prison-doors, till the American people, North and South . . . *recognize the essential manhood of the negro,* and his entire equality before the laws and in the sight of God, with the proud and cultivated Saxon race."[4]

A sense of gratitude also beckoned in the same direction. Friends of the Negro repeatedly emphasized that since the nation had accepted Negroes into the military service they should be recompensed for their conduct and valor, although there was wide disagreement over what these rewards should be. With characteristic bluntness, Senator Zachariah Chandler of Michigan gave this reasoning a practical and punitive twist which was too extreme or at least too blatant for most Republicans to espouse openly. A "loyal negro" was "better than a secession traitor either in the North or the South," Chandler told the Senate. "A secession traitor is beneath a loyal negro. I would let a loyal negro vote. I would let him testify; I would let him fight; I would let him do any other good thing, and I would exclude a secession traitor."[5]

A progressive racial policy also had other purposes. Hard experience had convinced most of the champions of the freedmen that it would take more than freedom to convert the slaves into productive citizens, more than emancipation to transform the South into Eden. Such drastic changes, they argued, could be accomplished only through a far-reaching social, economic, religious, and political revolution which should be initiated by Congress and carried out by unionists in the South. According to their plan the government and religious and philanthropic organizations ought to launch a massive effort to rehabilitate the slaves, providing them with Christian instruction, land, education, federal aid and protection, and a Freedmen's Bureau. Not only would such a program serve the interests of racial harmony, justice, and prosperity; it would also forge the Negroes into becoming a spearhead of southern nationalism and redemption, for they could be counted on to maintain loyalty to the Union, establish northern institutions and culture in the South, and elevate the section to the national standard of excellence.[6] Seldom has there been a happier union of national security, enlightened self-interest, and manifest destiny.

Some midwestern clergymen, editors, and politicians campaigned in other ways to win more respect and tolerance for Negroes. They continued to compare favorably the conduct of colored soldiers and civilians with that of Democratic "traitors," and, ironically, sometimes attempted to reduce racism with adroit appeals to religious and class prejudice, charging that only the Irish and "poor whites" were guilty of Negrophobia.[7] Specific facets of racial discrimination came under attack from a few of the bolder spirits. The Chicago *Tribune* complained that black criminals suffered heavier penalties than whites because of their color; the Milwaukee *Sentinel* assailed the ejection of Negroes from streetcars in New York City; and the Cleveland *Leader* helped to lead a successful drive to outlaw segregation on the city's streetcars, reprimanded Negro barbers who refused to serve men of their own race for fear of losing their white patrons, and denounced the local Academy of Music for barring persons of color. Two outstanding midwesterners set high examples of acceptance and understanding in Washington, D.C. To the delight of the Negroes and their white friends, President Lincoln conferred with Frederick Douglass on political matters, and, in 1864 and 1865, received colored persons at public receptions and allowed them to use the White House grounds. In a historic action in February of 1865, Salmon P. Chase, now chief justice of the Supreme Court, admitted a Negro lawyer from Boston to practice before the high tribunal.[8]

Using tactics of protest and reproach, midwestern Negroes did their part to improve their legal and social standing. In the early years of the war they had generally kept their peace, doubtless fearing a severe reaction from the white majority. In fact, a group of

Negroes meeting in Chicago had passed a resolution in 1862, stating that the "masses" of blacks believed that emancipation would "result in the migration of the colored people of the North to the South." By 1864, however, Negroes were increasingly criticizing discrimination and battling for equal rights. They formed an association in Chicago in 1864 to work for the repeal of the Illinois Black Laws, held a festival to raise money for the same purpose, and insisted that the city Board of Education scuttle its policy of racial segregation. In 1864 and 1865, Negroes in Ohio and Michigan formed state auxiliaries of the National Equal Rights League, founded in 1864 with the able John Mercer Langston of Ohio as president. In January of 1865, a delegation of colored men petitioned the Michigan legislature for equality, including the ballot, and complained that they were excluded from the secondary schools in Detroit and in other parts of the state. Negroes from several counties in Indiana met in the state capital in that same month and asked the legislature to repeal the worst of the Black Laws, to appropriate money to support "colored schools," and to allow Negroes to administer these schools.[9]

Meanwhile, a few Negroes sought admission, with varying degrees of success, to some of the schools, churches, streetcars, and other facilities traditionally off limits to men of their race.[10] Though Negroes were politically impotent, such activities, together with eloquent reminders that black men were fighting for the Union, grimly illustrated to the white population of the Midwest the gap between the dialectic and the practice of democracy.

Out of this torrent of words and action flowed some dramatic results. After hearing complaint that Negro military laborers were being paid less than whites, the President apparently directed the War Department to equalize the rates of pay. Almost without dissent Republican congressmen from the Midwest supported the creation of the Freedmen's Bureau (March 3, 1865) to help the freedmen adjust to freedom by providing them with supervision, care, education, and the opportunity to acquire land. With the same enthusiasm, House Republicans voted for a bill, never passed by the Senate, to provide southern homesteads for freedmen. Most of the proposals to erase some of the discriminatory provisions from federal laws usually had overwhelming approval of midwestern Republicans. With slight exceptions they backed measures that repealed the fugitive slave laws, deleted a requirement that only white persons could carry the United States mail, forbade in federal courts the exclusion of any witness on account of color, and killed the inert colonization program by withdrawing its appropriations. Though there was much less unanimity about raising the pay scale of Negro soldiers to that of white troops, most midwestern Republicans voted for such bills passed by Congress in 1864 and 1865.[11] Finally, a few of them made abortive efforts to enfranchise colored men in the District of Columbia, the Montana territory, and in the rebellious states.

These strides were paralleled by state actions in the Midwest. Republican legislators in Iowa repealed the Negro exclusion statute and stripped the word "white" from the poor maintenance law. Ohio Republicans wiped the last of the state's Black Laws from the books by making destitute colored persons eligible for relief and by striking out the "Visible Admixture Law," which barred from voting any person with a "visible and distinct admixture of African blood." A harder fought victory came in Illinois where the repeal of both the exclusion law and the ban on Negro testimony in state courts climaxed a long and bitter campaign. Some of the radicals called for broadening the franchise. Republican-dominated legislatures in Wisconsin and Minnesota responded in early 1865 by approving and scheduling referenda on constitutional amendments providing for Negro suffrage.[12]

The campaign for toleration also bore other fruit. Racial violence did not cease, but it continued to diminish. After the Negro exclusion law was repealed in Illinois, freedmen began to enter the state in somewhat larger numbers without arousing the accustomed furor. In some places long-standing racial barriers fell. When two colored shoemakers applied for admission to the Shoemakers Protective Union in Detroit, the Democratic Detroit *Free Press* moaned, "The darkey having forced himself into our churches [and] our schools . . . is now endeavoring to force himself into associations heretofore composed exclusively of white men." In 1864 and 1865 whites and Negroes attended fairs and public meetings together in Chicago, and colored women were received into the "Chicago Ladies Loyal League." Despite its unhappiness about certain aspects of race relations in the city, in 1865 the Cleveland *Leader* was generally satisfied: "An indication of the civilized spirit of the city of Cleveland is found in the fact that colored children attend our schools, colored people are permitted to attend lectures and public affairs," a situation that may have prevailed even before the war began.[13]

Reasons for the Republicans' mounting solicitude for the Negro in the late stages of the war have long been debated. It has frequently been maintained that only a handful of radical Republicans were sincerely interested in the welfare of the freedmen, and that the motives of even these men were often tainted by a thirst for power, by the needs of their party and northern business interests, by a desire to punish the South, and by fear of future rebellion. According to this interpretation, the majority of Republicans finally enlisted in the cause of Negro rights because it was politically essential to do so, not because it was right. By protecting and enfranchising the freedmen they hoped to win control of southern politics and tighten their grip on the national government.[14]

In recent years a number of historians have partially rescued the Republican program from this setting. While not denying the existence of base or expedient motivations, these scholars quite properly stress that idealistic concern for the Negro was not an insignificant impulse shared only by a few men of noble intellect; rather, it was a compulsive and complex force that powerfully shaped the minds and actions of the racial reformers and of the great body of Republicans. It has been variously maintained that "a genuine desire to do justice to the Negro . . . was one of the mainsprings of radicalism"; that the abolitionists were above all else righteous souls who sought during the war to achieve complete equality for Negroes and to secure land and education for southern freedmen; and that most Republicans were determined to secure varying degrees of rights for colored people to a considerable extent for idealistic reasons.[15]

In recapturing some of the forgotten spirit of Civil War radicalism, these fresh interpretations have done much to realign a distorted picture of the origins of reconstruction. But some scholars have gone considerably beyond this and have concluded that the chastening trial of war transfigured the national purpose from that of waging a war to save the Union into a moral crusade first for freedom and finally for equality. This school of thought is most succinctly represented by historian C. Vann Woodward, who writes that once emancipation was accepted as a goal of war the radicals then began a drive to commit the nation to a "third war aim"—equality.

"It cannot be said that the drive was as successful as the movement for freedom, nor that by the end of war the country was committed to equality in the same degree it was to freedom," he explains. "The third war aim never gained from Lincoln even the qualified support he gave to abolition. Without presidential blessing the commitment was eventually made, made piecemeal like that to freedom, and with full implications not spelled out until after the war—but it was made." In Woodward's opinion, radical Republicans intended to institute civil equality with the Thirteenth Amendment, but failing in this they later secured citizenship, equal protection under the law, and the ballot for Negroes, and finally granted all persons access to public accommodations.[16]

Even though this thesis does not pin down the moment when the commitment to equality was made or identify precisely what it consisted of, it still raises some grave questions so far as the Midwest is concerned. Was the dove of peace truly emerging from the experience of war to banish the anti-Negro feeling of the Midwest? In short, was there a popular commitment to equality as a war goal, and if there was, what was the character and extent of the obligation?

The idea that the Midwest accepted equality as an objective of the war imposes unity of purpose and resolution on a section lacking both. Midwestern Democrats—who polled approximately 44 per cent of the votes in the election of 1864—did not even assent to emancipation, much less to any form of racial equality. While they continued to denounce the abolition amendment, colored soldiers, Negro immigration into the North, and miscegenation, they also hotly opposed the creation of the Freedmen's Bureau, efforts to improve the condition of Negroes, bills to remove racial distinctions from state and federal laws, attempts to enfranchise men of color, and measures to reconstruct the Union.[17] Party needs as well as racial prejudice and constitutional scruples hardened their resistance. Democrats saw clearly that their hopes for ascendancy after the war might well be blasted if the freedmen were granted the right to vote and the traditional leaders of the South disfranchised. It is hardly surprising that the Democrats were the paragons of forgiveness, eager to welcome their wayward friends back into the Union with no strings attached, leaving the destiny of southern Negroes up to individual states.

On the other hand, the attitudes of the Republicans, except for Lincoln, were far more complex. While there is endless speculation about how Lincoln felt in the recesses of his heart and about what he would have done had he lived, it is usually agreed that he never gave his support to full equality for Negroes. Nor is there one shred of credible evidence that he ever modified his fundamental racial attitudes, in spite of his gentle nature, his kind feelings for Negroes, and his appreciation for their military prowess. Beyond signing the bills that came before him and aiding the struggle to equalize military pay rates, the President generally stood aloof from the campaign being waged in Congress for more rights and advancement for Negroes. Moreover, he never so much as hinted that the ballot be given to Negroes living in the North, and he apparently assumed no leadership in the battle to eliminate the Black Laws in Illinois and elsewhere in the Middle West.

Lincoln's policy for reconstruction was flexible but essentially conservative. Although he assented to the repeal of his colonization program in 1864, it is likely that he never gave up the idea completely. As prospects for deportation dimmed, he suggested at various times that an apprenticeship system ought to be established to prepare for racial coexistence. But it was the need to found a loyal political organization in the South, rather than his compassion for the Negro, that absorbed most of his attention, and the party he envisaged was to have a white base. At one time the President suggested that the Unionist government in Louisiana might consider enfranchising "some of the colored people . . . as, for instance, the very intelligent, and especially those who have fought gallantly in our ranks"; but he steadily turned down demands that equal suffrage be imposed on the South and used his influence in Congress to block such legislation. According to his lights, the freedmen were to be entrusted to the care of those conservative white southerners whom he hoped would control politics in the new South. As Kenneth M. Stampp has said, "The Negroes, if they remained, would be governed by the white men among whom they lived, subject only to certain minimum requirements of fair play."[18]

Behind the President stood a hesitant and divided party. On the one side, Republicans registered their impressive reforms in 1864 and 1865 mainly in the name of lofty principles: freedom, protection, justice, opportunity, and equality for Negroes. On the other, for all their earnestness and accomplishments, there is no reason to believe that full equality for Negroes ever became one of their war aims. Abstract belief in the egalitarian dogma was one of the strongest moral sinews in the Republican party, but there were sharp differences of opinion over how to interpret and apply the doctrine. Notwithstanding all their talk about equal rights, midwestern Republicans disagreed over what these rights were and over whether, when, and how they should be granted to Negroes.

These disagreements were partially reflected in the actions of the various states. On the matter of Negro rights, the states of Iowa, Minnesota, Wisconsin, and Michigan were usually more advanced than those of the lower Midwest. By far the most conservative state was Indiana, where Republicans and Unionists could not muster enough votes to eliminate any of the Black Laws, despite their control of the state legislature. In September of 1865, Governor Oliver P. Morton described the condition of Negroes in his state.

> We not only exclude them from voting, we exclude them from testifying in courts of justice. We exclude them from our public schools, and we make it unlawful and criminal for them to come into the state. No negro who has come into Indiana since 1850 can make a valid contract; he can not acquire title to a piece of land, because the law makes the deed void, and every man who gives him employment is subject to prosecution and fine.[19]

Another division prevailed in Congress where Senators Wade, Chandler, Howard, Howe, and Morton S. Wilkinson of Minnesota, and Representatives Julian, Ashley, Josiah B. Grinnell of Iowa, and John H. Farnsworth of Illinois pitted their radical ideas against the more moderate and conservative sentiments of James R. Doolittle, John Sherman, Henry S. Lane, and Lyman Trumbull, whose antislavery zeal was not matched at this time by his zest for Negro rights.

Beneath the blurred purpose and indecision, there were certain areas of fairly general agreement among midwestern Republicans. At rock bottom the consensus was that all men were entitled at least to "natural," or "inalienable," or "civil" rights—those considered vital to the true enjoyment of liberty. As in the past, they usually listed in this category the rights to testify in court, to trial by jury, to receive rewards for labor, to marry and have a family,

170

and to move at will. It was in this spirit that they repealed the exclusion laws in Iowa and Illinois, opened the courts in Illinois to
Negro witnesses, and outlawed in federal legal proceedings the
disqualification of witnesses because of color. Reluctance to legis-
late on matters traditionally regulated by the states and uncertainty
about how southern Negroes would be treated after the war helped
to forestall any action to guarantee these rights in the South. A few
optimists such as Representative Ebon C. Ingersoll of Illinois
felt that the Thirteenth Amendment would guarantee civil equality in the South, although it is difficult to follow his logic in
view of the inferior position historically assigned to Negroes in the
free state where he lived.[20] The belief that freedom was meaning-
less without civil rights would help later to persuade midwestern
Republicans to secure them through federal action, once it became
plain that the conquered states were denying them through the
enactment of Black Codes.

The Midwest's definition of equality seldom included political
rights for Negroes. During the Civil War, not a single midwestern
state granted men of color the right to vote, and state party organizations refused to come out for such a step. In Congress only a
few midwesterners spoke out for any form of Negro suffrage with
only Senators Wade, Wilkinson, and Howe classifying the franchise as a natural right. Most of the congressional champions of
broadening the franchise showed little interest in extending it in
the Midwest. Instead, they urged that black men be allowed to
vote in areas under the jurisdiction of Congress such as the District
of Columbia and in the emerging territory of Montana in recognition of their devotion to the Union. Armed with the ballot, southern
freedmen could be counted upon to protect their freedom and break
the sway of the planters.[21]

Despite these appeals and warnings, the Republican party was
not prepared for equality at the polls. Most of the midwestern Republicans who spoke on the subject not only denied that the franchise was an inherent right; they denied also that Congress had
the power to fix voter qualifications in any state, or that freedmen
were qualified to vote. Not even Salmon P. Chase, who was attempting to secure the ballot for southern freedmen, classified the
franchise as a natural right. The Chicago *Tribune* clung to this
familiar distinction when it rejected the claim "that the rights of

which slavery deprives the negro, the right to marriage, to the parental relation, to wages, to education, are on a par with the right to vote. . . . The former like office, is given by society through the law to such as society deems proper. The former," it concluded, "are necessary to make us freemen. But the elective franchise makes us rulers, and therefore should require at least one qualification of rulers—intelligence."[22]

Equally important, perhaps, most midwestern Republican leaders rightly sensed that a majority of their constituents strongly opposed Negro suffrage anywhere. On April 1, 1864, Republicans in the United States Senate passed a bill enfranchising all free adult males in the Montana territory, but, after being cautioned that such a position would damage their party in the fall elections, reversed themselves and restricted the franchise in Montana to white males; they decisively turned down a move to permit Negroes to vote in the District of Columbia; and in July of 1864 they easily defeated an attempt to insert a Negro enrolment clause in the reconstruction bill cosponsored by Senator Wade.[23] For all practical purposes the suffrage issue rested there until after the war.

Midwestern Republicans demonstrated much the same attitude toward promoting increased contact between the races. There was some bold talk about wiping out legal discrimination, but little action. In Washington their only major attempt to upset Jim Crow came in 1865 when they made common cause with their eastern colleagues in passing a bill forbidding the exclusion of any person because of color from the street railway lines in the District of Columbia.[24] Then, in the same Congress, they voted for laws that perpetuated racial segregation in the Union army and in the public school system in the district. On the home front most of the severe legal disabilities that fostered segregation went untouched, despite Republican-Unionist control of every state legislature in 1864 and 1865. Every state continued to bar black men from the militia as well as from the polls. Michigan, Ohio, Illinois, and Indiana retained their bans on interracial marriages. Colored children were still excluded from the public schools of Indiana, were not provided for in the education laws of Illinois, and were segregated into separate schools by statute in most parts of Ohio. In Iowa, Minnesota, and Michigan, state legislatures stood aloof while Dubuque, Detroit, St. Paul, and other cities and towns, by local action, shunted Negro pupils into separate schools.[25]

Only a few of the innumerable, subtle, extra-legal devices which drew the color line in the Midwest were discarded during the war, and the vast majority of Republicans were apparently satisfied with the status quo. At any rate, few of them sought to alter it. To be sure, there was some pressure to do away with some of the most flagrant aspects of segregation and a few breakthroughs were made, but, on the whole, these changes scarcely scratched the surface of white supremacy. Although customs still varied from area to area, in most places Negroes remained fundamentally as before—victims of discrimination in travel and restaurants, of social ostracism, and of economic subordination. Generally, the masses of the colored people of the Middle West still lived in segregated neighborhoods, worshiped in Negro churches, moved in a black society, and usually worked at menial or unskilled tasks for white employers.[26]

In searching for answers to the race problem in the nation at large, the people of the Midwest deliberately turned away from one suggestion that might have spared much anguish: that of reducing the concentration of Negroes in the South by diffusing them throughout all of the states or by settling them on the public domain in the West. The nation's powerful sense of guilt over its complicity in slavery never developed to the point of expiating its sin in such a manner. While it is true that recommendations for dispersal were frequently intended to embarrass the antislavery movement, there were repeated warnings and admissions by well-meaning men that racial antagonism mounted in proportion to the ratio of blacks to whites in a given area.[27] Such advice went unheeded. On the one hand, the Republican party abandoned its program of colonizing the Negroes abroad on the grounds that it was uneconomical and a concession to racial prejudice; on the other, it bowed to these same forces when it encouraged the freedmen to stay in the South although their labor was badly needed in the North and free land and opportunity awaited them in the West.

This may well have been one of the most tragic failures of Civil War statesmanship—particularly the discarded alternative of voluntary resettlement in the West. Perhaps never in American history has the federal government had a better opportunity both to mitigate racial intolerance in the South and to emancipate the freedmen from the heritage of slavery than that of transporting those who were willing to go into the vast, thinly-settled western territories. In December of 1863 Secretary of Interior John P. Usher made such a recommendation in his annual report to the President. Foreign colonization seemed to be a failure, he said, and there was "much prejudice . . . throughout much of the free States in regard to the introduction of colored persons therein," but Negro labor was in great demand in "a place where the objection to color does not exist," the "line of the Pacific railroad." The appropriations for colonization, he suggested, might "be more judiciously applied in transporting them to those fields of labor within the dominions of the United States where they are wanted, and where they will be welcomed. In this way the expense to which the Government is now subjected will be greatly diminished, and we shall have the satisfaction of placing these people in a position of usefulness, security, and peace."[28] But politics and prejudice dictated otherwise.

This is not to say that the freedmen were systematically restricted in the South or that no efforts were made to find places for them in the North. On the contrary, a small number of Negroes continued to leave the South, and some military commanders and reformers assisted them in finding employment in the free states and along the newly chartered Pacific railroad. Nevertheless, this kind of immigration was not sanctioned on a large scale by the federal government or by most of the humanitarian groups in the Middle West before the end of the war. In 1864 the Union general in charge of the Department of Mississippi counseled the "benevolent of the North" to "seek means to place them [freedmen] through the country" on farms, in factories, and in private homes as house servants. A Minnesota preacher wrote, "We all feel a great interest in the 'contrabands.' Agents are among us, all the time, asking aid to feed and teach them, *where they are.* This is a slow business." He proposed instead that about ten thousand Negroes be brought to Minnesota and compelled to work for wages for at least one year for employers who would pay for their passage. If they should break their contracts, he suggested that they be fined or imprisoned.[29] Yet, as these appeals imply, the Midwest continued to channel most of its philanthropy for Negroes into the South.

The truth was that most midwestern politicians and reformers were convinced that the people of the North still opposed having large numbers of Negroes move into their midst. Certainly Lincoln had no doubts on this score. Upon receiving a letter from Governor John A. Andrew of Massachusetts in February, 1864, protesting that military authorities in Virginia were forcibly detaining Negroes who wanted to emigrate to the Bay State where there was a need for their labor, Lincoln drafted a biting reply which revealed his views, although the letter may not have been mailed. "If I were to judge from the letter, without any external knowledge," he wrote, "I should suppose that all the colored people South of Washington were struggling to get to Massachusetts; that Massachusetts was anxious to receive and retain the whole of them as permanent citizens; and that the United States Government here was interposing and preventing this. But I suppose these are neither really the facts, nor meant to be asserted as true by you." Rather, Lincoln suspected that Andrew was trying to raise colored recruits to credit to the Massachusetts quota, and the President insisted that the army was only trying to be fair to the governor of unionist Virginia who wanted the Negroes for his regiments. "If, however," Lincoln went on, "it be true that Massachusetts wishes to afford a permanent home within her borders, for all, or even a large number of colored persons who will come to her, I shall be only too glad to know it. It would give relief in a very difficult point; and I would not for a moment hinder from going, any person who is free by the terms of the proclamation or any of the acts of Congress."[30]

Congress took much the same position. Following an investigation, the House of Representatives adopted a resolution in March of 1865 requesting the President to direct the revocation of a military order issued in July of 1864 stipulating that "no colored man should be allowed to leave Washington city, going North, without a pass," a directive allegedly designed to protect Negroes in the District of Columbia from being kidnapped by recruiters seeking substitutes for draftees. But it was one thing to brand such overt restrictions "an odious discrimination" and quite another to inaugurate a policy of dispersing the Negro population. In 1864 the Senate was twice put to the test. In April the Senate scorned an effort by Garrett Davis of Kentucky to expand the proposed abolition amendment so as to provide that Congress would distribute American Negroes among all the states and territories in proportion to their white population. Two months later Senator Waitman T. Willey, Republican of West Virginia, raised the issue in a much milder form when he offered an amendment to the freedmen's bureau bill, then being debated, stating that whenever the commissioner of freed-

175

men's affairs should be unable to find land for the former slaves in the South he should attempt to provide homes and employment for them by opening "a correspondence with the Governors and the various municipal authorities of the different States requesting their cooperation in this behalf." Such a system, he said, would solve the labor shortage in the free states and locate the Negroes "where they will have the benefit of free institutions, the benefit of kind and humane society, the benefit of the benevolence that would surround them, in aiding them to elevate themselves to independence and real freedom."[31]

Most of the Senate did not view the matter in this benign light. After the Willey amendment passed with some midwestern support, an unusual coalition of northern Democrats and radical Republicans raised serious objections. Charles Sumner said that the whole idea of organized migration "is entirely untenable; but even if it were at all tenable, it is out of place on this bill." Another Massachusetts radical, Henry Wilson, explained that the amendment would "have a bad influence in the country"; it would not secure work for the freedmen; and it would subject the whole bill "to the carping misrepresentation" of the Democrats. "I want as little correspondence with States where there are prejudices against [Negroes] as possible," S. C. Pomeroy of Kansas announced, because "there is always a political party to make a fuss about it, and it will become an unpopular thing." So persuasive were these arguments that the Senate finally threw out the amendment without a recorded vote.[32]

Indeed, one of the major reasons that many midwesterners could discuss the future of the black race in such enlightened terms was the growing conviction that the South would ultimately be the home of most American Negroes. In short, they could afford to do so because it seemed quite unlikely that they would be intimately involved in the problems of freedom. Midwesterners applied a familiar balm as they pressed for reforms stressing that the freedmen would not leave the South. As he pled for the repeal of the Illinois Black Laws in early 1865, Governor Richard Yates renewed his prophecy that the freedmen would live in the South rather "than seek the cold climates of the North, to face the strong competition of northern skilled free labor, to encounter the prejudice against his color, and the pauperism and neglect which would meet him on every hand."[33]

Paradoxically, the Midwest's aversion toward Negroes continued to be exploited for radical ends. Since 1861, antislavery men had held that emancipation was the best way to halt a Negro exodus from the South; now some concluded that other inducements would assist in keeping the freedmen there. For the most part this point was made by implication and indirection in a noble vein. In asking Congress for protection and land for freedmen in the South, Representative William B. Allison of Iowa said, "It is the duty of the government to give the colored man at least an equal chance with our race in the settlement and cultivation of the soil in his native land." The Contrabands' Relief Commission of Cincinnati recommended that the government provide the former slaves with education, supervision, relief, and a freedmen's bureau to insure their "future happiness and freedom, on the soil where they have suffered their degradation." Sometimes the connection was made with less subtlety. In January of 1865 the Columbus *Ohio State Journal* proclaimed that emancipation and the policy of the "Freedmen's Department" of tutoring the freedmen and setting them to work in Arkansas and Tennessee were effectively answering the race question. Not only were the fears of a Negro invasion receding, but the "way is being opened for those here now to remove Southward, without the danger of being sold into bondage."[34]

Thus, the Republicans' viewpoint on the race issue was varied and complicated. They quite earnestly and sincerely accepted much personal responsibility for the Negro, welcomed their role as the protector of the freedmen, embarked upon an unprecedented federal experiment in racial rehabilitation in the South, and moved, however awkwardly, toward granting a cramped, meager degree of equal rights to colored persons in the Midwest. Even so, they were far from embracing total equality and fraternity. To some extent, the reluctance of most midwestern politicians to strike for a fuller measure of equality stemmed from the fear of popular reaction. There were a few Republicans who were confident that the day of unstinting egalitarianism had finally dawned and exhorted their colleagues to act accordingly—before and after the political campaign of 1864. For the party to have taken such a position in the election would have invited disaster.

When the Senate briefly flirted with enfranchising the Negroes in Montana in the spring of 1864, Senator Doolittle declared that if the Democrats should nominate McClellan on a war platform and stake their battle "upon the basis of negro suffrage . . . no man can doubt for one moment as to the result, and the man is blind that does not see it." The much less cautious Lyman Trumbull was just as emphatic as he cried that this "needless proposition" would divide the people of the North in the coming election. "Shall that be the question to be discussed, instead of the vital one of appealing to the patriotism of the land to rally around the standard of the country and put down this wicked rebellion?" he asked. Sober counsel prevailed. Most Republicans and Unionists forsook the equality and reconstruction issues for the duration of the crucial campaign. Frederick Douglass described their apprehensions poignantly as he explained his lack of activity in the election of 1864: "I am not doing much in the Presidential canvass for the reason that Republican committees do not wish to expose themselves to the charge of being the 'N. . . . r' party. The Negro is the deformed child, which is put out of the room when company comes."[35]

Yet their qualms usually went deeper than political expediency. The chief reason that most midwestern Republicans did not support full equality was that they did not believe in it. Belief in white racial superiority survived almost intact both the antislavery crusade and the rhetoric of equal rights. The efforts of eastern abolitionists to challenge this creed made slight inroads in the Middle West. To most midwesterners of all parties, experience and the teachings of science still seemed to point irresistibly toward the innate inferiority of the black race, although they no longer doubted that Negroes possessed the ability to live under freedom. While many Republicans contended that the slaves would improve greatly under the influence of freedom and that they ought to be given the opportunity, only a few dared to say that they would ever pull abreast of the whites. Representative Ignatius Donnelly of Minnesota, for example, informed the House that blacks would profit from contact with civilization and wished them justice and "the fullest development of which they are capable." Then he added, "Not that I would rate them above or even equal to our proud, illustrious, and dominant race."[36]

Even among many of the radicals of the Midwest, it is hard to find during the Civil War any unequivocal commitment to racial equality. Unquestionably, there were some color-blind equalitarians in the Middle West, but many of the most dedicated advocates of equal rights and advancement wanted equality for Negroes, not because they believed the Negro race to be biologically or intellectually equal to the white, not because they had any intention of accepting them as their own social equals, but because they felt that all men ought to be equal before the law. As they crusaded in the name of equality, many radical politicians, religious leaders, and humanitarians continued to sound traditional midwestern attitudes toward the inferiority of Negroes.

Sometimes they voiced these views obliquely. Some of the same newspapers that most deplored Negrophobia referred to colored persons as "niggers" or "shades" and praised the white race for its superior intelligence and strength.[37] At times they were more direct. The radical Representative Josiah B. Grinnell of Iowa secured House approval of a resolution urging a more vigorous effort to enlist Negroes because of their proven value to the service, and because they would relieve "northern soldiers" from manual labor, and "lessen the number to be taken from their homes and from the industrial pursuits." In July of 1864, Senator Wilkinson of Minnesota, impassioned fighter for equal suffrage and rights, advised the Senate that he would prefer to see more "black soldiers enter into the contest than to have all our white men annihilated before the war shall be over." But it remained for General John A. Logan of Illinois, who was making his way from Democratic conservatism to radical Republicanism, to reduce this argument to its crassest form. Speaking in Springfield in 1864, Logan shouted that he "had rather six niggers . . . be killed than one of his brave boys."[38]

A somewhat more sophisticated brand of racism appeared in the unabated revulsion against commingling of the races. Hearing rumors that a dance had been attended by Negroes and white women, the leading Republican paper in Iowa exclaimed, "This is horrible if true" and then blamed the incident on a "Copperhead." Republicans met allegations that they promoted and practiced miscegenation with the hackneyed retort that slavery encouraged amalgamation, but that emancipation would discourage such odious tendencies. It was the Democratic slave owners and their northern friends who had long been guilty of trying "to bleach out the black race," they chortled. Not more than ten of the 700,000 mulattoes in the United States had Republican fathers, estimated the radical Chicago *Tribune*.[39]

Commenting upon the marriage of a white woman and a Negro man, an Iowa Republican indignantly wrote, "Copperheads and niggers have a perfect right to mix, but it is improper for any loyal man or woman to be parties to such a case, and we hope the press everywhere . . . will be prompt to condemn all such amalgamation." In a typical ambivalent fashion, a preacher from Ohio addressed the General Conference of the Methodist Episcopal Church in 1864 on a proposal to organize southern Negroes into a separate jurisdiction within the church. "He . . . was in favor of having no distinction in the Church. He did not favor amalgamation and never did. He looked forward to the time when the Africans would find homes and liberty in a warmer climate than ours." The government, he suggested, might send Negro troops to Mexico. "Let them go there, and the mongrel population of that country will have nothing to fear from amalgamation."[40]

Robert Dale Owen, George W. Julian, and Benjamin F. Wade epitomized the continuing blend of abstract egalitarianism and pragmatic racism that frequently existed in the psyche of midwestern radicals. A life-long Democrat, reformer Robert Dale Owen of Indiana, broke with his party on the slavery issue early in the war. In 1862 he personally appealed to Lincoln to emancipate the rebels' slaves, and in early 1863 Secretary of War Stanton appointed him to head the American Freedmen's Inquiry Commission. In this post he largely wrote the Commission's final report, submitted in June of 1864. This report, which has accurately been described as a "Radical Blueprint for Reconstruction," decried racial prejudice, called for the establishment of a federal bureau to protect and uplift the freedmen, championed political and civil equality for Negroes, and recommended that the southern states not be readmitted to the Union until they guaranteed equal rights to all of their inhabitants.[41]

But Owen set his edifice of equality on the quicksand of white paternalism and condescension. In contrast to the Democrats who usually said that the black race was consigned by God or nature to eternal degradation, the commissioners took a more humane outlook, conceding that Negroes were inferior to whites in some ways and superior in others. "The Anglo-Saxon race, with great force of character, much mental activity, an unflagging spirit of enterprise, has a certain hardness, a stubborn will [and] only moderate geniality. . . . Its intellectual powers are stronger than its social instincts. . . . It is a race . . . better fitted to do than to enjoy." Of the Negro race, they wrote, "Genial, lively, docile, emotional, the affections rule. . . . It is a knowing rather than a thinking race. . . . It is little given to stirring enterprise, but rather to quiet accumulation. It is not a race that will ever take a lead in the material improvement of the world; but it will make for itself, whenever it has fair play, respectable positions, comfortable homes." Furthermore, Negroes possessed more of the "Christian graces of meekness and long suffering." Even though the report stated that the "softening influence of their genial spirit" would improve the "national character," their analysis reinforced rather than corrected the stereotype of the carefree Negro, for it failed to attribute to him those characteristics deemed necessary to success in a progressive, materialistic society.[42]

The Commission dealt forcefully with the delicate question of interracial marriages. The "amalgamation of these two races," it suggested, led to degeneration and should be "discouraged by public opinion" and parental training. While acknowledging that such practices like "other evils of the kind" were beyond the legitimate reach of legislation, the report prescribed an old antidote to discourage such relations: emancipation. Turning to the fear of a Negro invasion of the North, Owen bluntly asserted that colored people had every right to emigrate northward and that no just man would object if they did so. Then, in a more practical tone, he predicted that climate and northern animosity would deter such a movement and attract half of the Negroes in the North into the South.[43]

George W. Julian was perhaps the most thoroughgoing radical congressman from the Midwest. Representing a safe Republican district with a sizable Quaker population, Julian was in the forefront of his party on nearly every question relating to slavery and the Negro, to the alarm of many of his more conservative colleagues in Indiana. Devoted democrat and implacable foe of land monopoly and political privilege, he was convinced that "independence, liberty, and equality" could be established only if the freedmen were enfranchised and were given the confiscated lands of the planters. Still, Julian also believed that the Negro "is excluded from the northern States and Territories by their uncongenial climate, by his attachment to his birthplace, and by Anglo-Saxon domination and enterprise." He also recoiled in disgust from the prospect of miscegenation. Republicans sometimes associated with Negroes, he admitted, but there were "no such *intimate* relations" as there were in the South where "slave mothers and slave masters . . . are brought on to the level of social equality in its most loathsome forms."[44]

Opinions such as these did not always receive publicity. Unlike many of his colleagues, Senator Benjamin F. Wade largely kept his personal views on race to himself. "Bluff Ben" Wade was one of the Midwest's most courageous and effective champions of freedom and equality. Priding himself upon his democratic principles and upon his hatred of aristocracy, he was an outstanding leader of the radicals, supporting abolition, a root and branch reconstruction of the South, and universal manhood suffrage. Eventually his career in the Senate would end partly because of his forthright advocacy of allowing black men to vote in Ohio. Still, in letters to his wife over a period more than spanning his congressional career, Wade consistently bared a deep-rooted personal antipathy toward colored people. Shortly after taking his Senate seat in 1851, Wade commented on the large number of Negroes in Washington, grumbled that their odor was pervasive, and complained that the food was "all cooked by niggers until I can smell and taste the nigger." His subsequent leadership in the cause of freedom and equality did not dull these sensibilities. While searching for a servant in Washington in 1873, he wrote, "For mere nigger power it will cost over $500 a year"; he preferred to hire "a white woman of the English or Northern European breed" because he was "sick and tired of niggers."[45]

At the close of the war it was abundantly plain that the Midwest's attitude toward the Negro race had changed in many ways, but that the white people of that region still were far from an acceptance of true equality. Four years of war had tempered the racism of the Midwest but had not purged it. Upon this most fragile foundation rested the radicals' hopes for future equality and racial amity. Small wonder that they would fail.

Notes

1. Edward McPherson, *The Political History of the United States of America, during the Great Rebellion* (rev. ed.; Washington: Philip and

Solomons, 1865), pp. 378–84; Dudley Taylor Cornish, *The Sable Arm: Negro Troops in the Union Army, 1861–1865* (New York: Longmans, Green, 1956), pp. 168–69.

2. *Congressional Globe,* 38 Cong., 1 sess., p. 2243.

3. *Ibid.,* pp. 823–24, 2242, 2989; *ibid.,* 37 Cong., 2 sess., p. 1780; *Leader* (Cleveland), January 16, 1864; *Western Christian Advocate* (Cincinnati), December 14, 1864, March 22, 1865.

4. *Tribune* (Chicago), November 19, 26, 1864, January 5, 1865; "Final Report of the American Freedmen's Inquiry Commission to the Secretary of War," May 15, 1864, in U.S., War Department, *The War of the Rebellion: A Compilation of the Official Records of the Union and Confederate Armies* (128 vols.; Washington, D.C.: Government Printing Office, 1880–1901), 3d ser., IV, 380–82 (hereinafter cited as *Official Records*); Chase to Alfred P. Stone, May 23, 1864, in Robert B. Warden, *An Account of the Private Life and Public Services of Salmon Portland Chase* (Cincinnati: Wilstock, Baldwin, 1874), p. 595; *Western Christian Advocate* (Cincinnati), December 14, 1864.

5. *Congressional Globe,* 38 Cong., 1 sess., p. 3349.

6. "Final Report of the American Freedmen's Inquiry Commission to the Secretary of War," May 15, 1864, in *Official Records,* 3d ser., IV, 361, 370, 379–80, 382; *Congressional Globe,* 38 Cong., 1 sess., pp. 143, 821, 1186–87, 1744–45, 2038–39, 2116, 2235, 2242, 2250, 3349; *ibid.,* 38 Cong., 2 sess., p. 1002; *Leader* (Cleveland), November 19, 1863.

7. *Congressional Globe,* 38 Cong., 1 sess., p. 1072; *Times* (Dubuque), May 4, 1864; *Tribune* (Chicago), July 15, 30, 1864.

8. *Tribune* (Chicago), January 6, 9, 1864; *Sentinel* (Milwaukee), June 27, 1864; *Leader* (Cleveland), June 27, July 1, 1864, February 22, 1865; Benjamin Quarles, *Lincoln and the Negro* (New York: Oxford University Press, 1962), pp. 198, 205–7, 232–34.

9. *Free Press* (Detroit), January 26, 27, 1865; *Indiana True Republican* (Centreville), January 26, 1865; *Tribune* (Chicago), April 22, 1862, October 6, November 23, 1864; James M. McPherson, *The Negro's Civil War: How American Negroes Felt and Acted during the War for the Union* (New York: Pantheon Books, 1965), pp. 252–54, 287–89.

10. *Free Press* (Detroit), May 9, 1864, January 26, 27, 1865; *Leader* (Cleveland), May 21, July 1, 1864, March 7, 1865; *Crisis* (Columbus), July 27, 1864.

11. *Congressional Globe,* 38 Cong., 1 sess., pp. 2253, 3261, 3263, 3350, 3402, and Appendix, p. 201; *ibid.,* 38 Cong., 2 sess., pp. 63, 1348, 1418; McPherson, *The Political History of . . . the Great Rebellion,* pp. 277–78; James G. Randall and Richard N. Current, *Lincoln the President: Last Full Measure* (4 vols.; New York: Dodd, Mead, 1945–55), IV, 319–20.

12. *Acts and Resolutions Passed at the Regular Session of the Tenth*

General Assembly of the State of Iowa (Des Moines: F. W. Palmer, 1864), pp. 6, 41; Arthur Charles Cole, *The Era of the Civil War, 1848–1870* (Springfield: Illinois Centennial Commission, 1919), p. 388; George H. Porter, *Ohio Politics during the Civil War Period* (New York: Columbia University, 1911), pp. 201–2; Leslie H. Fishel, "Northern Prejudice and Negro Suffrage, 1865–1870," *Journal of Negro History,* XXXIX (January, 1954), 9. Repeal of the "Visible Admixture Law" was a hollow victory since the state constitution of Ohio continued to bar Negroes from voting.

13. *Free Press* (Detroit), May 9, 1864, March 8, 1865; *Leader* (Cleveland), March 7, 1865; *Tribune* (Chicago), February 26, 1864, February 14, 1865; Cole, *The Era of the Civil War,* p. 336.

14. A concise summary of this school of thought is in Kenneth M. Stampp, *The Era of Reconstruction, 1865–1877* (New York: Alfred A. Knopf, 1965), pp. 4–9.

15. The three points of view expressed in this sentence are to be found, in the order given above, in *ibid.,* p. 105; James M. McPherson, *The Struggle for Equality: Abolitionists and the Negro in the Civil War and Reconstruction* (Princeton, N.J.: Princeton University Press, 1964), pp. 221 ff.; W. R. Brock, *An American Crisis: Congress and Reconstruction, 1865–1867* (New York: St Martin's, 1963), pp. 18–20. See also Jacobus tenBroek, *The Antislavery Origins of the Fourteenth Amendment* (Berkeley: University of California Press, 1951), pp. 129–54.

16. C. Vann Woodward, "Equality: The Deferred Commitment," *The Burden of Southern History* (Baton Rouge: Louisiana State University Press, 1960), pp. 74–78. For a modification of this view, see Woodward's "Seeds of Failure in Radical Race Policy," *Proceedings of the American Philosophical Society,* CX (February, 1966), 1–9.

17. *Congressional Globe,* 38 Cong., 1 sess., pp. 554, 709–12, 766, 783–84, 839, 863, 1075–78, 1304–6, 1395–96, 1457, 1590–91, 1991–95, 2047–48, 2802–3, 2915, 2958–59, and Appendix, p. 55; *ibid.,* 38 Cong., 2 sess., pp. 87, 125, 150, 216, 219, and Appendix, p. 85; *Enquirer* (Cincinnati), May 28, 1864; *Times* (Chicago), February 3, 1864; *Free Press* (Detroit), February 5, March 23, 1864, February 17, March 7, 1865; *Democratic Herald* (Dubuque), May 21, October 9, 1864; *Crisis* (Columbus), January 27, April 13, December 14, 1864.

18. "To Michael Hahn," March 13, 1864, in Roy P. Basler (ed.), *The Collected Works of Abraham Lincoln* (9 vols.; New Brunswick, N.J.: Rutgers University Press, 1953), VII, 243; Ludwell H. Johnson, "Lincoln and Equal Rights: The Authenticity of the Wadsworth Letter," *Journal of Southern History,* XXXII (February, 1966), 83–87; Stampp, *The Era of Reconstruction,* pp. 46–48.

19. William Dudley Foulke, *Life of O. P. Morton, Including His Important Speeches* (2 vols.; Indianapolis: Bowen-Merrill, 1899), I, 449.

20. *Congressional Globe,* 38 Cong., 1 sess., p. 2990; *ibid.,* 2 sess., p. 142, and Appendix, p. 72; *Tribune* (Chicago), January 7, 1865.

21. N. P. Banks to William L. Garrison, January 30, 1865, N. P. Banks Papers (Illinois State Historical Society, Springfield); Chase to Lincoln, April 12, 1865, in *Official Records,* 1st ser., XLVII, 428–30; *Congressional Globe,* 38 Cong., 1 sess., pp. 1745, 2242, 2250–51, 2348, 3349; *ibid.,* 38 Cong., 2 sess., pp. 968, 1002, and Appendix, p. 67.

22. Chase to William T. Sherman, January 2, 1865, William Tecumseh Sherman Papers (Manuscript Division, Library of Congress); *Tribune* (Chicago), January 7, 1865; *Congressional Globe,* 38 Cong., 1 sess., pp. 1844, 2240.

23. *Congressional Globe,* 38 Cong., 1 sess., pp. 1361, 1704–5, 1745–46, 1843–44, 1846, 2351, 2544, 3449.

24. *Ibid.,* p. 3127, and Appendix, p. 142; *ibid.,* 2 sess., pp. 604, 1334.

25. Eugene H. Roseboom, *The Civil War Era, 1850–1873* (Columbus: Ohio State Archaeological Society, 1944), pp. 193–95; Emma Lou Thornbrough, *The Negro in Indiana: A Study of a Minority* (Indianapolis: Indiana Historical Bureau, 1957), pp. 203–4; Cole, *The Era of the Civil War,* pp. 336–37; Earl Spangler, *The Negro in Minnesota* (Minneapolis: T. S. Denison, 1961), pp. 33–35; U.S., Department of the Interior, *Report of the Commissioner of Education . . . for the Year 1870* (Washington, D.C.: Government Printing Office, 1875), p. 188; *Democratic Herald* (Dubuque), February 20, June 5, 1864; *Free Press* (Detroit), January 26, 27, 28, 1865.

26. Thornbrough, *The Negro in Indiana,* pp. 347, 367–68; Cole, *The Era of the Civil War,* pp. 336–37; Spangler, *The Negro in Minnesota,* pp. 55–57; William Ghormley Cochrane, "Freedom Without Equality: A Study of Northern Opinion and the Negro Issue, 1861–1870" (Ph.D. dissertation, University of Minnesota, 1957), pp. 357–58; *Democratic Herald* (Dubuque), January 23, 1864; *Free Press* (Detroit), March 8, 1865; *Illinois State Journal* (Springfield), December 1, 1864; *Indiana True Republican* (Centreville), December 8, 1864.

27. *Congressional Globe,* 37 Cong., 2 sess., Appendix, pp. 83–84; *ibid.,* 38 Cong., 1 sess., pp. 1884, 2141.

28. *Congressional Globe,* 38 Cong., 1 sess., Appendix, p. 26.

29. John Eaton, *Report of the General Superintendent of Freedmen, Department of the Tennessee and State of Arkansas for 1864* (Memphis: n.p., 1865), p. 80; L. G. McMasters to Lyman Trumbull, June 4, 1864, Lyman Trumbull Papers (Manuscript Division, Library of Congress).

30. "To Edwin M. Stanton," February 17, 1864, in Basler (ed.), *The Collected Works of Abraham Lincoln,* VII, 190; "To John A. Andrew," February 18, 1864, in *ibid.,* p. 191; "To Edwin M. Stanton," February 25, 1864, in *ibid.,* p. 204.

31. *House Executive Document No. 79,* 38 Cong., 2 sess. (Washington, D.C.: Government Printing Office, 1865); *Congressional Globe,* 38 Cong., 2 sess., pp. 1114, 1418, 1425, 3329.

32. *Congressional Globe,* 38 Cong., 1 sess., pp. 3329–35, 3337.

33. *Ibid.,* p. 1188; *Illinois State Journal* (Springfield), January 3, 1865; *Journal* (Indianapolis), February 21, 1865; *Ohio State Journal* (Columbus), January 23, 1865.

34. *Congressional Globe,* 38 Cong., 1 sess., p. 2116; *Ohio State Journal* (Columbus), January 23, 1865; *Leader* (Cleveland), November 19, 1863; *Report by the Committee of the Contrabands' Relief Commission of Cincinnati; Proposing a Plan for the Occupation and Government of Vacated Territory in the Seceded States* (Cincinnati: Steam Printing House, 1863), pp. 10–14.

35. *Congressional Globe,* 38 Cong., 1 sess., pp. 1706, 1745–46, 1843–46; Douglass to Theodore Tilton, October 15, 1864, in Philip S. Foner (ed.), *The Life and Writings of Frederick Douglass* (4 vols.; New York: International Publishers, 1950–55), III, 424; William Frank Zornow, *Lincoln & the Party Divided* (Norman: University of Oklahoma Press, 1954), pp. 164–68.

36. *Congressional Globe,* 38 Cong., 1 sess., pp. 2038–39, 2235.

37. *Tribune* (Chicago), October 2, 1864; *Nonpareil* (Council Bluffs), April 9, 1864; *Times* (Dubuque), March 15, August 9, 1864; *Sentinel* (Milwaukee), February 17, 1865; *Illinois State Journal* (Springfield), June 23, 1864, April 10, 1865.

38. *Congressional Globe,* 38 Cong., 1 sess., pp. 161–62, 426–27, 3488; *Illinois State Journal* (Springfield), April 27, 1864.

39. *Iowa State Register* (Des Moines) [January, 1864], quoted in Robert Rutland, "The Copperheads of Iowa: A Re-Examination," *Iowa Journal of History and Politics,* LII (January, 1954), 19; *Sentinel* (Milwaukee), October 15, 1864; *Tribune* (Chicago), April 3, 1864; *Times* (Dubuque), March 11, April 14, 1864; *Illinois State Journal* (Springfield), February 23, March 3, 23, 1864.

40. *Nonpareil* (Council Bluffs), April 9, 1864; *Tribune* (New York), May 7, 1864.

41. John G. Sproat, "Blueprint for Radical Reconstruction," *Journal of Southern History,* XXIII (February, 1957), 25–44; "Final Report of the American Freedmen's Inquiry Commission to the Secretary of War," May 15, 1864, in *Official Records,* 3d ser., IV, 370, 380–82.

42. "Final Report of the American Freedmen's Inquiry Commission to the Secretary of War," May 15, 1864, in *Official Records,* 3d ser., IV, 378–79.

43. *Ibid.,* pp. 373–78.

44. *Congressional Globe,* 38 Cong., 1 sess., pp. 1188, 2250–51; *ibid.,* 38 Cong., 2 sess., Appendix, p. 67.

45. Wade to Mrs. Wade, December 9, 1851, March 9, 1873, Benjamin F. Wade Papers (Manuscript Division, Library of Congress). See also Hans L. Trefousse, *Benjamin Franklin Wade: Radical Republican from Ohio* (New York: Twayne Publishers, 1963), pp. 284–90, 311–13.

Bibliographical Essay

This bibliographical essay is highly selective. It makes no effort to describe every item cited in the notes, which are provided in considerable detail. Rather, this discussion points out only those sources that proved particularly fruitful to this study.

Manuscripts

Manuscript collections are one of the best sources of midwestern attitude toward slavery and the Negro. Several collections warrant special attention. The Robert Todd Lincoln Papers in the Library of Congress are extremely valuable, for they contain numerous letters written by midwestern Democrats and Republicans as well as pamphlets and newspaper clippings pertaining to the politics of the Middle West. Various Republican points of view are expressed in the papers of Lyman Trumbull, Elihu B. Washburne, Salmon P. Chase, John Sherman, and Richard Yates, five large collections which include a multitude of letters from editors, major and minor politicians, military officers, and ordinary citizens. The first four of these collections are located in the Library of Congress, the fifth in the Illinois State Historical Society.

The outlook of moderate and conservative midwestern Republicans and Unionists is further delineated in the James R. Doolittle Papers (Wisconsin State Historical Society), which mirror the bitter division within the Republican party and make plain Senator Doolittle's humanitarian and racial reasons for favoring Negro colonization. Letters in the Thomas Ewing Papers at the Library of Congress cast additional light on the fierce opposition to radical policies. Detailed and incisive political commentary by Senator John Sherman is provided in the papers of his brother, General William Tecumseh Sherman (Library of Congress), a collection which also reflects the General's consistently low opinion of Negro soldiers and radical measures. The Lew Wallace Papers (Indiana State Historical Society) are also profitable.

Among the sources that explain much about the character of radical politics in the Midwest and in the nation are the papers of John Fox Potter and Timothy O. Howe (Wisconsin State Historical Society), the Salmon P. Chase Papers (Cincinnati Historical Society), and the George W. Julian Papers (Indiana State Historical Society). The diary of Indiana humanitarian Calvin Fletcher (Indiana State Historical Society) indicates the depth and sincerity of the conviction that God had established abolition and justice for the Negro as the price of Union victory. Also helpful are the collections of Zachariah Chandler and Benjamin F. Wade, both in the Library of Congress.

There is an abundance of manuscript material relating to Negro soldiers and to the freedmen. The Edwin M. Stanton Papers at the Library of Congress contain much correspondence on this subject. Records in the Civil War Division of the National Archives are invaluable. Among the files of the Adjutant-General's Office, which include the important letterbooks of General Lorenzo Thomas, is a vast amount of data concerning the enlistment of Negro recruits, the attitudes of white soldiers toward the slaves and colored troops, and the steps taken by the federal government and by the Union army to deal with the freedmen. The records of the secretary of war are also of assistance.

Of the manuscript collections that illuminate the activities, opinions, and disagreements of the various wings of the Democratic party in the Midwest, the papers of Moses M. Strong (Wisconsin State Historical Society), Charles H. Lanphier (Illinois State Historical Society), Alexander Long (Cincinnati Historical Society), William H. English, Charles B. Lasselle, and Allen Hamilton (Indiana State Historical Library) are the most serviceable. The most important of these is the Hamilton collection, which includes perceptive and sometimes prophetic letters from William S. Holman. Correspondence from Samuel S. Cox and Clement L. Vallandigham in the Manton S. Marble Papers at the Library of Congress is almost as rewarding.

Government Documents: Federal and State

As the text indicates the proceedings of Congress which are recorded in the *Congressional Globe* are vital to this study. Some facet of the race issue was discussed almost daily while Congress was in session, and the reports of these debates yield rich rewards. *The Official Records of the War of the Rebellion* is, among other things, a voluminous compilation of documents dealing with Negro troops and the freedmen, and it also contains the influential preliminary and final findings of the American Freedmen's Inquiry Commission. Also utilized with success were the relevant publications of the reports of congressional committees and cabinet officials. The legal and social status of midwestern Negroes is partially defined and described in the legislative journals and statutes of the various states.

Newspapers and Periodicals

The newspapers of the Midwest are filled with editorials, articles, news stories, and anecdotes bearing on politics, emancipation, and race. They are indispensable, for the press shaped and reflected the attitudes of midwesterners and also told a great deal about the racial mores of the region. Except where indicated, the newspapers mentioned below were consulted for the entire period of the war.

Nowhere is the delicate blend of humanitarianism, abstract egalitarianism, and racism more clearly revealed than in the moderate and radical antislavery presses. While midwestern editors strongly disagreed about Negro rights, every journal that I consulted continued to express belief in Negro inferiority in one way or another. The Cincinnati *Western Christian Advocate,* a Methodist weekly, was a strident voice of radicalism which advocated legal and political equality for Negroes late in the war. After initially opposing federal interference with slavery and criticizing Negro immigration and labor competition, the Cincinnati *Catholic Telegraph* gradually moved to the support of emancipation and equal rights. Of the Republican presses, the radical Chicago *Tribune* and the Cleveland *Leader* provided a wealth of material. Representative George W. Julian's political organ, the Centreville *Indiana True Republican,* often took a radical stand. The radical New York *Tribune* frequently reported political and racial news from the Middle West and criticized the section's hostility to Negroes.

Most midwestern Republican editors were moderates in that they generally supported the President's policies, increasingly praised colored soldiers, pled for toleration for colored people, called for more rights for Negroes, and yet did not advocate complete equality. Following this pattern, with slight variations, were the Terre Haute *Wabash Express* (1862), Council Bluffs *Nonpareil* (1863–65), *Howard Tribune* (Kokomo), Battle Creek *Journal* (1861–63), Milwaukee *Sentinel,* Dubuque *Times,* Springfield *Illinois State Journal,* Indianapolis *Journal,* and Columbus *Ohio State Journal.*

Democratic editors who remained true to their party usually resisted emancipation and condemned the Negro. The Columbus *Crisis,* Chicago *Times,* Detroit *Free Press,* Dubuque *Herald* (1861–62), Dubuque *Democratic Herald* (1862–65), and Cairo *Gazette* (1861–62) were vociferously anti-Negro, and they frequently reprinted excerpts bearing the same stamp from other Democratic journals in the Midwest. Scattered issues and short runs of the following newspapers were also read with profit: Chicago

Sonntags-Zeitung (Republican), St. Paul *Pioneer* (Unionist), Milwaukee *See-Bote* (Democratic), Cincinnati *Enquirer* (Democratic), *The Liberator* (abolitionist), New York *Times* (moderate Republican), New York *Herald* (erratic Democrat), and *Harper's Weekly* (Republican).

Some periodicals are helpful. The *Ladies' Repository* (Cincinnati), a Methodist publication with wide circulation, is worthy of special mention. Magazines which were not published in the Midwest but contain articles of interest are the *Congregational Quarterly, Harper's New Monthly Magazine,* and *Atlantic Monthly.*

Published Correspondence, Diaries, Memoirs, and Autobiographies

Roy P. Basler (ed.), *The Collected Works of Abraham Lincoln* (9 vols.; New Brunswick: Rutgers University Press, 1953), is a basic source of information on Lincoln and almost every aspect of the problems of slavery and race. Charles Sumner, *The Works of Charles Sumner* (15 vols.; Boston: Lee and Shepard, 1870–73); Edward L. Pierce, *Memoir and Letters of Charles Sumner* (4 vols.; Boston: Roberts Bros., 1887–93); Sarah Forbes Hughes (ed.), *Letters and Recollections of John Murray Forbes* (2 vols.; Boston: Houghton Mifflin, 1899); and Jessie Ames Marshall (ed.), *Private and Official Correspondence of General Benjamin F. Butler during . . . the Civil War* (5 vols.; Norwood: privately printed, 1917), include much relevant material. Candid appraisals of northern racial attitudes and acute observations on the strategy of Democrats and Republicans are set forth in Philip S. Foner (ed.), *The Life and Writings of Frederick Douglass* (4 vols.; New York: International Publishers, 1950–55). *The Sherman Letters* (New York: Charles Scribner's Sons, 1894) is of assistance but must be used with care since portions of the letters were deleted by the editor, Rachel Sherman Thorndike.

Yielding salient information on the measures of the Lincoln administration and on northern politics are the diaries of two cabinet members and of one of the President's closest friends: Howard K. Beale (ed.), *Diary of Gideon Welles: Secretary of the Navy under Lincoln and Johnson* (3 vols.; New York: W. W. Norton, 1960); David Donald (ed.), *Inside Lincoln's Cabinet; The Civil War Diaries of Salmon P. Chase* (New York: Longmans, Green, 1954); and Theodore Calvin Pease and James G. Randall (eds.), *The Diary of Orville Hickman Browning* (2 vols.; Springfield: Illinois State Historical Library, 1927–33). A few pertinent entries are recorded in Tyler Dennett (ed.), *Lincoln and the Civil War in the Diaries and Letters of John Hay* (New York: Dodd, Mead, 1939), and Howard K. Beale (ed.), *The Diary of Edward Bates, 1859–1866* (Washington, D.C.: Government Printing Office, 1933).

Except for testimony on politics the bulk of the memoirs and autobiographies of prominent midwesterners are of little value. In most of these accounts white attitudes toward the Negro receive scant attention, and the opposition to abolishing slavery and arming the freedmen disappears in the spirit of emancipation, probably because the memory of the Midwest's wartime racial animosity faded in the light of efforts to establish equality during reconstruction. A notable exception is John Mercer Langston, *From the Virginia Plantation to the National Capitol* . . . (Hartford: American Publishing Company, 1894), the reminiscences of a Negro abolitionist who describes race relations in Ohio and also relates the prejudice he encountered in securing permission to recruit colored troops in the state. Other works that deserve notice are *John Sherman's Recollections of Forty Years in the House, Senate and Cabinet: An Autobiography* (2 vols.; Chicago: Werner, 1895); George W. Julian, *Political Recollections, 1840–1872* (Chicago: Jansen, McClurg, 1884); and Francis B. Carpenter, *Six Months at the White House with Abraham Lincoln* (New York: Hurd and Houghton, 1867), a short account that includes some vital information on the Emancipation Proclamation.

Regional, State, and Local Studies

A great and growing body of literature deals with the Midwest during the Civil War. A good general survey of the region is Henry Clyde Hubbart, *The Older Middle West, 1840–1880* . . . (New York: D. Appleton-Century, 1936). I have drawn heavily from the thorough but conflicting analyses of anti-administration Democrats by Wood Gray, *The Hidden Civil War: The Story of the Copperheads* (New York: Viking Press, 1942), and Frank L. Klement, *The Copperheads in the Middle West* (Chicago: University of Chicago Press, 1960).

A number of state histories cover the war years, but until recently most of these accounts have minimized the political importance of the race issue and have failed to recognize the extent and usually the existence of white supremacist sentiment among antislavery men. An example is Kenneth M. Stampp, *Indiana Politics during the Civil War* (Indianapolis: Indiana Historical Bureau, 1949), an otherwise authoritative work. Other excellent studies which touch somewhat more heavily on the Negro question are Arthur Charles Cole, *The Era of the Civil War, 1848–1870* (Springfield: Illinois Centennial Commission, 1919); George H. Porter, *Ohio Politics during the Civil War Period* (New York: Columbia University, 1911); and Eugene H. Roseboom, *The Civil War Era, 1850–1873* (Columbus: Ohio State Archaeological and Historical Society, 1944). Midwestern Negrophobia is more adequately stressed in Emma Lou Thornbrough, *Indiana in the Civil War Era* (Indianapolis: Indiana Historical Bureau, 1965); Harry E. Pratt, "The Repudiation of Lincoln's War Policy in 1862—Stuart-Swett Congressional Campaign," *Journal of the Illinois State Historical Society,* XXIV (April, 1931); Eugene H. Roseboom, "Southern Ohio and the Union in 1863," *Mississippi Valley Historical Review,* XXXIX (June, 1952); Robert Rutland, "The Copperheads of Iowa: A Re-Examination," *Iowa Journal of History and Politics,* LII (January, 1954); Emma Lou Thornbrough, "The Race Issue in Indiana Politics during the Civil War," *Indiana Magazine of History,* XLVII (June, 1951); Charles R. Wilson, "Cincinnati's Reputation during the Civil War," *Journal of Southern History,* II (November, 1936); and Leslie H. Fishel, "Wisconsin and Negro Suffrage," *Wisconsin Magazine of History,* XLVI (Spring, 1963). Other contributions to a better understanding of midwestern politics are Robert S. Harper, "The Ohio Press in the Civil War," *Civil War History,* III (September, 1957); Olynthus B. Clark, *The Politics of Iowa during the Civil War and Reconstruction* (Iowa City: Clio Press, 1911); and Frank L. Klement, *Wisconsin and the Civil War* (Madison: State Historical Society of Wisconsin, 1963).

The life of the Negro in the Midwest and white racial attitudes in many of the states of the region are treated in several monographs. By far the most valuable is Emma Lou Thornbrough, *The Negro in Indiana: A Study of a Minority* (Indianapolis: Indiana Historical Bureau, 1957), a model of exhaustive research and outstanding scholarship. Several other studies were consulted with varying degrees of benefit: Norman Dwight Harris, *The Study of Negro Servitude in Illinois, and of the Slavery Agitation in that State, 1719–1864* (Chicago: A. C. McClurg, 1904); Charles T. Hickok, *The Negro in Ohio: 1802–1870* (Cleveland: Francis C. Butler Publication Fund, 1896); Frank U. Quillen, *The Color Line in Ohio: A History of Race Prejudice in a Typical Northern State* (Ann Arbor, Mich.: George Wahr, 1913); Earl Spangler, *The Negro in Minnesota* (Minneapolis: T. S. Denison, 1961); Charles H. Wesley, *Ohio Negroes in the Civil War* (Columbus: Vanguard Press, 1962); Leola Nelson Bergmann, "The Negro in Iowa," *Iowa Journal of History and Politics,* XLVI (January, 1948); Leslie H. Fishel, "Northern Prejudice and Negro Suffrage, 1865–1870," *Journal of Negro History,* XXXIX (January, 1954); Mason M. Fishback, "Illinois Legislation on Slavery and Free Negroes, 1818–1865," *Transactions of the Illinois State Historical Society* (January, 1904); and James H. Rodabaugh, "The Negro in Ohio," *Journal of Negro History,* XXXI (January, 1946).

Biographies, General Works, and Monographs

Biographies of public figures in the Middle West supply information on political affairs and on some aspects of the slavery controversy but usually play down or ignore the race issue during the Civil War. Important exceptions to this general rule are Hans Trefousse, *Benjamin Frank-*

lin Wade: Radical Republican from Ohio (New York: Twayne Publishers. 1963); David Lindsey, *"Sunset" Cox, Irrepressible Democrat* (Detroit: Wayne State University, 1959); and William Dudley Foulke, *Life of O. P. Morton* (2 vols.; Indianapolis: Bowen-Merrill, 1899). Richard W. Leopold, *Robert Dale Owen: A Biography* (Cambridge, Mass.: Harvard University Press, 1940) discusses the activities and reports of the American Freedmen's Inquiry Commission. Touching with varying emphasis on many key points is the single most important biographical source of this study, James G. Randall, *Lincoln the President* (4 vols.; New York: Dodd, Mead, 1945–55), the fourth volume of which was completed by Richard N. Current. Current also lights some of the enigmatic corners of Lincoln's mind in *The Lincoln Nobody Knows* (New York: McGraw Hill, 1958). Lincoln's racial attitudes and policies are also treated in Benjamin F. Quarles, *Lincoln and the Negro* (New York: Oxford University Press, 1962).

A few of the early histories of the Civil War are of value. Edward McPherson, *The Political History of the United States of America during the Great Rebellion* (Washington, D.C.: Philip and Solomons, 1865) provides material of interest on the slavery and equality controversies. Observations on northern opinions of the Negro and some good interpretations are in Horace Greeley, *The American Conflict* (2 vols.; Hartford: O. D. Case, 1865–66) and James G. Blaine, *Twenty Years of Congress: From Lincoln to Garfield* (2 vols.; Norwich: Henry Bill, 1884). Henry W. Wilson penned a contemporary description of northern racial views in *The Rise and Fall of the Slave Power in America* (3 vols.; Boston: Houghton Mifflin, 1872–77). Part of the Democratic side of the story is told in Samuel S. Cox, *Three Decades of Federal Legislation, 1855–1885* (Providence: J. A. and R. A. Reid, 1886), even though Cox had apparently forgotten that he and his party had opposed emancipation and the arming of Negro soldiers for racial as well as constitutional reasons. Among the more recent general histories, Allan Nevins, *The War for the Union* (2 vols.; New York: Charles Scribner's Sons, 1959–61), awards the most space to the race question, but James G. Randall and David Donald, *The Civil War and Reconstruction* (2d ed.; Boston: D. C. Heath, 1961) is also helpful.

Several studies focus attention primarily upon the Negroes' experience in the war. Parts of this story are in James M. McPherson, *The Negro's Civil War: How American Negroes Felt and Acted during the War for the Union* (New York: Pantheon Books, 1965), and Benjamin F. Quarles, *The Negro in the Civil War* (Boston: Little, Brown, 1953). The best examination of Negro soldiers is Dudley T. Cornish, *The Sable Arm: Negro Troops in the Union Army, 1861–1865* (New York: Longmans, Green, 1956). The trials of the freedmen and the efforts of the federal government to resolve them are discussed in Bell I. Wiley, *Southern Negroes, 1861–1865* (2d ed.; New York: Rinehart & Co., 1953).

An excellent work on northern racial attitudes and the life of the Negro in the North in the ante bellum period is Leon F. Litwack, *North of Slavery: The Negro in the Free States, 1790–1860* (Chicago: University of Chicago Press, 1961). The conclusions and assumptions of American scientists on racial characteristics are related in William R. Stanton, *The Leopard's Spots: Scientific Attitudes toward Race in America, 1815–59* (Chicago: University of Chicago Press, 1960). James M. McPherson recounts the abolitionists' efforts to secure equality and opportunity for Negroes in *The Struggle for Equality: Abolitionists in the Civil War and Reconstruction* (Princeton, N.J.: Princeton University Press, 1964), but he underestimates their ambivalence on race. Some of the chinks in the abolitionists' egalitarian armor are explored by William and Jane H. Pease, "Antislavery Ambivalence: Immediatism, Expediency and Race," *American Quarterly,* XVII (Winter, 1965), and Thomas F. Gossett, *Race, The History of an Idea in America* (Dallas: Southern Methodist University Press, 1963). Gossett clearly shows that in the nineteenth century most American intellectuals and scientists believed in the inherent inferiority of the Negro race. The response of white Union soldiers to Negro troops is described in Bell I. Wiley, *The Life of Billy Yank: The Common Soldier of the Union* (Indianapolis: Bobbs-Merrill, 1952). Also of use is Leslie H. Fishel, "Northern Prejudice and Negro Suffrage," *Journal of Negro History,* XXXIX (January, 1954). William Ghormley Cochrane, "Freedom without Equality: A Study of Northern Opinion and the Negro Issue, 1861–1870" (Ph.D. dissertation, University of Minnesota, 1957), lacks depth, but it contains useful information. Also suggestive are Lee Allen Dew, "The Racial Ideas of the Authors of the Fourteenth Amendment" (Ph.D. dissertation, Louisiana State University, 1960), and Leslie H. Fishel, "The North and the Negro, 1865–1900: A Study in Racial Discrimination" (Ph.D. dissertation, Harvard University, 1954), an outstanding study.

The opposition of northern labor to Negro competition receives varying degrees of attention from Bernard Mandel, *Labor: Slave and Free: Workingmen and the Anti-Slavery Movement in the United States* (New York: Associated Authors, 1955); Emerson David Fite, *Social and Industrial Conditions in the North during the Civil War* (New York: Macmillan, 1910); Sterling D. Spero and Abram L. Harris, *The Black Worker: The Negro and the Labor Movement* (New York: Columbia University Press, 1931); Charles H. Wesley, *Negro Labor in the United States, 1850–1925* (New York: Vanguard Press, 1927); and Williston H. Lofton, "Northern Labor and the Negro during the Civil War," *Journal of Negro History,* XXXIV (July, 1949).

The Negro colonization movement has received elaborate attention. Two studies of this subject, especially for the ante bellum period, are P. J. Staudenraus, *The African Colonization Movement, 1816–1865* (New York: Columbia University Press, 1961), and Frederick Bancroft, "The Colonization of American Negroes, 1801–1865," in Jacob Cooke, *Frederick Bancroft, Historian* (Norman: University of Oklahoma Press, 1957). Of value for the war years are Robert H. Zoellner, "Negro Colonization: The Climate of Opinion Surrounding Lincoln, 1860–65," *Mid-America*, XLII (July, 1960); Walter L. Fleming, "Deportation and Colonization: An Attempted Solution of the Race Problem," in J. G. deRoulhac Hamilton (ed.), *Studies in Southern History and Politics Inscribed to William Archibald Dunning* (New York: Columbia University Press, 1914); Warren A. Beck, "Lincoln and Negro Colonization in Central America," *Abraham Lincoln Quarterly*, VI (September, 1950); Paul J. Scheips, "Lincoln and the Chiriqui Colonization Project," *Journal of Negro History*, XXXVII (October, 1952).

A number of other monographs are useful. Lincoln's consummate flexibility and a dark picture of the radicals are portrayed in T. Harry Williams, *Lincoln and the Radicals* (Madison: University of Wisconsin Press, 1941). A comprehensive investigation of the election of 1864 with some emphasis on the race issue is in William F. Zornow, *Lincoln & the Party Divided* (Norman: University of Oklahoma Press, 1954). John Hope Franklin, *The Emancipation Proclamation* (New York: Doubleday, 1963) is a detailed account of that order. Useful for the backstage controversy over the Thirteenth Amendment is Lawanda and John H. Cox, *Politics, Principle, and Prejudice, 1865–1866: Dilemma of Reconstruction America* (New York: Free Press of Glencoe, 1963). The influence of the American Freedmen's Inquiry Commission report is the subject of John G. Sproat, "Blueprint for Radical Reconstruction," *Journal of Southern History*, XXIII (February, 1957). Lawanda Cox, "The Promise of Land for the Freedmen," *Mississippi Valley Historical Review*, XLV (December, 1958), raises some important points and questions about the drive to supply the freedmen with land. Stressing the radicals' idealistic motives but also conceding the lack of a popular northern belief in racial equality are William R. Brock, *An American Crisis: Congress and Reconstruction, 1865–1867* (New York: St Martin's, 1963), and Kenneth M. Stampp, *The Era of Reconstruction, 1865–1877* (New York: Alfred A. Knopf, 1965), a work which emphasizes the pragmatic nature of Lincoln's reconstruction policy. C. Vann Woodward, "Equality, America's Deferred Commitment," in *The Burden of Southern History* (Baton Rouge: Louisiana State University Press, 1960), is a masterful essay on the ingredients of the egalitarian impulse.

Acknowledgments

I have acquired many obligations while writing this book. My greatest debt is to Charles P. Roland, whose vision, insights, and wise understanding were indispensable sources of encouragement and direction. I am also deeply grateful to William R. Hogan for his constructive criticism of the entire manuscript and for providing me with the opportunity to finish this study. I am indebted to Bennett H. Wall and William R. Wyatt for reading portions of the manuscript.

Financial aid supplied by the Southern Fellowships Fund enabled me to conduct research in parts of the Midwest and in Washington, D.C. The John T. Monroe Scholarship awarded by Tulane University permitted me to prepare the manuscript for publication. I appreciate the efforts of the staffs of the Reference Department of Howard-Tilton Memorial Library, Tulane University; State Historical Society of Wisconsin Library, Madison; Illinois State Historical Library and Illinois State Archives, Springfield; Indiana State Historical Society and Indiana State Library, Indianapolis; Indiana University Library, Bloomington; Cincinnati Historical Society, Cincinnati; Western Reserve Historical Society, Cleveland; Kansas State Historical Society, Topeka; and the Library of Congress and National Archives, Washington, D.C.

I wish to acknowledge permission from the Organization of American Historians to reprint parts of my article, "The Northwest and the Race Issue, 1861–1862," *Mississippi Valley Historical Review* (September, 1963). Extracts on page 82 from *The Life of Billy Yank: The Common Soldier of the Union,* by Bell Irvin Wiley, copyright 1952 by the Bobbs-Merrill Company, Inc., reprinted by permission of the publishers. Passages on pages 45 and 50 from *Inside Lincoln's Cabinet: The Civil War Diaries of Salmon P. Chase* and *The Sable Arm: Negro Troops in the Union Army, 1861–1865,* by Dudley T. Cornish, copyrights 1954 and 1956, respectively, by Longmans, Green and Company, Ltd., used by permission of David McKay Company, Inc. Quotations on pages 65, 150, 152, and 178 from *The Life and Writings of Frederick Douglass* (4 vols.), edited by Philip S. Foner, copyright 1950–1955 by International Publishers Company, Inc., reprinted by permission of the publishers.

Finally, I owe more than I can say to my wife, Jean, who edited and typed the manuscript through its many stages. Without her perseverance and generous support this book would never have been completed.

☙ Index ☚

108; Methodists support Union party, 121

Cincinnati *Catholic Telegraph:* policy of, 87; endorses Union ticket, 121–22; on opposition to emancipation, 128; predicts Negro exodus from North, 130–31; advocates white supremacy, 130–31; on emancipation ending labor competition, 130–31

Cincinnati *Commercial,* 83, 129

Cincinnati *Enquirer,* opposes emancipation, 6, 14

Cincinnati *Western Christian Advocate:* 59; on equality, 163

Clay, Cassius M., predicts Negro exodus from North, 58

Clay, Henry, exploits fears of Negro influx, 6

Cleveland, 112; spring elections, 1863, 83–84; race relations, 166–67

Cleveland Convention, Frémont nominated by, 141

Cleveland *Leader:* supports abolition, 5; on Negro immigration, 58; on elections of 1862, 62; praises Emancipation Proclamation, 79; racial views of, 86–87; enlistment of Negro soldiers, 105; attacks racial discrimination, 164; on race relations in Cleveland, 166–67

Cleveland *Plain Dealer,* opposes emancipation, 14

Coffin, Levi, 87

Colfax, Schuyler: on elections of 1862, 63; on reaction to Lincoln's peace terms, 147–48; explains Niagara peace terms, 148

Colonization, Negro: effect of war on, 22; Republican opposition to, 22, 25; motives behind movement, 23–24; arguments for, 23–24; as deterrent to Negro immigration, 24–25; Republican party converted to, 25; provisions for, 25; supported by Ohio legislature, 28–29; advocated by Lincoln, 39, 43–45; advocated by Joseph A. Wright, 44; advocated by John P. Usher, 44; as means of allaying fears of Negro influx, 44; contract signed, 44; criticism of, 45; as political stratagem, 45; analysis of Lincoln's support for, 45; issue in elections of fall, 1862, 57; rejected by Republicans, 65; in South,

supported, 65; urged by Lincoln, 66–67, 73; unpopularity of, 74; failure of, 95; Lincoln supports, in Caribbean, 97; in Florida, discussed by cabinet, 97; on Isle à Vache, 97–98; abandoned by administration, 112; effects of Negro mobilization on policy of, 112; endorsed by War Democrats, 127; failure of, 160; appropriations withrawn, 166; Lincoln's views on, 169

Columbus, Kentucky, 105, 108

Columbus, Ohio, spring elections, 1863, 83–84

Columbus *Crisis,* 6; predicts Negro immigration, 4, 122; on racial violence, 9; opposes emancipation, 14; elections of 1862, 64; promotes peace, 78–79; on motives of egalitarians, 126; reaction of, to Lincoln's peace terms, 146

Columbus *Ohio State Journal:* suggests emancipation, 5–6; fears emancipation, 17; and emancipation issue, 1862, 56; on Emancipation Proclamation, 79; on election issues, fall, 1863, 128; on deterrent to Negro immigration, 177

Compensated emancipation: advocated by Lincoln, 66–67, 73; debated, 74; Democrats object to, 74, 77

Confederacy, 5, 36, 40, 119, 122–23, 150, 160–62; effects of refusal of, to consider peace, 152

Confiscation Act of 1862, 46; provisions of, 13, 25; significance of, 36; and use of freedmen by army, 42; effect on War Democrats, 53

Congress, United States, 22; special session of July–August, 1861, 6; war aims resolutions, 9; emancipatory measures, 13; recognizes Haiti and Liberia, 25; and militia law, 1862, 25; racial legislation, 25, 85; Midwestern representation in Thirty-eighth, 61–62; debates Lincoln's program, 73–74, 76; prohibits Negro suffrage in Idaho territory, 85; authorizes employment of Negroes in armed forces, 98; debates Negro soldier bill, 103–4; and Thirteenth Amendment, 137–38, 141–44, 154; and Negro rights (1864–1865), 161–62, 165–66, 170–72; action of, on Negro

egy, 148–52; Democratic strategy, 146–47, 151–52; analysis of, in Midwest, 153–54; significance of, in Midwest, 154; Democratic vote in Midwest in, 168; Republican campaign tactics in, 178; racial equality issue in, 178

Emancipation: Democratic opposition to, 4, 6–7, 14–15, 35–36, 54–55, 61, 64, 74, 76–79, 125–26, 141–44, 151, 153–54, 168; Republicans on, 5–9; economic opposition to, 16–17; Republican arguments for, 1862, 16–17; Republican attitudes toward, 1862, 36–40; Lincoln develops policy of, 1862, 40–47; used by Democrats, in elections of 1862, 54–55, 60; as campaign issue, fall, 1862, 54–55, 58–60, 62–63; and Republicans, in elections of 1862, 55–57; churches' support of, 1862, 59; charged as part of Africanization scheme, 60; role in election results of 1862 evaluated, 62; Greeley on Northern attitudes toward, 63; Lincoln on effects of, 66; as source of discontent, 81–82; attitudes of army on, 82; Lincoln favors gradual, 97; turning point in movement for, 118–19; influences in movement for, in 1863, 118–23; influence of religion on movement for, 119–20; willed by God, 120; effect of prosperity on movement for, 120–21; Republican and Unionist arguments for, 1863, 120, 128–31; movement assisted by loyalty issue, 121; supported by churches, 121–22; movement accelerated by declining fear of Negro influx, 122; movement accelerated by economic prosperity, 122; movement aided by improving racial attitudes, 123; issue in elections of fall, 1863, 129; effects of, predicted, 130–31; movement in Maryland and Missouri, 132; leaders of movement for, 137; effect of elections of fall, 1863, on movement for, 137; support for, in Midwest, 138; moral urgency of movement for, 138–39; seen as instrument of Southern regeneration, 139; utopianism in movement for, 139; as instrument of national uniformity, 139; gains adherents in Midwest, 140; limitations of commitment to, 141; movement wanes in summer of 1864, 145; as condition of peace, 146–

53; issue in elections of 1864, 146–54; and Negro rights movements, 162–63

Emancipation Proclamation: provisions of, 74–75; analysis of, 75; Democratic reaction to, 76–79; exploited by Peace Democrats, 78; moral justification of, 79–80; Republicans' reception of, 79–84; effects considered, 81–82; reaction of Union army to, 82; Lincoln on effects of, 83; revolutionary nature of, 84; Republican press on, 86–87; Lincoln on legitimacy of, 95; announces decision to accept Negro soldiers, 98; John Brough on impolicy of, 120; Lincoln on opposition to, 128; Lincoln refuses to extend, 128–29; unpopularity of, in Ohio, 129; and Midwestern attitudes toward, 131–32; Lincoln on effects of, 131–32. *See also* Emancipation, Preliminary Emancipation Proclamation, Thirteenth Amendment.

Episcopal church, conservatism on slavery, 59

Ewing, Thomas: on emancipation, 18; on elections of 1862, 62; on Emancipation Proclamation, 81

Faran, James J., on reconstruction, 144

Farnsworth, John H., 170

Foote, Andrew H., on emancipation proclamations, 82

Fort Sumter, 4

Fort Wayne, 123; anti-Negro violence in, 88

Fort Wayne *Sentinel,* 88

Fredericksburg, battle of, 75

Freedmen: problems concerning, 41, 95–97; policy for providing for, 42–45, 96, 98, 106, 108–11; migration of, into free states, 42, 109–10, 166, 174; praised by Republicans, 84; Lorenzo Thomas instructed to provide for, 105; Lorenzo Thomas on disposition of, 106; utilization of, in South, 106–7; sent by army to Midwest, 108; detained in South, 109; remain in South, 110; analysis of federal policy concerning, 110; effect of providing for, in South, 111–12, 177; effect of activities of, on racial attitudes, 123–24

Freedmen's aid organizations, 65, 87–88,

124–25, 130, 161–66, 169–73, 177–82; and the war, 16; attitudes of, toward slavery, 16; antislavery strategy of, 17; and Negro immigration, 18–22, 56–58, 60–61, 63–67, 84–87, 128, 130–31, 176, 181; oppose exclusion laws, 26–27, 85–86; tactics on emancipation, fall, 1862, 55; charge Democrats with Negrophobia, 57; accused of hiring freedmen, 60; accuse Democrats of hiring Negro immigrants, 61; oppose Negro immigration into Illinois, 61; evaluate elections of 1862, 62–65; reappraise race problem, 64–65; attitudes of, toward Lincoln's antislavery program, 74; reception of Emancipation Proclamation, 79–83; tactics on emancipation issue, 1863, 83–84; accuse Democrats of being pro-Negro, 85; oppose colored soldiers, 99–100; campaign for Negro soldiers, 101–3; urge enlistment of Negroes to save whites, 102, 179; and Negro soldier bill, 103; on retaining Negroes in South, 106–7; arguments for emancipation, 1863, 120, 124, 129; accuse Democrats of disloyalty, 124; attempt to abate racial prejudice, 124–25, 130; praise Negro soldiers, 124, 129, 132; use Negro substitutes, 125; accused of political egalitarianism, 126; political tactics of, fall, 1863, 127–31; victory of, in elections, fall, 1863, 131; support emancipation movement, 137–40, 153–54; win elections of 1864, 153; response of, to Thirteenth Amendment, 154; egalitarian efforts of, 161–66; efforts of, to aid Negroes, 161–66; arguments of, for Negro suffrage, 171; reject Negro suffrage, 172; accept segregation, 173; analysis of racial attitudes of, 177–82; charge Democrats with practicing miscegenation, 179–80; opposition of, to racial equality and miscegenation, 179–82. *See also* Emancipation; Negro immigration; Negro soldiers

Republican (Union) party, 45; composition of, 3; attitude toward slavery and Negro, 3–4; political strategy of, 1860, 4; press attitudes toward Negroes, 8; antislavery program of, 13, 15–16; divisions in, on emancipation, 15–16, 36–38; converted to emancipation, 17; ra-

cial measures of, 25, 160–61, 165–66; divided on Negro soldiers, 41; effects of Preliminary Emancipation Proclamation on, 52; accused of egalitarianism, 54–55, 60, 76–77; exploits loyalty issue, 54, 56–57; tactics in fall elections, 1862, 55–57; of Michigan, on emancipation, 56; press, campaign tactics, fall, 1862, 56–58, 61; supported by Midwestern churches, 59; advice to, from Chicago *Tribune,* 63–64; debates Emancipation Proclamation, 74; discusses reaction to Emancipation Proclamation, 80–83; freedmen problem confronts, 95; press hails L. Thomas' policy, 111; benefits from disloyalty charges, 121; dissension in, 1864, 140; radicals in, attempt to replace Lincoln, 140–41, 150; platform calls for abolition amendment, 141; and reaction to Lincoln's peace terms, 147–50, 152; effect of dissension in, on Lincoln, 149; radicals support Lincoln, 1864, 153; lacks plan of racial adjustment, 160; disagreements within, over race problem, 162; motives of, debated, 167–68; division in, over racial equality, 169–73; and Negro resettlement, 176; campaign tactics, 1864, 178. *See also* Republicans, Midwestern

Rhode Island, 58

Richardson, William A.: leads opposition to emancipation, 14; advocates white supremacy, 15; opposes enlistment of Negro soldiers, 55; on elections of 1862, 64; leads attack on Republicans' racial policies, 76

Richmond, 36, 145

Riddle, Albert G.: predicts Negroes will go South if freed, 20; on race problem belonging to South, 21

Robinson, Charles D.: reaction to Lincoln's peace terms, 147; Lincoln's letter to, 148–49

Rosecrans, William S., 108

St. Louis, 110

St. Paul: spring elections, 1863, 84; anti-Negro violence in, 89; freedmen sent to, 110

Santo Domingo, 98–99

Saxton, Rufus, 42